THE ENCYCLOPEDIA OF GAMES

THE
ENCYCLOPEDIA
OF
GAMES

COMPILED BY BARB WHITER

HINKLER
BOOKS

First published in 2000
This edition published in 2003 by
Hinkler Books Pty Ltd
17–23 Redwood Drive
DINGLEY VIC 3172
Australia

Reprinted 2003

ISBN 1 8651 5867 4

Compiled by Barb Whiter

Printed and bound in Australia

CONTENTS

INTRODUCTION

It is human nature to play games. People have been playing them since prehistoric times, either to meet a need or to satisfy an interest. In the course of history, hundreds of games have been created. The more popular of these have evolved to become either simpler or more complex. Some games make us laugh. Others test us mentally or physically. But all have developed as a way of enjoying our time and keeping our minds active and alert.

The development of games continues today and is underlined by the rapid growth of the computer game industry. Many computer games have their roots in traditional games that involve a race against time or the outwitting of foes. The Encyclopedia of Games is about the games that have been played by generations of people and that have stood the test of time. These are games that stimulate the imagination and, very often, teach social skills – essential for children.

Here are games with their origins in the cosy parlours of Elizabethan England and the ancient palaces of the Far East. Whatever their source, games continue to hold an important place in our lives. The games in this book provide countless ways to amuse and entertain, as well as ways to improve mental and physical skills. From Marbles to Mah Jong, Hangman to Hazard, Badminton to Backgammon, The Encyclopedia of Games offers hours of fun. Start playing now.

FAMILY GAMES

In the eighteenth and nineteenth centuries family games, or parlour games as they were mainly referred to then, were particularly popular before radio and television were invented for entertainment. As the parlour has gone from our house plans, most families will today play these games in a family room or rumpus area – some need lots of room to work well, others can easily be contained on the top of a table.

Many of the games that follow are suitable for collective family fun, or for children to play by themselves, whether at home at parties for instance, or at kinder or school. It's well documented that playing games is a vital part of any child's development, bringing together practice with a combination of numbers, language, socialisation and motor skills.

INDOOR GAMES

'Parlour games' is a term still used to describe a range of indoor games which adults and children alike will enjoy. We have included information especially when very young children (say three to five years) will enjoy the game, although we encourage parents to play any of the games they find enjoyable, as their children will try to learn games their parents love.

Most of the following games which have been designated as indoor games will be equally easy and fun to play out of doors on a sunny day, but often they lend themselves better to being contained by a room or two inside.

BALLOON RACE

Players: two teams of three or four are best
Age: from three up
Equipment: balloons for the number of players in two different colours; two lengths of string

1 Lay string out on the floor as start and finish lines.

2 Each player is given a balloon; each team member has the same colour.

3 One child from each team begins and has to get from the start to the finish line holding the balloon between their knees (without help from hands!). If the balloon is dropped they must return to the start and begin again.

4 As soon as one child crosses the finish line the next child in the team may begin. The quickest team is the winner.

BEAN RACE

Players: two teams of three or four players
Age: five to eight years
Equipment: spoons, small containers, twenty beans

1 Line up the players in two teams. Place a spoon, a small container (perhaps an ice-cream container) and 10 beans on the ground, about 2 metres (6 ft 7in) in front of each team.

2 At the word 'Go!' the first child in each team runs to the spoon and puts the beans, one at a time, in the container using only the spoon and one hand.

3 When all 10 beans are in the container, they are tipped back out on the floor and everything else is left as it was. The player runs back to their team and the second player in each team sets off to do the same thing.

4 The winning team is the one whose members finish first.

BEETLE

Players: two to eight (or more and divided into teams)
Age: from five up
Equipment: one dice to share, a sheet of paper and pencil for each player

1 Each part of the beetle corresponds to a number on the dice. A completed beetle needs a body (1), a head (2), legs (3, six times or, if this makes the game too long, only throw a 3 twice and add three legs on one side of the body at each throw), eyes (4, twice), feelers (5, twice) and 6 for a tail.

2 Each player takes a turn to roll the dice and must begin with a one to enable the beetle's body to be drawn first. A player who does not throw a one must pass the dice and throw again on their next turn, continuing until a one is thrown.

3 As soon as a one has been thrown and a beetle body drawn, other parts may be added as the numbers are achieved. Only when a head has been drawn can the eyes and feelers be added.

4 The first player to complete a beetle shouts 'Beetle!' and wins the game.

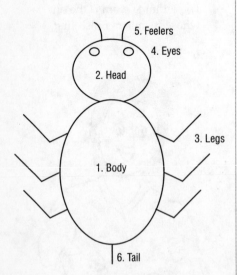

5. Feelers
4. Eyes
2. Head
3. Legs
1. Body
6. Tail

BIRD'S NEST

Players: minimum of four, or four teams of two or, three players in each team for a party
Age: from five up
Equipment: four different coloured hard-boiled eggs that have been painted bright colours after boiling or dyed with food colouring as they boil, a piece of cardboard with scoring circles marked from 90cm (35½ in) inwards (see illustration), lollies for the winning team.

1 Once the target, or nest, has been drawn and placed on the floor, four points need to be marked around it, about 2 metres (6ft 7in) out from the nest.

2 Each team takes one point around the nest and chooses a coloured egg.

3 The first player in each team takes the egg and gently rolls their egg into the nest. Then the score is written down for that team.

4 Play continues, with each member of each team taking a turn before the scores are added up. A sweet treat is in store for the team who gets the highest score and therefore keeps their egg the safest!

BLIND MAN'S BLUFF

Players: six or more
Age: any age
Equipment: a blindfold

1 Select one player to be the 'blind man', blindfold them, lead them to the centre of the room and turn them around three times. This makes the blind man dizzy and unsure of where they are facing.

2 All the other players scatter around the room and stay quiet.

3 The blind man can then search for the other players, who are not allowed to move their feet but can twist away from the blind man's prying hands to escape being touched.

4 When the blind man reaches a body, its identity has to be established by touch only. If the blind man is correct in his choice that person becomes the next blind man; if wrong, the blind man must try to catch another.

Variations: In Blind Man's Staff (or Stick) the blind man carries a stick and the rest of the players walk around in a circle close enough so the stick can reach them. When the blind man points the stick, the player closest takes the end of the stick and everyone stops walking. The blind man says, 'Who's there?' and the person, disguising their voice, answers, 'It's me'. If the blind man can now identify the player, that player becomes the next blind man, but if the choice is incorrect the game continues with the same blind man.

For adult parties only perhaps, Seated Blind Man's Bluff has all players, except the chosen blind man, seated on chairs in a tight circle. The blind man sits on the lap of one of the players and, without touching the body further, has to identify that lap. Usually the sat-upon player will giggle which can help the blind man. If the blind man guesses correctly, the two change places, otherwise another lap must be sat upon.

BUZZ AND BUZZ-FIZZ

Players: two upwards, but the game is greater fun with more players
Age: equal fun for everyone who knows their five (and seven) times tables and knows what multiples are!
Equipment: none, just great concentration

1 Choose a number to replace with the word 'Buzz' – it is often five.

2 Players sit in a circle and the game starts with the first player calling out 'one'; the next 'two'; the next 'three' – but the player who would say five says 'buzz' instead of the number.

3 If the number is a multiple of five, such as fifteen, you would also say 'buzz'.

4 If the number contains five but is not a multiple of it, such as 51, you would say 'buzz-one'.

5 If two are playing, the game is over when one player hesitates too long or forgets to say 'buzz'. If there are more than two players, the player who hesitates or forgets is out of that round.

6 To heighten the fun, this game must be played quickly, without hesitation.

Variations

When lots of people are playing Buzz, it is even more fun if a forfeit is added. This means that the player who has to say 'buzz', also has to stand up and sit down quickly, or clap once or twice, which creates great havoc! Imagine the fun when the person who has to say 55 or 'buzzbuzz' has to stand up and sit down quickly twice or clap twice or more!

Fizz is the same game, but uses seven and multiples thereof as the trigger number. This is rather difficult on its own, but how about the game of Buzz-Fizz? It can be terrifying for those not concentrating. Consider the following sequence which will happen with Buzz-Fizz. After four comes: 'buzz', 'six', 'fizz', 'eight', 'nine', 'buzz', 'eleven', 'twelve', 'thirteen', 'one-fizz', 'one-buzz' and so on.

All games of Buzz, Fizz, or the complicated Buzz-Fizz work well when everyone keeps a clear head and concentrates. Knowing the times tables and being good at mental arithmetic helps lots too!

1

2

3

4

Buzz!

CALENDAR TARGET

Players: from one to many
Age: from six up
Equipment: one counter for each player, large wall calendar

1 Lay one of the pages of a large wall calendar down flat on the floor.

2 Each player sits about 1 metre (3ft 3in) away, for the youngest, and up to 2 metres (6ft 7in) if all players are around eleven or twelve years old.

3 The players throw their counter in turn and their score is represented by the date on which the counter lands. If the counter lands on two dates, the lowest scores.

4 There should be a target score to reach, such as 100 for each game, so no one gets bored!

The counter resting between 5 and 12 would only score 5 for the player, but the counter sitting at 21 would score 21 for that player.

CHARADES

Players: six or more ensures two good-sized teams
Age: anyone and everyone who enjoys acting and dressing up
Equipment: it is usual to provide a box of old clothes and props

1 Each team chooses a two- or preferably three-syllable word to act out to the opposing team, syllable by syllable, and then finally as a whole.

2 For example, if the word 'indulgent' is chosen, the team would split it into 'in', 'dull' and 'gent'.

3 Using the playing conventions which take the form of sign language, the appropriate number of fingers are held up for the number of syllables in the word. To identify which syllable is being acted at any time, the relevant finger is indicated.

4 The clothing and props box can be used liberally or rarely – that is up to the participants.

5 There are really no winners or losers, just much fun and noise, with everyone enjoying themselves.

Children usually love the game, because they are able to dress up.

Variations: Not really variations, but for those who love words and acting, similar games are Dumb Crambo, The Game and In the Manner of the Word. All good fun for families, and for adults after a dinner party!

CODES / MORSE CODE

Players: minium of two
Age: probably from seven up, as there is quite a lot to learn
Equipment: pencil and paper, something to tap on such as a pipe, a torch, a mirror

1 Introduce your children to the ideas of secret codes with a really simple one. Pick a key letter such as 'O'. It's good to use a common letter, as you will be using it a lot. If the letter used is Q or Z, the sentence will obviously look like a code and could be easier to break!

2 First, write down the secret message you are about to code. For instance – THE WINTERSTONN FAMILY ALL HAS TO MEET AT THE BRIDGE TONIGHT.

3 Now add the key letter to the end of every word and write the whole sentence as one long word. Here's our example:
THEOWINTERSTONNOFAMILYOAL LOHASOTOOMEETOATOTHEOBRID GEOTONIGHTO.

4 It still looks easy to read, so now you need to camouflage it even further. Divide it into groups of three letters and write it again: THE OWI NTE RST ONN OFA MIL YOA LLO HAS OTO OME ETO ATO THE OBR IDG EOT ONI GHT O.

5 With practice, you'll be able to create a whole new family language!

MORSE CODE

1 Perhaps your children are ready for something more difficult than the above example of secret code?

2 Introduce them to Morse Code. It's a classic signalling code that represents the alphabet and can be used with light or sound. It's named after an American electrician, S.F.B. Morse, who devised it in the mid-1800s.

3 Each letter is represented by a dot, dash or combination thereof, so there is a little bit to learn before your children can start sending messages. However, once they do, there will be no stopping them. We've included the code below.

A . -	J . - - -	S ...
B - ...	K - . -	T -
C - . - .	L . - ..	U .. -
D - ..	M - -	V ... -
E .	N - .	W . - -
F .. - .	O - - -	X - .. -
G - - .	P . - - .	Y - . - -
H	Q - - . -	Z - - ..
I ..	R . - .	

4 Messages in Morse Code can be transmitted by sound, so tapping clearly and slowly on a pipe or a wooden tabletop will transmit the sounds needed for someone else to be able to write down and decipher the code.

5 Morse Code can also be transmitted by flashing a light towards the message taker. Try using a torch at night, in the dark. Short flashes are dots, while long flashes are dashes. The message needs to be transmitted clearly and slowly, especially when everyone is learning the code.

6 If your children have enjoyed learning the simple code and Morse Code, maybe they're ready for semaphore signals. For this you need a set of flags or two brightly coloured handkerchiefs attached to sticks. The code can be found in books at the library, or on the internet.

DINO TRACKS

Players: as many as you like – this is a great game for parties
Age: six and older
Equipment: two paper dino footprints for each player

1 This is a very simple game for younger children which will create some giggling, as each player tries to stand on their own dino footprints.

2 Everyone stands in line at one end of the room, standing on their dino footprints. The aim is to shuffle across the room to a line already marked on the floor, keeping the footprints under their feet.

3 If anyone touches the floor with their feet, they must return to the beginning and start again.

4 The winner is the person who first crosses the line with their dino footprints, without having touched the floor with their own feet. (A hint – it's okay to use your hands to balance if you shuffle and one foot doesn't come with you, for instance. However, the player must then get that wayward foot and footprint back in line, so they can continue.)

DUMB CRAMBO

Players: six or more
Age: everyone enjoys this game
Equipment: none

1 Players divide into teams. One team leaves the room and the other team thinks of a word, which is usually a verb. When the other team returns they are not told the word (of course!) but a word that rhymes with it. For instance, the word chosen is 'deal', and the opposing team is told 'steal'. This is the only time the teams talk.

2 The team leaves the room again, this time to choose three words which rhyme with 'steal' to mime as their guesses. Perhaps they would try 'heel' and then 'reel'. As these are incorrect, the members of the first team boo, hiss and stamp their feet in disgust. They would then mime 'deal' to huge applause from the other team.

3 Although only one word is said in Dumb Crambo, there is great fun to be enjoyed with the mimes, so it becomes a noisy game!

EARTH, AIR, FIRE AND WATER

Players: six or more
Age: older children and adults
Equipment: a large handkerchief or scarf, knotted into a ball

1 One player is chosen to stand in the centre of a circle of the other players, who are all seated.

2 This central player holds the handkerchief or scarf which has been knotted into a ball.

The player counts to ten and then throws the ball into the lap of one of the players, calling out either 'Earth', 'Air', Water' or 'Fire' at the same time.

3 If the call is 'Earth', the person in whose lap the ball has fallen must instantly name an animal which lives on the earth; if the call was 'Water' a fish must be named; if the call was 'Fire', something that can withstand fire, such as rock, must be named. And if 'Air' was called, a bird must be named.

4 The player only gets a count of ten by the central player to complete his turn – he then gains control of the ball and becomes the central player. However, if he cannot name an acceptable item from the correct category he pays a forfeit, to be determined by the rest of the players. This can be anything from a missed turn to a few lollies.

ELVES, GNOMES AND GIANTS

Players: as many as possible, but at least twelve
Age: children probably love the noise and bedlam more than adults
Equipment: none

1 The principle is the same as Scissors, Paper, Stone (see page 31) but this is a rowdy team game! Players are divided into two teams, with one other person being selected to act as an umpire. Teams form at opposite ends of a large, cleared room.

Members decide whether to be elves (same gesture as scissors – two fingers making the shape of a 'V'), gnomes (paper – an open hand) or giants (stone – a clenched fist). As with the other game, elves beat gnomes; giants beat elves and gnomes beat giants. If both teams make the same choice, the round is tied.

2 When the umpire calls for the game to begin, each team rushes towards the other, shouting their identity and displaying the appropriate gesture. The winning team stays in the middle of the room and the losing team retreats to their original position when everyone considers again what to be in the following round.

3 For example, if the game was a draw because both teams were giants, both teams stay in the middle of the room and are forced to decide secretly what their next choice will be, using nods and winks and clever gestures. To win, a team must win two rounds in a row.

EVERYBODY OUT

Players: any number
Age: any age
Equipment: none in particular, just one person who has a good imagination

1 Although anybody can play this game, it's probably a good one for ten- to twelve-year-olds at a party.

2 Everyone playing should be dancing around to music. Every now and again, DJ (or parent) stops the music and calls out something that will eliminate some of the dancers.

It may be something like 'Everybody out . . . who's wearing something blue.'

The next one may be 'Everybody out . . . who had pizza yesterday.' And so it goes until there is one final dancer left on the floor.

Tip: When you know the guest list for the party, make sure there is something on your elimination list applicable to each guest, so nobody feels left out!

FIND THAT LETTER

Players: two to ten
Age: older children and adults
Equipment: a newspaper for each player, pen or pencil each and paper for a score sheet

1 Everyone needs a space to rest their newspapers on a table, for this race against both the clock and other players.

2 Each player takes one page of the newspaper and on the word 'Go', has 1, 2 or 3 minutes to find and cross out every occurence of a single letter, such as 'k', or a word such as 'the', 'and', or 'man'.

3 The length of time chosen for each search will depend upon the age of the players involved – for instance, one minute is long enough for young children, while adults might want to create larger scores by trying for 3 minutes.

4 Words or letters are counted after the time has elapsed and these are scored for each player (usually one point per word or letter).

5 Each player takes a new page of newspaper and a new letter or word is chosen. Then the game continues until a player reaches 50 points and is the winner. Alternatively, the player with the highest score after a set number of pages, say five or ten, wins.

FIVE SENSES

Players: any number
Age: for any age
Equipment: each of the five games needs specialised equipment – see each separate game

1 Each of the following games may be played over a short time, or a longer time. They can be part of a range of games played at a party, or they can amuse children on rainy days, weekends or school holidays. They are all good for creating conversation and learning about the five senses.

2 Smell: gather together five or six herbs and/or spices with distinctive smells. Each player is allowed to smell them carefully once. Then they are blindfolded in turn and one of the herbs or spices is once again held under their nose. The player must then identify the smell. Each correct answer earns a point and the winner is the player who successfully identifies the most smells, and gains the most points.

3 Taste: divide players into teams of two. One player is blindfolded and the other player gives him small tastes of different foods, such as grains of sugar, a piece of cheese, a drop of mustard or a lick of mayonnaise. The blindfolded player guesses each one and is scored one point for each correct answer. Then the two players exchange places and the player who was previously the taster feeds his companion the same foods, and his score is recorded. It is best if the foods are not fed in the same order. The winner is the player who gets the highest score.

4 Touch: small objects are placed into paper bags – perhaps grapes, a sponge, soap and broad beans. Each player is blindfolded and must identify the various objects by feeling them. Their score is recorded and the winner is the person who correctly named the most objects.

5 Hearing: have a selection of unbreakable objects, such as a spoon, a book, a coin, a screw and a ball waiting. Then each player is blindfolded and asked to guess what objects are being dropped, one at a time, on the ground or floor. Scores for correct answers can be recorded.

6 Sight: this game also tests memory well! Put ten or more unrelated objects on a tray. For example, keys, a clock, a book, a computer disk, some biscuits and a photo. Cover them. Give each player a pen or pencil and a piece of paper. Then take the cover off the tray. Give the players 30 seconds to look at the contents of the tray, cover the items again and give the players 1 minute to write down every item they remember. Scores can be recorded as one point for each correct answer.

7 Finally, if all five games have been completed, you can add up all the scores for each player and declare an overall winner, with a suitable treat for their effort. Or, you can declare winners in each section.

FLUTTERING FEATHERS

Players: eight to ten
Age: all the family
Equipment: a feather or two, or something else light, such as a tissue

1 Everyone sits close together on the floor and one person takes the feather or tissue and blows it up in the air.

2 The other players must keep it afloat by their breath – a hint here, the biggest blow doesn't always work!

3 The person who allows the feather or tissue to sink to the ground must pay a penalty, which could be to sing a song, write a poem or do a dance!

GOING BLANK

Players: four or more
Age: adults who have good general knowledge and a quick brain
Equipment: none

1 This game could have been the original Trivial Pursuit®. One player is chosen as the Inquisitor and chooses three categories for the questions, such as flowers, makes of cars and animals.

2 Players sit in a circle surrounding the Inquisitor while that player points a finger at them and demands an immediate answer to the question.

3 Players do not have to be asked in turn, but the Inquisitor has to be very alert, as a player cannot be asked more than three questions from one of the categories.

4 Players should try not to 'go blank' as this will mean they are out of the game! In theory, the winner will be the last one still in, or the last ones in after the Inquisitor has asked three questions of each other player from each category.

19

HOT POTATO

Players: six or more
Age: from three up
Equipment: a large, soft beach ball or similar

1 Stand everyone in a circle and nominate one person to hold the 'hot potato' or beach ball. (This is a great birthday party game for small children, and the birthday child could start the game holding the hot potato.)

2 Play some music and ask the child to begin passing around the hot potato.

3 When the music stops the child holding the hot potato has to do a simple forfeit. This could be hopping on the spot and counting to five, running around the inside of the circle, closing eyes and touching nose, touching the sole of their left foot with their right hand, etcetera!

4 Continue until everyone has performed a forfeit.

HOW? WHEN? AND WHERE?

Players: four to six are best for this game
Age: older children with good vocabularies and adults
Equipment: none

1 One player is chosen to ask the questions, and they leave the room.

2 The other players sit in a line and choose a word with many meanings, such as 'reel'.

3 The person outside is called in and goes down the line of players, asking each 'How do you like it?' Then he walks down a second time, asking 'When do you like it?' And the third time he asks 'Where do you like it?'

4 Some of the answers for the above, using 'reel' as an example could be, 'How do you like it?' 'Small and round.' (For a fishing reel). 'When do you like it?' 'When I'm dancing.' (Another person in the line may be thinking of a dancing reel). 'Where do you like it?' 'On a river bank.' (Back to thinking of a fishing reel.)
Multiply these answers by the number of people playing and the questioner may well be confused!

5 However, from the complete set of answers, which should have an element of truth contained in them and of course a few laughs, the questioner should be able to work out what the word is.

6 You can score by crediting the questioner with 1 point if he gets the answer correct at the end of the questioning, or 5 points if he succeeds in guessing the correct answer after two series of questions, or 10 points if he guesses after only asking everyone 'How?'. Or just score 1 point whenever the questioner gets it right and the winner is the person with the highest score once everyone's had a turn at being the questioner.

I HAVE NEVER

Players: three to six
Age: probably best for adults
Equipment: none

1 The aim of each player of this game is to declare something they have never achieved, on the basis that everyone else playing will have achieved it. If a player's 'I have never . . .' proves to be unique a point is scored, and the first player to score three points wins. This game is harder than it sounds.

2 Examples could be 'I have never eaten seafood' or 'I have never worn a suit'. It is important that everyone is honest about their claims, but there is scope for challenging those claims which seem too outrageous.

I have never scuba dived

IN THE MANNER OF THE WORD

Players: four or more
Age: older children and adults will enjoy this game
Equipment: none

1 A similar game to Charades and Dumb Crambo, In the Manner of the Word uses acting and word skills to create a fun and uninhibited game.

2 One person leaves the room and the players that remain choose an adverb, such as 'slyly', 'greedily', 'naughtily' or 'amusingly'.

3 The other player returns to the room and has to guess what the adverb is. They can ask questions that the others answer 'in the manner of the word' or they can ask one or more of the players to act out a situation, such as cleaning a car or eating an apple 'in the manner of the word'. Of course, this creates amusing situations where the combinations seem quite hilarious, such as cleaning a car naughtily or greedily or eating an apple slyly!

4 If they guess correctly they score 1 point and the turn moves to someone else. If there is no correct guess after each player has acted out a situation, the turn moves to someone else but no point is scored.

Variations: Instead of the player going out of the room and the other players choosing an adverb, one player chooses an adverb and then acts out 'in the manner of the word' situations at the other players' request. The first player to guess correctly scores 1 point, but if no one guesses correctly after the player has acted a situation for each player, the player who chose the adverb receives 1 point.

Another variation is playing 'In the Manner of the Word' as a team game. Two players think of an adverb and they are given situations to act 'in the manner of the word' by the remaining players. Again, the player who guesses correctly scores 1 point, or if no one guesses the adverb after each has had a situation acted out, both players receive 1 point.

JOURNALISTS

Players: good as a party game
Age: older children
Equipment: pencil and paper for each child

1 The easiest way to play this game
is to get every child to write down
the most important events that have
taken place throughout the year. They
have 3 minutes to finish.

2 Once everyone has a list of events,
it's easy to find the winner – he's
the one with the longest *verified* list!

3 There are ways to make this game
even more interesting. Everyone
still writes down the most important
events of the year, but this time when
scoring, one person reads out their list
and whoever has the same items must
cross them through on their own list.
At the end of one list, players are asked
if they have any other items remaining
which haven't been crossed off. The
person with the most items left is the
winner. If more than one person has
the same number of items left, they
may have 1 minute extra to think of
other interesting items to add to their
list. The person who has extra items
after the one minute tie-break is the
winner.

4 This game can also be made
slightly more difficult by stating
that all the events must be in Australia,
Europe, America or Africa. Or all the
events must be on a theme such as
sport, or the environment.

LIKES AND DISLIKES

Players: six or more, preferably those who know each other well
Age: adults only
Equipment: pencil and paper

1 This is a fun and easy game! Each player writes a list of five things they like and five things they do not like on a piece of paper – anything at all can be included. Perhaps a typical list would look like this:

Likes:	red wine
	sleep
	fishing
	warm weather
	Christmas
Dislikes:	computers
	heavy traffic
	politicians
	cooking
	barking dogs

2 The pieces of paper are folded and collected and one player reads out the lists one after another, while everyone guesses who wrote each list. There are really no winners or losers but it can be a lot of fun.

3 A tip. If everyone in the group is well known to you, more subtlety in your selections is advisable as, if this is the case, they will know you equally well.

LOST ON THE MOON

Players: as many as you like
Age: from six up
Equipment: cushions, a big doona or a rug, ten toy squeakers (can be purchased from a craft shop), a blindfold

1 Arrange several cushions of different shapes and sizes over the floor and scatter ten toy squeakers on and between the cushions.

2 Cover the 'moonscape' with the doona or rug and line up all the players at one end.

3 Each player takes it in turn to walk blindfolded over the doona. If they tread on a squeaking 'moon alien', they must return to the beginning and start again.

4 There should be some treats ready for the moonwalkers who make it through without squashing a moon alien.

MOONROCK GRAB

Players: minimum of three, but multiples of three are fine too
Age: from six up
Equipment: a 3 metre (9ft, 9in) piece of rope for each group of three children playing, pieces of foil rolled into 'rocks' for each player, a treat for the winner

1 Each group of three players is given a rope to hold on to which has been knotted tightly to make a circle. Players form a triangle and hold the rope with their left hands.

2 Three foil 'rocks' are placed just out of reach and the first person to prevail over their companions and pick up their rock is the winner.

3 For a large party, you could also have a championship playoff, of the winners of each round. They could play off for an extra treat.

MORA

Players: two
Age: children and adults
Equipment: none

1 A simple game suitable for children who can add up to ten. It can be played nearly anywhere, so is great for entertainment on a car or train journey, or for a rainy day.

2 The object is for both players to guess how many fingers will be 'thrown' or displayed in total by both players.

3 Preferably standing or sitting opposite one another, each player keeps their hand closed into a fist against their chest. On the count of three, or another signal, they throw a chosen number of fingers (or keep the fist closed for zero) while calling out the number of fingers they think will be the total thrown by both players.

4 If the player says 'Mora' it means that the player thinks ten fingers will be thrown.

5 If neither player guesses correctly, the round is void; if one player guesses the right number they win that round, and if both players guess the right number the round is a draw.

Variation: Also see Scissors, Paper, Stone on page 31 for another easy to play hand and finger game.

Another variation is a game called Shoot, where the players do not guess the number of fingers thrown, but whether the number will add up to an odd or even number (zero is considered an even number). Players can use both hands, so they can each throw a maximum of ten and, as they throw their hands out, they call out 'Odds' or 'Evens'. Scoring is as in Mora.

MURDER IN THE DARK

Players: to make it really scary, eight or more is best
Age: older children and adults
Equipment: pencil and paper; a dark house!

1 Tear up a slip of paper for each player. On one write X for the murderer and D for the detective. Each player picks a piece of paper out of a hat. The murderer (who chose the piece of paper with an X) must not say anything, but the detective must announce their identity to the other players.

2 Now the lights are turned off in the house.

3 There is a choice in what happens next. One set of rules says that the detective stays in the room where the slips of paper were chosen, and everyone else disappears into the darkness. Others play that the detective goes out of the room, or maybe adjoining rooms, and the rest of the players stay where they are.

4 Whichever way is chosen to play, the aim is that the next step is the murderer finds a victim and whispers 'You're dead', upon which the victim must scream, and fall to the ground if they are good at acting!

5 When the scream is heard, everyone stays still except the detective who switches on the lights, finds the 'body' and notes where everyone else is located.

6 Everyone is now questioned by the detective and must answer truthfully – only the murderer can lie – but they must admit they are the murderer if directly challenged.

7 After all the evidence is assembled and suspects have been questioned, the detective is allowed two guesses at the murderer's identity. And then there could be time for another game!

MY LITTLE BIRD

Players: as many as possible (it is a good birthday party game)
Age: any age will enjoy it except very young children
Equipment: none

1 Choose one player as the leader and everyone else either stands or sits in a circle so they can see this person.

2 The leader begins the game by saying 'My little bird is lively, is lively' and continues by naming something followed by the word 'fly'. For example, 'My little bird is lively, is lively. Cats fly.'

3 If whatever the player names can fly – such as magpies – all the players raise their arms and wave them about. If whatever the leader names cannot fly – as with cats, above – the players should remain still.

4 Players who wave their arms at the wrong time are out. The last player left in the game wins and becomes leader next time.

PASS THE ORANGE

Players: two teams of four or six is best
Age: children and adults
Equipment: two oranges

1 To win, the team must pass an orange up and down the row of team members using only their feet, which may sound easy, but is actually surprisingly difficult to achieve!

2 To begin, each team sits in a line on the floor facing the other team.

3 The first player holds the orange between their feet and passes it to the next team member, who accepts it by using only their feet.

4 This continues until someone drops the orange. The person who dropped it must pick it up, no matter where it has rolled, by using only their feet. This could mean they are bouncing around the floor on their bottom! When they pick up the orange it must be returned to the first player and play begins again.

5 The first team to get the orange up and down their row, wins.

Variation: This variation could have begun at teenage parties a few decades ago, but it has been played by a great number of people. Instead of team members using their feet to manoeuvre the orange, it became popular to use the neck and chin – no hands! – to pass the orange along the team. It can be interesting!

PICTURES

Players: two teams of three or four is best
Age: children and adults
Equipment: large blackboard and chalk or drawing pad and pens

1 Best played with two teams, however small. One team decides on a phrase, which could be the title of a book, play, film or television show, a quotation or a proverb. They tell one member of the other team and this player has to communicate the phrase just by drawing to his other team players.

2 It is the speed of the guess that will ultimately decide the winning team.

3 When a correct guess has been made, the teams reverse roles.

4 No talking is allowed in Pictures, so a player can tell their team what the phrase is by drawing an arch for a play, a camera for a film, and a face with an open mouth for a song. Quotation marks " " mean it is a quotation or proverb, and a book is – a book.

5 The number of words in the phrase is indicated by a string of dashes; to indicate syllables, the word needs to be circled and divided with dashes and a dot between syllables.

PLUS AND MINUS

Players: one to four
Age: six to twelve years
Equipment: counters in two different colours, enough for one of each colour for every player, a rectangular scoring target, pen/pencil and paper for scoring

1 There are two things to decide before anyone begins to play this game. Firstly which colour counter represents Plus and which represents Minus. For instance, if you have yellow and blue counters, the yellow could be Plus and the blue Minus.

2 The other thing to decide is what score is the winning score. A hint – if there are only two young players, perhaps 20 would be a high enough score. But if there are four twelve-year-olds, you may want to stretch the winning score to 50, or even 100.

3 The scoring rectangle needs to look like the following illustration. Each numbered rectangle needs to be

quite big, say 30cm (11^1/$_2$ in) deep and 20cm (7^1/$_2$ in) wide.

4 Now each player takes it in turn to throw both their Plus and Minus counters onto the rectangle. If the Plus counter lands on the 8 and the Minus counter lands on the 2, his total score for the throw is 6. However, if a player scores 1 with the Plus counter and 6 with the Minus counter, his score is minus 5. You can now see why 20 is a good starting score to aim for! If a counter lands between two rectangles, the lowest number is taken for both Plus and Minus.

5 The winner of this game is the player who reaches the prearranged score, and the score must be reached exactly. If the winning score is 20 and the player scores 22, he needs to keep throwing until the scores the exact 20 (perhaps this condition could be ignored for very young players).

| 1 | 2 | 3 | 4 | 5 | 6 | 7 | 8 | 9 | 10 |

RUMOURS

Players: two equal teams, with as many people as possible
Age: children and adults
Equipment: none, but there is a need for an organiser (probably an adult) to begin each rumour!

1 Each player takes it in turn to be their team's leader.

2 Each team sits in a circle a little away from the other team.

3 The organiser whispers the same message to each team leader.

4 Each team leader then goes back to their team and whispers the message to the player on their right. This whispering continues around the circle. Each player is only told the message once; nothing is repeated.

5 The last player of each team tells the organiser the message as they heard it. The leader (or the organiser) tells everyone the message as it began.

6 The team that kept the message most correct wins the game.

SARDINES

Players: four or more
Age: children and adults
Equipment: none specifically, but a house with lots of nooks and crannies would be great

1 This is a variation of the old favourite, Hide and Seek, and someone has to be chosen to go off and hide first.

2 After this person leaves the room, they are usually given 5 minutes in which to find a suitable place to hide before the rest of the players split up and go in search of the person hiding. (It is important the first person to hide finds a hiding place where all players can join them – that is why the game is called Sardines.)

3 The first player to find the person who is hiding waits until any other player is out of sight and then joins the hiding player without saying a word to anyone else.

4 The two wait quietly for the next player to find them and so on until all but one of the players has joined the group.

5 The last player to discover the hiding place of the group is the next sardine.

SCISSORS, PAPER, STONE

Players: two (or for many players which could be divided into teams, see Elves, Gnomes and Giants on page 16)
Age: from around seven or eight up
Equipment: none

1 Determine how many rounds will be played. (It is fascinating, but you can also just time yourselves to say, 15 minutes.)

2 This game can be played anywhere – in the car, on a train, sitting inside on a wet day or outside on a warm day.

3 Both players decide whether to represent scissors (two fingers making the shape of a 'V'), paper (an open hand) or stone (a clenched fist) where the point of the game is that scissors cut paper; paper wraps stone and stone blunts scissors. Therefore, scissors win over paper, paper beats stone and stone beats scissors. If both players choose the same shape in a round, it is declared a draw.

4 If there is room, the players put one hand behind their backs and count to three when they produce it with their representation for that round.

Scissors

Paper

Stone

SLEEPING LIONS

Players: as many as can lie down comfortably wherever the party is!
Age: four to eight years
Equipment: none

1 This is a perfect indoor party game to play after everyone's been running around shouting or singing – it's very, very quiet!

2 Choose one person to be 'It' if there are eight or less children. If there are more, chose two people to both be 'Its'.

3 Everyone else becomes a 'sleeping lion' by lying down flat on their back and being as still as possible. They aim to keep a straight face and not laugh out loud, despite what the It or Its say or do to them.

4 Now the person or people chosen as It try to make the sleeping lions laugh any way they can – such as pulling funny faces – but they mustn't touch the sleeping lions at all.

5 Any lion who laughs is out and the last one (or two) lions left take their turn to be It in the next round.

SPOOF

Players: two or more
Age: older children and adults
Equipment: for each player, three small objects such as coins or buttons

1 This is another game which can be played just about anywhere. Spoof relies on bluffing the other players into some false thinking – but only sometimes. If the same bluffing is used every time, a player will get caught out!

2 Each player in every round has the choice of keeping any number, or none, of the three items he possesses in his clenched fist and then must guess the total number which may be displayed. Hence, if two people are playing, the total cannot be more than 6; if three are playing, 9; four would be a maximum of 12, etcetera.

3 Moving clockwise, each player calls out the number of items they think is the total of items in all players' hands – every call must be a different number.

4 When everyone has guessed, all closed fists are opened and the total items are counted. The player who guessed correctly, or nearest, is the winner.

5 It can be seen where bluffing could be useful. If a player calls first and has 3 in their hand, they might guess 4 if only two are playing. But that player could be bluffing and only be holding one, hoping that the other player has 3!

SUN AND RAIN

Players: two
Age: six to twelve years
Equipment: large wall calendar, two dice, 30 counters in two different colours – black or grey for rain and yellow for the sun would be good!

1 Use a page from a large wall calendar which has a month with 30 days and place it on a table or floor. (No calendar available? That's okay; simply draw one up on a large piece of card.)

2 The first player, let's say he's the sun, throws the dice. If the sum of the two numbers is even, such as ten, he puts a yellow counter on the first day of the month. If he throws an odd number, he misses a turn.

3 Then the other player, representing rain, throws the dice and the opposite holds true. If his total is an odd number, he can put one of his counters on the first day of the month, or the second day if the first is already taken. If he gets an even number as total, he misses a turn.

4 When the month is completed, the counters are added up and the winner is the player with the most counters on the dates.

TELEGRAMS

Players: two
Age: seven to ten years
Equipment: old newspapers, white paper, scissors, glue-stick each

1 Players exchange telegrams which they have made by cutting up words, phrases and sentences from the newspapers, and sticking them on to the sheets of paper.

2 The first player is chosen to send a message and the other player replies. There should be a time limit of only two minutes or so, otherwise the player waiting will become bored.

3 Telegrams can also be played as a party game, with teams of two or three all creating messages at once and passing them around a circle clockwise. When the message is received, a reply is decided upon and created. This message then returns, anti-clockwise.

4 This is an excellent game for a rainy day!

THE FARMYARD

Players: as many as possible
Age: from three up, with an older storyteller
Equipment: none

1 This is a great game for a three- or four-year-old's birthday party, but it does need a little preparation on the part of the storyteller.

2 The children are seated in a circle around the storyteller. Each child is given the name of a farmyard animal and asked to make the noise that animal makes as a test. For example, a pig – oink, oink. If the story is complicated and there are not enough children to have an animal each, they can double up with a pig and a cow, for instance.

3 Tell the children they need to make their animal sounds every time their animal is mentioned in the story.

4 Tell a story about a day on the farm and mention all the animals at least once, more if possible.

5 Encourage the children to be as loud as they like with their animal noises and keep the story simple and funny too.

THE HAT GAME

Players: up to eight
Age: any age
Equipment: a hat and some cards

1 This sounds such an easy game! However, it can be much harder to play than to read about. Try it and see.

2 Place a hat on the ground and mark a line about 2 metres (6ft 7in) away.

3 Players take it in turns to throw their cards into the hat from behind the marked line. A reward of a few lollies could be made available for those who manage to pop a card in the hat.

THE PHRASE GAME

Players: at least four
Age: older children and adults
Equipment: pen/pencil and paper

1 Many people think this is the best family game ever. It is similar to Charades, In the Manner of the Word and Dumb Crambo in that it involves words and acting out. The only way to find out if your family thinks it is the best game is to play!

2 First of all, divide the players into two equal teams. Then a decision needs to be made as to whether the game is to be the single actor version or the team acting version. It is probably best to begin with the single actor version, which is as follows.

3 Both teams secretly compile a list of phrases, one for each member of the opposing team. The phrases could be titles of books, films, songs, plays or proverbs.

4 Game conventions insist on no words being used at all so the member chosen to act out the phrase uses a form of sign language. A film is indicated by winding an old-fashioned movie camera; a book by opening your hands together, palms upwards; drawing a rough arched shape is a play; pulling sound from your open mouth indicates a musical or opera; drawing a square in the air means a television programme, and drawing quotation marks in the air indicates a proverb.

Film

Book

Play

5 One team gives the first player from the other team one of the phrases chosen and that player acts out the phrase to their team-mates without using any words. While the team-mates are guessing, the other team members make it hard to concentrate by shouting or sniggering.

6 When the phrase has been guessed, or the team has given up, the round is over.

7 It is swap-over time now while the second team gets its revenge. The game goes on until either the phrases run out or a time limit (previously set) is over.

8 In the other (rowdier) version, players still compete in two teams, but this time one person is chosen as quizmaster. This quizmaster compiles the list of phrases and gives the same phrase to one team member of each team at the same time.

9 These players return to their teams and act out the phrase in front of their team. The person who guesses correctly dashes to the quizmaster for the next phrase until all the phrases have been acted out and the team who reaches the end of the list first is the winner.

10 As expected, this version is much more noisy, and there are more opportunities to cheat as everyone tries to listen to the other team guess as well as watching their own 'actor'. In reality the game is so much fun, and players are usually so caught up in guessing they do not cheat. It is up to the quizmaster to ensure everyone plays fairly.

11 Just a hint – there is no fun if everyone chooses really easy, safe phrases, so try to think of some difficult titles of books and plays to get more fun out of The Phrase Game.

Second syllable

Three words in title

A small word such as 'a'

THROWING THE HANDKERCHIEF

Players: as many as you like
Age: all the family, good for children's birthday parties
Equipment: a handkerchief

1 This is a simple, easy game, suitable for many young children at a noisy birthday party. Adult supervision is good, so everyone gets a turn in the centre and everyone gets to throw and catch the handkerchief.

2 One child stands in the centre of a circle of seated players.

3 The seated players throw the knotted handkerchief from one side to the other and the person in the middle tries to catch it. When they succeed in doing so, they take the place of the player who last threw the knotted handkerchief.

4 The player who threw the handkerchief then enters the circle and the game begins again.

TOWERING CARDS

Players: one to four
Age: older children and adults
Equipment: one or two packs of cards and a carpeted floor

1 This is a great rainy day game for the whole family. Everyone taking part has a pack of cards and a spot on the floor. Play begins by placing four cards on their edges and resting them against one another to make a four-walled 'room'.

2 Two cards are placed on top to create a roof. Then players try to build another room on top and so on, until the tower falls.

3 There's only one winner – the player who builds the highest tower that stays up when the others fall.

WHAT'S MY LINE?

Players: up to eight or ten
Age: seven to ten years
Equipment: several slips of paper, pencil and a box

1 This game is based on one of the earliest TV game shows and is terrific at an indoor party for children over seven years.

2 Firstly, the host must organise a box with several slips of paper (around double the number of guests) inside, with different tasks written on them. These could include 'mowing the lawn', 'chopping wood', 'cleaning windows', or 'putting up a tent'.

3 One by one, each child picks out a slip of paper, reads the task and acts it out in front of the other children.

4 The other children must try to guess what was being done straight away, or, if that doesn't work, by asking questions which can only be answered 'Yes' or 'No'. Usually it's best to keep a time limit of one or two minutes for each bout of questions, otherwise some children won't get a chance to act, before they are tired of the game!

5 If this game sounds familiar, it's because it's similar to Twenty Questions, for adults!

WINKING

Players: four or more
Age: older children and adults
Equipment: a pack of playing cards

1 With four players, select four cards from the pack, one of which must be the Ace of Spades. (However many are playing there must be an equal number of cards chosen, including the Ace of Spades.)

2 Lay one card in front of each player and ask them to look at the card, but not to declare it, and not to let anyone else see it. The person who draws the Ace of Spades is the Murderer.

3 The Murderer commits the murder by catching the eye of another player and sending a calculated 'deadly' wink in their direction. The victim waits a few seconds (so as not to give the game away) and then slumps dead on the playing table.

4 If any other player spots the wink, they reveal the identity of the murderer and a new game begins.

5 If no one guesses correctly, the murderer can continue.

6 A hint: you must participate in this game to get the most out of it. If you stare at the table so as not to get 'murdered' you also won't see the murderer winking someone else to death. If you are the murderer you can't just wink at random; you need to have the attention of only one person. It is a great game for friends to play together.

WRONG!

Players: as many as you like
Age: can be tailored for any age group
Equipment: a prepared short story

1 The aim of this game is to spot the deliberate errors in a story that is read out to the group.

2 Whoever writes the story needs to include many things suitable for the age group who will be listening. For instance, most older children and certainly adults will know that if you go to an antique shop you will not buy a new dinner service or a new table. For younger children you could include the phrase, 'and she went to bed in her party dress', or something equally as obvious!

3 The first player to spot a mistake calls out 'Wrong!' and earns a point. If someone calls out and there is not a mistake, they have a point taken away. The player with the most points at the end of the story wins the game.

YES-NO BEANS

Players: as many as you like
Age: older children and adults
Equipment: 5 beans or any other small item such as buttons

1 Everyone begins with 5 beans each.

2 The players circulate around a room asking each other questions to which no one must answer 'yes' or 'no'.

3 Whenever a player is tricked into saying 'yes' or 'no' that person accepts a bean from the player who asked the question.

4 The winner is the person who gets rid of his 5 beans first.

WRITTEN GAMES

Obviously these games, as well as those under the heading Word and Spoken games, will increase any child's literacy, spelling, writing and reading skills while they are having lots of fun. Many of the following games are as good for one or two to play, as when there is a whole tribe of children who need to be shown how to entertain themselves.

Another great point is that little equipment is usually necessary – often just a pencil (or pen for older children) and some scrap paper for each player is all that is needed.

ACROSTICS

Players: one can play, but it is more fun with friends, say up to six
Age: older children and adults
Equipment: pencil and paper

1 Acrostics is a word-building game. A word of at least three letters is chosen, but four or five letters is more challenging! Each player writes the word in a column on the left-hand side of a piece of paper and then writes the same word, but with the letters reversed down the right-hand side of the paper.

B.............................D
R.............................A
E.............................E
A.............................R
D.............................B

2 Each player fills in the space between the columns with words starting and ending with the letter at either side. For example, the above word, 'bread', could have board, Riviera, extreme, arbour and dumb inserted between the columns.

3 Depending upon the choice of rules, which will probably be decided by the ages and abilities of those playing, the winner could be the first person to fill in all the words (with real words!) or the player with the longest or most original words. Perhaps you could eliminate people who have the same words and the winner or scorer of points is the person or persons left with the more original words.

ALPHABET RACE

Players: two or more
Age: adults and all children who know their alphabet
Equipment: pencil and paper

1 Each player lists all the letters of the alphabet on a piece of paper which is kept in front of them. Another piece of plain paper is to be used as a board by everyone.

2 Choose who goes first (highest dice roll or a coin-toss) and that person writes down a word on the piece of paper being used as the board, spacing the letters carefully, and then marking them off their own alphabet list. (Hence, words with double letters cannot be used, such as 'letter', because each alphabet only has one 't'.)

3 The next player continues, adding a word to the board, intersecting with the original word by using at least one letter, and crossing off the letters used on their alphabet list. (They only cross off the letters added by them, not the letters used from the first player's word.)

PLEAD

O   J

A   E

DRIFT

In the illustration above, the first player put down PLEAD, the second added 'oad' to 'l' to make load, the first player added 'rift' to the 'd' and the second player added 'je'.

4 This play continues until everyone has used as many letters as they can on the board, using every letter only once of course. If a player is stuck when it is their turn they can say 'pass' and hope that someone else will put down something they can use next turn.

5 The first player to finish off their alphabet wins, but because everyone starts with only 26 letters it is difficult to use them all. In this case, the player with the least number of letters left is declared the winner.

Variation: The rules of Alphabet Race can be varied endlessly, but agree to any changes with co-players before the game is started. Some people double or even triple the number of vowels available to each player, or just double the whole alphabet, except maybe Q, X and Z!

ANAGRAMS

Players: two is fine, but there is a team version for six or more
Age: older children and adults
Equipment: pencil and paper

1 For two players, one player is chosen to draw up a list of categories, which could include breeds of cats, mammals, birds, football teams, film stars or just about anything they want to include. Five categories are about the right number.

2 Then each player devises an agreed number of anagrams (between two and five) for each of the categories. It is a good idea to put a time limit on this – 30 minutes is about right.

Breeds of cats	Hill Can Chi – Chinchilla
	Sees Mia – Siamese
	Xer – Rex
Mammals	Gan Kooar – Kangaroo
	Mussop – Possum
	Alako – Koala
Birds	Pigame – Magpie
	Borin – Robin
	La Rosel – Rosella

3 When the lists are ready, each player spells out every anagram in a category and the opposing player writes each one down.

4 The players solve the anagrams within the time limit they have set – again usually 30 minutes. The winner is the player who solves the most anagrams within the time frame, over all the categories. The prize is that they get to complete the list of categories for the next game.

Variation: For a team game one player is designated as the question master and they get to devise the categories and the anagrams. For a planned party this would be done in advance. This also means that the categories can be tailored to match the individuals playing the game.

BATTLESHIPS

Players: two
Age: older children
Equipment: pencil and paper

1 In this game of luck, each player begins by drawing two 10 × 10 grids, numbering the squares from 1 to 10 down the left-hand side, and labelling them from A to J along the top. Each player uses one grid for their 'home fleet' and the other is for their opponent's 'enemy fleet' – this one stays blank for the moment.

2 Each player has a fleet consisting of one battleship (made up of four squares), two cruisers (three squares each), three destroyers (two squares each) and four submarines (one square each).

3 Each player now places the individual ships of their home fleet on their home grid, shading in the squares used and/or using a 'b' for battleship, a 'c' for cruiser, a 'd' for destroyer and an 's' for a submarine. The squares that make up each ship must touch each other and can do so either horizontally, vertically or diagonally. However, no two ships can touch each other, even by a corner. Once all ships are marked, a coin is tossed to determine who starts.

4 Each player takes it in turns to try to hit the enemy fleet by calling out a reference for the square in which they think the ship is located, such as B4 (part of a cruiser on the home grid below) or J3 (a miss). Each player marks his blank enemy grid with a cross for misses, and adds the letter of the vessel for a hit. All direct hits must be declared by the enemy and the type of vessel given.

5 The winner is the first player to destroy the enemy fleet by guessing each position and marking them off on their 'enemy' grid.

	A	B	C	D	E	F	G	H	I	J
1		■								
2						■	■	■	■	
3										
4		■		■						
5		■				■				
6		■							■	
7										
8					■					
9	■		■	■						
10					■					

Example of a home grid deployment.

	A	B	C	D	E	F	G	H	I	J
1							X			
2		X								X
3										
4										
5		C	X				S			X
6		C								
7		X		X						
8									X	
9				D	X					
10				X						

Diagram showing opponent's guesses and their outcomes for the above deployment.

BOXES

Players: two
Age: from eight up
Equipment: pens of two different colours and paper

1 Mark out a square grid of dots on a piece of paper – usually 10 in a row and 10 columns is about the right size for a quick game.

2 Each player uses a pen of a different colour (to avoid any arguments!) and takes it in turn to draw a line between any two dots – the aim is to form a box. When a player completes a box they mark it with their initial and can add another line to the grid. (This may mean that they get to claim another box and sometimes many boxes. That is acceptable because, even when they have finished, they still have to place another line and that is when their opponent has a turn!)

3 When all the boxes have been enclosed, each player's boxes are counted and the one with the most is the winner.

Hints: Towards the end of the game, strategy and cunning come into play. The idea is to look for the move which will limit your opponent's opportunity to gain more boxes than you. Look for the move allowing them to complete one or two boxes instead of a whole row!

Variation: Bored with the game? Played it to death? Well, just reverse the rules, and the winner is the person who has the least enclosed boxes! It is harder than you think to change your mindset.

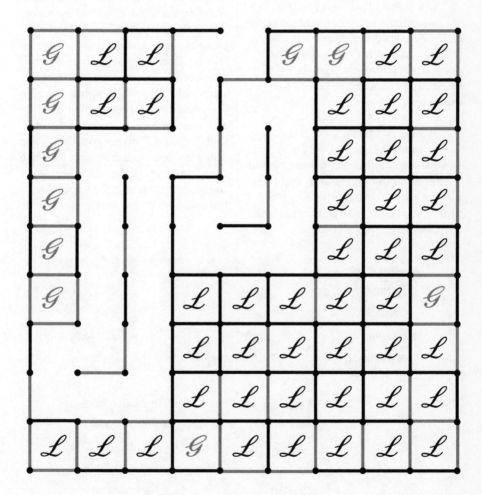

CATEGORIES

Players: three or more
Age: can be tailored to be played by children and adults, but is usually thought of as an adult game
Equipment: pencils and paper

1 One person is chosen (or turns are taken) to select a list of up to eight categories. They can be as varied as possible and as difficult as you like! Try actors, composers, parts of the body, colours and horse breeds for example.

2 A letter of the alphabet is chosen at random (open a book, a newspaper or a dictionary and point to a letter without looking at it) and then players have 10 minutes in which to write down as many words beginning with that letter in each category.

3 Once the ten minutes is over, each player's list is allotted points. One point is scored for a valid word which is also on someone else's list and 2 points are given for a word that no one else listed. A player can rest on their laurels after one round or agree on a score to aim for, such as 20 points.

Variation: This version is a little more difficult. Each player writes the letters of the alphabet down one side of a piece of paper and just one category is chosen. Everyone then writes down one word within the category starting with each letter of the alphabet within a set time limit – maybe 10 or 15 minutes. Perhaps agree beforehand that X, Q and Z do not count! A player will achieve a perfect score if they use every letter of course, but otherwise the scoring system is the same as for the straightforward version.

Categories	G	S
parts of the body	gum	stomach
countries	Greece	Spain
colours	grey	sapphire
dog breeds	Greyhound	Maltese

	Category animals	Category cities/towns
A	antelope	Amsterdam
B	bear	Bucharest
C	cheetah	Cairo
D	dog	Denver
E	elephant	Edmonton
F	fox	Florence
G, etc.	geese	Gosford

CONSEQUENCES

Players: two or more
Age: older children and adults; develops and nurtures imaginative play in all
Equipment: pencil and paper

1 This is a great game for all the family as there are no winners or losers, just lots of fun. Plus, each game only takes around 20 minutes. It is also easy to learn because each game follows a set format.

2 Variations exist and home rules can be used with a changed format if desired, but the following 'script' is the most common:
i)   (one or two adjectives)
ii)   (female name – which could be a real person, or a celebrity or a fictional character) met
iii) (one or two adjectives)
iv)   (male name) at
v)   (the place where they met)
vi)   he . . . (what he did)
vii) she . . . (what she did)
viii) he said . . .
ix)   she said . . .
x)   and the consequence was . . .
xi)   and the world said . . .

3 Players sit in a circle and each take a pencil and a piece of paper and writes one or two adjectives to describe a female character on the top of the paper. They then fold it over so it cannot be seen and pass the paper to the person on their left. For each phrase this continues, so the paper keeps being folded down and passed on.

4 When the story is complete, the final player passes the story to the left again and then each story is read out – usually to much hilarity!

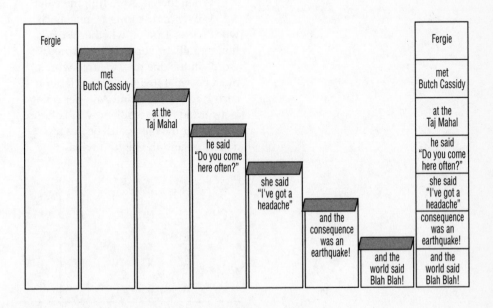

51

Variation: Children especially like to play a simpler version of Consequences called Picture Consequences. First, each player draws a head (any head, human or animal), adds a long neck and then folds the paper so the neck is showing. This is passed along to the player on their left and a torso is drawn, the paper folded again, and then legs and, finally, feet are added. There are some rather strange results from this, usually very amusing!

CROSSWORDS

Players: two or more, or this game can be played in teams
Age: older children and adults
Equipment: pencil and paper

1 Each player begins by drawing a grid of squares, 5 × 5, on a sheet of paper. If there are more than two players, a grid of 7 × 7 helps to make it more interesting.

2 Taking turns, each player calls out a letter of the alphabet and this letter is placed in the square of the player's choice. The aim is to form words that may read either across or down. Rules for accepted words need to be agreed before beginning, but generally they must be at least two-letter words and not abbreviations or proper nouns. Once the letter is in place on the grid it cannot be moved.

3 When the grids are full, the game is over and scoring begins. Each word scores 1 point, whether it reads horizontally or vertically. To score two words in the one row, the two words must be separated by another letter if each is to score a point. Another point is awarded if the whole row or column is used for the one word. Scores are added up and the highest wins.

S	P	A	D	E	2
O	I	N	O	C	1
W	A	G	E	R	2
T	A	X	B	M	1
U	H	Q	L	F	0
1	1	1	1	0	10

CRYSTALS

Players: two is best
Age: older, imaginative children and adults
Equipment: graph paper, different coloured pen for each player

1 The aim of this game is to create symmetrical shapes known as crystals. A crystal is made up of atoms (or single squares) and players must observe certain rules of symmetry in scoring their crystals at the end of the game. Whether a crystal is legitimate or not is determined by visualising four axes through its centre: horizontal, vertical and two diagonal axes. It should be possible to visually fold each crystal along each of the axes to provide mirror images. Players do not score points for the number of crystals they 'grow' but for the squares each crystal covers. A minimum crystal is made up of four squares, and the atoms forming the crystal must be joined along their sides.

2 Draw a border around a square 20 rows by 20 squares across on the graph paper for two players (increase to say 30 × 30 for more players).

3 Each player in turn shades in any one square of their choice in the one colour for each player.

4 As a strategy, for several turns both players would not try to grow a crystal but would place single atoms around the playing area to establish potential sites. Further along it is easier to see which atoms are best to grow and so they will be added to.

5 When a player believes they have created a crystal, they declare it and circle the area it covers.

6 A player can block their opponent's attempts at crystal growing but, as this does not grow him any crystals, it is best to limit these blocks to necessary ones.

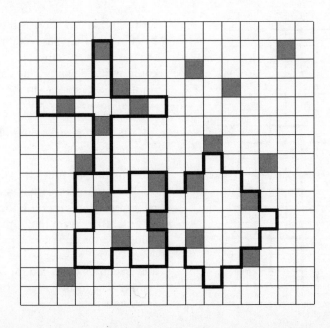

7 Play ends when there are no blank squares, or players agree no more crystals can be formed.

8 To score, players decide which crystals are legitimate and count the number of squares in each. A crystal that is not symmetrical does not score. Adding up the squares, the player with the most wins the game.

GEOGRAPHY RACE

Players: as many as possible – best for large groups
Age: adults and children who are good at geography
Equipment: pencil and paper and a reference atlas

1 Firstly, the players should be formed into two teams. If possible they should sit in parallel rows facing each other.

2 The first person in each team is given a pen and paper, and a person acting as the umpire chooses the name of any well known city or town around the world, specifying a compass direction from that city – north, east, west or south. For example, the umpire could say, 'Cities or towns to the west of Los Angeles.'

3 The signal is given to begin and the first person in one team could write 'Tokyo'. As soon as the player has finished they pass on the paper to the next person in their team who could write 'Beijing'. Play continues until the last member in the team has written down a town.

4 As soon as one team finishes the game is over.

5 The umpire now checks both teams' answers (that is where the reference atlas is useful if there is a dispute!). The team that finished first gains a bonus of 5 points. In addition, every correct answer scores 1 point, and 1 point is deducted for an incorrect answer. The team with the highest score wins.

GUGGENHEIM

Players: three or more is probably best, although two can play
Age: can be tailored for children or adults
Equipment: pencil and paper

1 This is a similar game to Categories, but slightly more complicated.

2 Instead of choosing only one letter for each round, the players choose a keyword of four or five letters, such as 'skate'. This word is written across five columns on a piece of paper (see illustration) and, still using up to eight categories, players try to find words for each of the categories beginning with the letter heading each column.

3 Scoring is the same as in Categories. One point is scored for a valid word which is also on someone else's list, and 2 points are given for a word that no one else listed. A winner can be declared after one round, or agree a score to aim for, such as 20 points.

Category	S	K	A	T	E
girl's names	Sue	Kate	Anita	Tammy	Elise
pleasures	swimming	kissing	art	talking	eating
drinks	squash	Kahlua	Amaretto	tequila	eggnog
plants	sunflower	Kangaroo paw	azalea	tree fern	epacris

HANGMAN

Players: two or more
Age: children and adults
Equipment: pencil and paper

1 This is a popular, easy game for two or more players.

2 One player thinks of a word, but does not tell any other player, just writes down the same number of dashes as there are letters in the word.

3 The other player/s now begin guessing letters in the word, calling one letter out at a time. If the guess is right, the first player writes in the letter above the correct dash (or dashes if the letter appears more than once in the word).

4 If the guess is incorrect, the first player begins to draw the gallows and the hanged man – one line represents each wrong letter. See illustration.

5 The other players can guess at the hidden word at any time. The player who correctly identifies the word is the person to choose the next word.

6 To make the game more difficult, longer words may be chosen, or even use the title of a film, television show, book or play. The person choosing the phrase can give a clue as to the category.

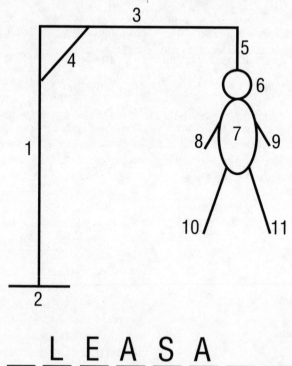

_ L E A S A _ _

(PLEASANT)

HEADLINES

Players: three or more
Age: usually adults only, although some older children may see the point
Equipment: pencil and paper

1 There are no winners or losers as such, this game is played purely for fun. The aim is to create amusing, tabloid newspaper-style, attention-grabbing headlines.

2 For instance, the first player begins by writing down the word 'divorce'. The next player adds 'filmstar' before or after the first word, the third player adds 'lovenest', again either before or after and you could already have 'Divorce filmstar's lovenest!' (It is acceptable to add grammatical extras such as an 's' as the game progresses.)

3 If there are many players, every player can be given a different coloured pen, or one could write in capital letters, and you can go on as long as you like. Keep in mind it is the quick, short and pithy headline you require!

LEGS

Players: from three to ten or so
Age: children and adults, although probably best for adult entertainment after dinner
Equipment: pencils and paper

1 This may seem a really simple game, but to win is difficult.

2 Each player has a pencil and paper and one player is chosen to select a letter of the alphabet at random.

3 Next, set a timer for 2 minutes or maybe someone needs to make a note of the time and the time to stop. Everyone gets those 2 minutes to write down everything with legs (or, in fact, can have legs) they can think of which begin with that letter.

4 If there was a lot of time, everyone would probably think of lots of items, and people and animals which have legs form most of the easy letters of the alphabet. However, the trick is not to dry up when everyone else is writing. Another trick is also to think of unusual or more unlikely answers.

5 Why? Well, when the 2 minutes writing time is up, one person begins by reading out their list (see example on page 56). Anyone who has the same word crosses it off their list; and the next player reads their list and so on until all lists have been read out. All players add up the words left on their list and the winner of the round is the person with the most words. These no doubt will be the most uncommon words.

6 To complete a game the participants can agree on a score to reach, say 20, or a time limit – most rounds will only take around 5 minutes, depending upon the number of players and how much laughter takes place.

settee	setter
sofa	sparrow
soldier	spider
sailor	stag
sow	shepherd
sentry	stallion
scuba diver	sloth
seat	skink
settle	skunk
scullerymaid	spunk
sideboard	

Depending upon what other players have written down, this player could obtain a high score as many words would count as unusual in this list.

LOTTO

Players: as many or as few (although four is probably a minimum) as you like
Age: everyone loves it
Equipment: pencil, cards and numbered discs

1 My grandmother played this at her Senior Citizens' Club in the 1960s as Housey-Housey; others will know it as Bingo (the gambling form of the game), and still others who go to fairs and fetes will know it as Tombola.

2 Lotto cards and numbered discs can still be bought – you will need the numbers 1 to 90 inclusive – or you can make them yourself. The cards must be nine rows across and three rows deep (see illustration next page) and within the horizontal rows must be five numbers and four blank spaces. Each vertical row contains certain numbers: row one must only contain numbers between 1 and 10; the second row between 11 and 20 and so on until the last vertical row, which contains the numbers 81 to 90. When you are placing numbers on the cards for your players, be sure to make every card include a different set of numbers.

3 You can also make the discs – just cut out lots of circles and number them 1 to 90. Perhaps make a few spares in case some numbers go missing.

4 Now to play. One person is chosen as a caller. They take one disc out of a bag or box at a time and call out the number to the players. Any player who has the number marks it off their card (using a pencil is best because then the cards have the opportunity

	13		30		54	65		81
2		22		44	56		78	
	15		31	49		67		86

of being used again!). The first person to mark off their fifteen numbers on their cards calls out 'Lotto' and wins the game.

5 Those players who are used to Bingo callers will enliven the game by shouting out 'Clickety-click' when the caller says '66'; or 'Two little ducks' for 22.

NOUGHTS AND CROSSES

Players: two
Age: anyone can play, but it is hard to win
Equipment: pencil and paper usually, but can be played on earth or sand for instance by marking a grid with a stick

1 Some people call this game Tick-Tac-Toe, but most know it as Noughts and Crosses. It is thought that a game similar to Noughts and Crosses was played in Roman times as markings have been found at archaeological sites which represent the two by two grid we draw to play this easy, but frustrating game.

2 So, first draw that grid, using a parallel pair of vertical and horizontal lines. Then, each player takes it in turn to place either an O or an X in any of the nine spaces. The object is to get three Os or three Xs in a row – vertically, horizontally or diagonally. By the way, the player who starts the game usually has an advantage so, to be fair, players should begin alternately.

3 As a hint for a winning strategy, whether you play first or second, put your mark in a corner. Whatever your opponent does, put another mark in another corner. It often means that there are two chances at drawing a line of three marks.

4 As each game usually only takes a minute or less, it is best to agree to a number of games or a time limit, or adding the times each player wins to an agreed total. When neither player wins a game it is considered to be a draw.

PYRAMIDS

Players: two can play, but it is best played in teams of, say, four players each
Age: can be tailored to young children's vocabularies, so very good for children and adults
Equipment: pencil and paper

1 Each player, or one player from each team, needs a piece of paper and a pen or pencil. The aim is to make a word pyramid beginning with one base word of about six letters which is added to one letter at a time (see illustration).

2 One person chooses a word – let us assume it was CHAIRS. On the sheet of paper this word is written with lots of space between each letter. Then the aim is for each team to write as many words as they can under every column, with each word being one letter longer than the previous word. All words must begin with the letter at the top of the column.

3 It is much easier if you just look at the illustration!

4 Hint: it is sometimes hard to find a two letter word to start you off – abbreviations may be used, such as 'ma' and 'pa', or foreign words such as 'la'.

5 There is a time limit placed on teams, usually 5 minutes, and the winning team or player is the one which has most words written down that are correctly spelt!

C	H	A	I	R	S
ca	he	at	in	re	so
cat	hot	ate	ink	rip	set
coat	here	able	inch	ripe	site
catch		apple			swipe
					seated

QUIZZES

Players: at least three, but more is better
Age: can be tailored to be suitable for any age
Equipment: pencil and paper for each player

1 It is easy to create a quiz. If you know the ages and interests of those taking part you can tailor the questions to that, or, if a mixture of ages and interests is evident in the people playing, go for a general knowledge quiz.

2 Thinking about your players, make up to ten questions per game. If there is time and interest, you can have another ten questions ready to go.

3 Ask the questions out aloud. Players write down their answers and, at the end of the quiz, each correct answer is awarded a point. If there are six or more players, it is probably good to divide into two teams whose members can quietly confer about answers.

4 Trick questions are allowed, such as: 'What was the name of the Prime Minister of Australia in 1934?' Most people will scratch their heads and come up with answers such as 'Robert Menzies', but the answer you require is 'The same as it is now!'

SHORT STORIES

Players: minimum of two, better with three or more
Age: older children and adults
Equipment: pencil and paper

1 This sounds as if it is an extremely easy game, but it is not! A good vocabulary is needed, so younger children may not enjoy it.

2 The aim is simple. In 2 minutes, each player has to write the longest sentence they can, using words consisting of only one, two or three letters. The sentence must make sense.

3 When you and your family and friends have played this game often, you may wish to alter the rules to make it even harder. Reduce the time limit to maybe 1 minute, or stipulate that every word must be three letters long, or both!

Short Stories example:

I met him and we ran up to her so she saw the dog and cat we had in a bag, but as we ran the dog and cat got out of the bag, so we got a rat.

SPOOF WORDS OR THE DICTIONARY GAME

Players: any number can play
Age: adults and children; the game can be tailored for younger children
Equipment: pencil and paper

1 Depending upon the number of players, the first thing is to agree to how many points must be scored to finish the game perhaps 20 for four or so players?

2 Choose one player to select an unusual word from the dictionary. They announce it to the rest of the players, and then write down the correct definition.

3 Every other player now writes down what they think is a believable meaning for the word and gives their definition to the first player who chose the word.

4 When this player has collected the definitions, they add in the correct definition, shuffle the papers, then number them.

5 Then, in a level voice (trying not to laugh at any definition!), the player reads out all the definitions, while the rest of the players vote for what they think is the true definition.

6 Each player amasses scores by being awarded two points if they are correct, and another point for every vote their own definition receives. A game finishes when one player reaches the agreed number of points.

SPROUTS

Players: best for two
Age: children and adults
Equipment: pencil and a large piece of paper

1 This is a game for the creative as well as those who love a challenge as it is an easy game to learn and play, but quite difficult to win.

2 Begin by drawing seven or eight dots on the paper, well apart from each other. (You could begin with five dots – the more dots the longer the game.)

3 Taking it in turn, the players draw a line joining any two dots, or joining a dot to itself, and then place another dot anywhere along the line they drew.

4 There are only three rules to keep in mind: i) a line cannot cross itself or any other line; ii) no line can be drawn through a dot; iii) no dot can have more than three lines leaving it.

5 The winner is the player to draw the last legal line.

Grey lines = first player
Black lines = second player
Dash line = disallowed move

SQUIGGLES

Players: two
Age: any age
Equipment: paper for each person and pens in two different colours

1 Each player takes a minute to scribble quickly on their piece of paper – the more weird and abstract the squiggle the better it is!

2 Players then exchange pieces of paper and within 2 minutes they must use every bit of each squiggle to make a picture.

3 Artistic ability is useful, but so is ingenuity and imagination. If a third person is available they could judge which is most the inventive overall. Otherwise, the two players must judge their own efforts against their opponent's and have a good laugh!

TELEGRAMS

Players: any number
Age: older children and adults
Equipment: pencil and paper for each player

1 Either choose a word of around fifteen letters long, such as 'strawberries', or each player chooses a letter in turn until there are fifteen letters chosen.

2 Everyone must use the letters in the order given to create a fifteen- word telegram which must make sense. The word 'Stop' may be used for punctuation.

3 The winner is the first player to complete a telegram or, if a time limit is set, the player whose telegram is judged the best at the end of that time.

For example: Send Trunks Right Away Stop Will Be Entering Race Stop Running In Easy Sue

THE POETRY GAME

Players: any number up to around ten, but probably best with four or five
Age: adults will probably enjoy this more than children
Equipment: pencil and paper

1 The wonderful thing about The Poetry Game is that you do not have to be 'good' at poetry or even like poetry – it is played purely for fun.

2 Each player is given a pen and piece of paper upon which they write two lines of poetry which do not have to rhyme, but should scan and have the same rhythm.

3 Papers are then folded to hide the first line and passed to the next player, who reads the second line and writes two more lines. The third line should rhyme with the second line but it is not necessary for the fourth to do so.

4 The game continues with each player having a turn to see the last line and writing two more lines of the poem passed on to them. If there are many players, probably stop at eight or ten lines, and then all the poems are read out to much laughter!

TRANSFORMATION

Players: three or more
Age: any age depending upon word chosen
Equipment: pencils and paper

1 The aim of the game is to alter one word to become another by only altering one letter at a time in the least number of steps.

2 For beginners and young children, begin with DOG and change it to CAT.

> DOG
>
> COG
>
> COT
>
> CAT

3 Staying at this level will mean families will be able to play together, but once you become ambitious (or good at the game!) you will want to progress to six and seven letter words – which can be much more difficult.

WORD AND SPOKEN GAMES

There's some family fun to be had with this range of indoor games. They include the perennial favourite, I Spy, and its many derivatives. Many are for adults only after a good dinner, but there are also plenty for children of all ages and mixed groups.

ANALOGIES

Players: at least four
Age: adults only
Equipment: none

1 Players need to know each other well, or make sure they choose characters that are fictitious, famous or absent as offence can occur in this after-dinner game.

2 One player begins by thinking of someone who would be known to all the other players. The rest of the players try to guess the identity of the chosen person by making analogies.

3 Firstly, they think of categories, such as buildings, flowers, meals, furniture, smells – anything that may help with descriptions. So, a question to the first player could be 'What species of flower would the person be?' For a homely, contented mutual friend who was not at the dinner party, the first player may answer, 'Daisy', and so on.

4 Especially with friends, it is a trap to confuse what the person likes with their real character, so a person who loves champagne at parties, may really be a soggy teabag person without it!

5 Be aware you may lose friends over this game unless you only choose the names of celebrities, but it would not be as much fun!

ASSOCIATIONS

Players: three or more
Age: can be played by children and adults, but groups should have the same standard of ability with words
Equipment: a dictionary for the wary

1 This game must be played quickly, with no player hesitating, otherwise it loses its point, which is to create a long chain of associated words.

2 Sometimes the associations are only in the mind of one player and, if so, they may be challenged and then lose a life if the association cannot be proved. (Note: if the association is proved, the challenger loses a life.) If a player hesitates at their turn, this means a lost life, too. In addition, if a player says they cannot think of any association, they are out of the game.

3 The game continues until only one player is left, and this person is declared the winner.

Associations example:	
Player one:	'Book.'
Player two:	'Page.'
Player three:	'Wedding.'
Player four:	'Why wedding after page?'
Player three:	'Because brides can be attended by a page or pages.'
Player four:	'That is a life of mine gone! 'White.'
Player five:	'Black.'
Player one:	'Coal.'
Etcetera.	

BOTTICELLI

Players: three or more
Age: adults
Equipment: none

1 A wide general knowledge is required by everyone who plays this intriguing game.

2 One person chooses a famous personality, real or fictional, living or dead, and preferably one they know something about. They tell the other players the initial of the surname of the person they have chosen, for instance, 'H' for Ernest Hemingway.

3 Taking it in turn, each of the other players must think of someone whose name begins with 'H' and ask a question of the first player without naming the person they have brought to mind. If the player thought of Adolf Hitler, the question could be, 'Are you a warring European dictator?'

4 If the first player recognises the description, they would reply, 'No, I am not Adolf Hitler.' If, however, the first player does not recognise the description, the player who asked may then ask a direct question which must be answered truthfully 'yes' or 'no', such as, 'Are you in the armed services?'

5 The game continues, with each player asking a veiled question, trying to beat the first player's general knowledge and be allowed to ask a direct question.

6 The first player to guess the correct identity of the personality wins the round and chooses the next character. If nobody guesses correctly after a set time limit, say ten minutes of questioning, the player tells the rest of the players the answer and chooses again for the next round.

COFFEE POT

Players: this is a good game with two, but better with four or six
Age: adults
Equipment: none

1 Like its name, Coffee Pot is a perfect after-dinner game. It is fun, easily learned and comes with guaranteed laughs.

2 The aim is for one player to think of a verb, for example, 'walk' or 'kiss' and they then say a sentence with the word in it – substituting 'coffee pot' for the actual verb. Using 'walk' they may say, 'I wanted to go for a coffee pot yesterday, but it was raining.'

3 The other players can then try to guess the verb and, if one is successful, they then take over. If not, everyone gets to ask questions of the first player, such as, 'Would your sister coffee pot?', 'Can I coffee pot?', 'Do you coffee pot every day?', and so on.

4 If the word is not guessed after every other player has put two questions (or one if there are a lot of players) the player who thought it up gets a point and the next player thinks of a coffee pot verb, and play begins again.

GHOSTS

Players: can be played with two, but great fun with four or more
Age: adults and older children with a good vocabulary
Equipment: pencil and paper for scoring and a dictionary for challenges

1 The rules for Ghosts are more easily explained by running through what could be a game. There are four players in our pretend game. The aim of the game is to contribute to the spelling of a word that you have in mind (although each player may be thinking of something different), but no player wants to complete a word as this would cost 'a life'. If, in fact 'a life' is lost three times, that player is out of the game and then becomes a Ghost!

2 One player begins by calling out a letter, say 'c'. The player has to have a word in mind, but of course is unlikely to be challenged on the first letter. The next player may call out 'h' and have the word 'chicken' in mind. This is good because, even if the rest of the players guess what it is and continue with the spelling, the word does not end with the originator.

3 However, unless a player has a wide and general vocabulary, they would not know that 'chi' is a word – in fact, it is the twenty-second letter of the Greek alphabet. However, assuming that the third player does know that, and says 'e' instead of the predicted 'i', the letters are now 'che'.

4 The fourth player then says 'a' and the first player is in trouble, because there are only two words in the English language beginning with 'chea'. Both are five letter words – cheap or cheat – so player number one has to say either of these letters and will then lose a life for finishing a word.

5 Any player may challenge another to tell them the word they were thinking of when they said a letter, which will stop people not knowing any words but not wanting to go out! However, if the player can name a legitimate word, the challenger loses a life, otherwise a life is lost by the challenged player.

6 Use the paper and pencil to mark down lives lost, or people will try to stay in longer than they should – it is guaranteed!

GRAB ON BEHIND

Players: as many as possible
Age: can be tailored to children as well as adults
Equipment: none

1 This game is also called First and Last, as will become obvious, and it is a game which can be enjoyed by a great number of people.

2 Players decide on a category, such as flowers, cities, car makes, dog breeds, birds or mammals.

3 The first player calls out a word in the chosen category. The next player follows with another word in the same category, but it must start with the letter with which the first player's word finished. Play continues around the group in this form, with players having to think of their word within only 5 or 10 seconds, and not repeating any which have gone before.

4 Anyone who fails to think of a word quickly enough (the rest of the group will usually tell when time is up) or calls out an incorrect word, drops out.

5 The last player to stay in wins.

Grab on Behind example:	
Category is Australian birds:	
Player one:	eagle
Player two:	egret
Player three:	tern
Player four:	nightjar
Player five:	rosella
Player six:	apostlebird
Player seven:	darter
Etcetera.	

GUESS WHAT?

Players: as many as you like, but four to six would be ideal
Age: from four and up
Equipment: cards with simple words naming animals, such as DOG, CAT, PIG, COW, HEN; or, for a variation, verbs such as JUMP, HOP, SLEEP

1 One child leaves the room and the others are shown a word card which is also read out to them.

2 The child is brought back into the room and the other children mime the meaning of the word.

3 The child has three guesses as to the animal or action and then someone else takes a turn to leave the room. A new word is chosen, the child comes back in and the new word is acted out.

4 There is not a specific winner, but everyone has fun.

I LOVE MY LOVE

Players: three or more
Age: adults only
Equipment: none

1 This is not a truth game. It is a make up game, or truth and fiction can be mixed, but the game could become less fun if truth is allowed to interfere with the fun!

2 Taking it in turns around the dinner table or lounge room with coffee and liqueurs after dinner, each player completes the sentence 'I love my love because she/he is . . .', and adds an adjective beginning with A and moving through to Z. So, a game could begin:

'I love my love because she is angelic.'

'I love my love because he is balding.'

'I love my love because he is co-operative.'

'I love my love because she is devious.'

3 The fun comes from players thinking of words which are less than flattering about their partners but, remember, it is not a truth game but played just for fun!

4 There can be winners and losers if desired. A player who hesitates too long in finding a word for their letter of the alphabet, or uses the wrong letter for their turn is out of the game. The winner is the last person left in.

Variation: If you have many dinner parties and tire of the basic game, try this one. Still using the alphabet, you say, 'I love my love with a T, because he is timid, his name is Tim and he comes from Tibet.' The next player follows with, 'I love my love with an H, because she is half-witted, her name is Helen and she comes from Honolulu.' Each player must find a descriptive adjective, a name and a place for their love to come from. As before, truth has little to do with the game!

I Packed My Bag

Players: two or more
Age: any age
Equipment: none

1 This game requires a good memory. Children are usually very good at it so love it.

2 It is very simple to play and can be a lot of fun. The first player starts the round with 'I packed my bag'; then the next player says, 'I packed my bag and put in . . .' and adds an item or items, such as an apple or five books.

3 It continues in this vein with each player having to remember what has gone before them and adding another item of their own on their turn.

4 If anyone omits an item or places it in the wrong order, that person is out of the round, so the winner is the one who remembers most and can repeat it.

Variation: Some people think this variation is easier, while others do not. It is the same game but a rule is made that each person has to add something in alphabetical order. It could go like this, 'I packed my bag and put in two apples, eight books, one pack of cards, ten dominoes . . .' etcetera.

I Spy

Players: two or more
Age: children love it, adults scream after only minutes
Equipment: none

1 Most people have played this game at one time or another. It is a very simple game that children can play for hours, especially on long car journeys, and it is guaranteed to send adults mad.

2 One player chooses an object in the room, or in the car or through the car window and says, for example 'I spy with my little eye something beginning with T.'

3 The first person to guess the spied object correctly then has to have a turn. Good luck!

INITIAL ANSWERS

Players: good for large groups
Age: any age, but a good vocabulary is a help
Equipment: none

1 Everyone sits in a circle and the first player thinks of a letter of the alphabet followed by a three letter word beginning with that letter. The player then says, 'H plus two letters is a farmyard animal'. The next person has to try to guess the word – hen – and then states their own clue, 'H plus three letters is part of the foot' – heel – and so it continues around the circle.

2 Of course, as the game continues, each word has to have one more letter than the previous word and any player who fails to think of a word or fails to guess a word drops out.

3 The last person left in the game is the winner. Choose a new letter for the next round.

INITIAL LETTERS

Players: as many or as few as you like
Age: older children and adults
Equipment: none

1 Everyone sits in a circle and one player puts a question – either as serious or as silly as desired – to the other players. Each player in turn must answer within five seconds with a two-word reply, beginning with the initials of their name.

2 So, for instance, if the question was 'What's your favourite animal?' lucky Ingrid Eastman could say 'Indian elephant', but all Tom Griffith can think of is 'tall giraffe'. It would be up to the group to adjudicate on that one, but it is probably all right!

3 Any player who cannot answer within the time limit, or gives a wrong or inadmissible answer drops out of the round; the winner is the last person standing.

4 When everyone has answered the first question, the second player asks a question and so the game continues.

NUMBER ASSOCIATIONS

Players: as many as possible
Age: adults, although older children may enjoy the game too
Equipment: none

1 One player leads by calling out any number between one and twelve.

2 As soon as the number is heard the other players call out an appropriate association, for example, if the number called is seven, any player could call out 'year itch'.

3 The first player to call out an appropriate association scores a point. Others may challenge and, if the player calling the numbers agrees, the person challenged loses a point.

4 An association may not be repeated and, at the end of the game, the winner is the person with the most points.

NUMBER PLATES

Players: two or more
Age: anyone can enjoy this – for a while
Equipment: none

1 A simple game to save sanity on a car journey. The driver could begin by calling out a number of letters, say seven.

2 Each player then writes down a word consisting of that number of letters, perhaps 'racquet' or 'runners'.

3 Then the players have to keep a keen eye out on the traffic, checking each number plate on the vehicles they see. Parked cars count, too, if you can read them quickly.

4 Whenever a letter in their word is seen it is crossed off and the first player to cross off all seven letters is the winner.

Variations: There are several. One is to list all the letters of the alphabet and cross them off as they are seen – the winner crosses all letters off first. Alternatively, write the numbers one to 100 and cross them off as they are seen.

Another variation is to make up phrases using the letters on the car number plates. So, perhaps seeing PYU would have the children saying Pick You Up; NHH would inspire No Hens Here, and so on. There is no winner here and you'll probably ask them to be quiet before they have finished having fun, but quite a few kilometres (or miles) of the journey will have passed by then!

If you and your family are involved in any way with flying or the emergency services you could use the number plates to practise the Phonetic Alphabet. Using the examples above, PYU would be Papa Yankee Uniform and NHH would be November Hotel Hotel.

PYU • 123

PROVERBS

Players: three or more
Age: adults only
Equipment: none

1 This is a game that will really test your brain power for, not only do you have to know many proverbs, but you have to be sure of the word order too.

2 To explain the game – one player leaves the room while the others decide upon a well-known proverb, for instance, 'A stitch in time saves nine'. The player returns and begins to ask each of the other players, one at a time, any question. Each player must use one word of the proverb, in the correct order, in their answer. So the first player asked replies incorporating an 'a' in their answer; the second player uses 'stitch', and so on. A round for the proverb mentioned above could run like this:

Q: Are you a good cook?

A: Yes, I love following a recipe and enjoying the results.

Q: What talent do you wish you had?

A: I would love to be able to stitch my own clothes.

Q: Where would you most like to go on holiday?

A: I would like to visit London and include Europe in my travels too.

Q: Who is the person you most admire in the world, living or dead?

A: I will keep my answer to the current time and say Nelson Mandela.

Q: What are you having for breakfast tomorrow?

A: Cereal with yoghurt because it saves time.

Q: What do you like to do to relax?

A: I go to the cinema and I read a lot. In fact I have read nine books in the last month!

This last reply should give away the proverb to an astute game player.

TABOO

Players: three or more is best
Age: children and adults
Equipment: none

1 This game is harder than it sounds to play. Put simply, all players agree to make 'taboo' a small word such as 'and', 'the', 'it' or 'on' and then one player is chosen as a questioner.

2 This player puts questions to all the other players about absolutely anything in order to make them use the taboo word. Of course, anyone who does immediately drops out of the game, as does anyone who hesitates for too long in their answer. The last player left in is the winner.

Variation: Harder again is the version of Taboo where only one letter of the alphabet is chosen as a taboo letter, so every word using that letter is taboo. Good luck with this version!

TRAVELLER'S ALPHABET

Players: as many as possible
Age: probably best for adults
Equipment: none (or perhaps an atlas for verification)

1 This is the game for every real or armchair traveller. However, a good general vocabulary is also required to complete the game well.

2 The aim is for each player to finish the sentence 'I am going on a journey to . . .' with the appropriate letter of the alphabet, so the first player begins with A, the second begins their sentence with B, and so on. (When this game has been played for a while, you may want to start at Z and work backwards, or perhaps start in the middle of the alphabet at M.)

3 The next part of the game includes answering the question 'What will you do there?' This must be answered with a verb, adjective and noun all beginning with the same letter as the place you are journeying to.

4 For instance: 'I am going on a journey to France. I shall find fancy fish.' (It does not have to make much sense!)

5 If a player cannot respond they are eliminated. If a player gives an inappropriate or incorrect answer (by using two nouns and no adjective for example) they can be challenged by another player. If the player who put up the challenge cannot compose a more appropriate sentence, the challenged player may stay. If they do, of course, the challenger is out of the game.

TWENTY QUESTIONS

Players: four or more
Age: children or adults, best for groups with similar levels of general knowledge
Equipment: none

1 Some people may know this game as Animal, Vegetable or Mineral, as these categories are the only clues given in this classic guessing game.

2 It is a fairly simple game for those who have a good general knowledge. One person thinks of an object and tells the others whether it is animal, vegetable, mineral or a mixture. Everyone playing must know the exact meanings of the categories to enable the game to flow smoothly:

Animal – includes animal products such as butter or wool, and includes people and animals;

Vegetable – includes anything organic which is not an animal, such as paper and tomato sauce;

Mineral – means things which have never been alive, such as the sun, a television or wallpaper;

Mixture – means the object includes more than one of the above, but it is usual to say what the main element is.

3 The rest of the players are allowed twenty questions, including direct challenges or guesses to find out what the word is (although if the guess is incorrect that person is out of the game.) The player who guesses correctly within the twenty question limit chooses the next word, but if no one guesses the word within the twenty questions, the same player can choose another word.

Variation: Play the game in reverse. One player leaves the room and the rest choose an object. When the player returns they have twenty questions in which to guess the answer. To add a really adult element, include a new category called abstract, which would include non-material things such as the landscape, a sense like touch, smiling, deceitfulness, etcetera.

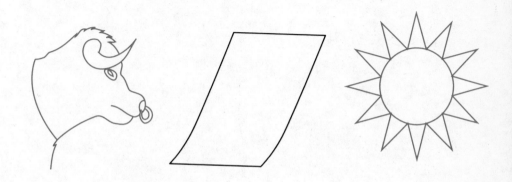

WHO AM I?

Players: four or more, but around ten is best
Age: any age
Equipment: pen/pencil and paper to begin

1 Friendships and family ties can be made or broken with this game, so be careful!

2 Each player writes their name on a piece of paper, folds it over so it cannot be seen, and places it in a container. Then, one by one, everyone draws out a name. The game involves assuming the character and mannerisms of the person whose name is on the paper, and the other players have to identify who each person is portraying.

3 This can be played in an informal way while preparing a dinner party perhaps, or more formally after dinner sitting around having a few drinks! Whichever way it is done, it can be rather daunting to see how your friends and family see your mannerisms!

CARD GAMES

Card playing families were far more common in the early and mid-twentieth Century, before television, computer games and the Internet took over so much of our leisure time. However, because card games have been around for centuries, they are still a favourite pastime, especially for holidays and rainy days when camping. Europe was introduced to card games back in the 1400s and these early games probably had their origins in China.

A pack of cards is such a wonderful, value-for-money investment! It can keep one person or many people occupied for hours. There are hundreds upon hundreds of card games to play just for fun or, for the more ambitious, just to win! For those who like to have a little gamble, there is also a variety of games, which do not necessarily have to be played for money. Counters, or similar pieces, can be used just as well.

The selection of card games we have included here will hopefully encourage new players, and perhaps introduce regular card players to a couple of new games. If you play a particular game and the rules here are slightly different to the ones you are used to, stay with the rules you know. Most rules for card games were not written down for many hundreds of years, hence they vary from country to country and often from family to family.

A FEW TERMS FOR NEW CARD PLAYERS:

Standard pack: has 52 cards and two Jokers. The cards are divided into four suits – two red and two black which have 13 cards in each suit.

Suits: spades ♠ (black), hearts ♥ (red), clubs ♣ (black) and diamonds ♦ (red).

Ranks: for each suit cards normally rank in this descending order: Ace, King, Queen, Jack, 10, 9, 8, 7, 6, 5, 4, 3 and 2, although for some games the Ace is scored as 1. The King, Queen and Jack are known as court or picture cards.

Wild card: a card which may represent any card the holder chooses.

Trump card: a card of any suit which takes precedence over any card of any other suit: hence to trump.

Trick: a number of cards to which each player has contributed one, the player with the best card winning the trick.

Discard: in a trick-taking game, any card played which is not of the suit led or a trump.

Tableau: the dealt cards, especially in Patience games.

GAMES FOR ONE

There have been several books written about card games for one player, known as games of Patience, but here are some of the best. Settle down for a few hours of enjoyable solo fun! By the way, if you have heard that card games for one are called Solitaire, that is also correct, but only in America. There is another game in Britain, Europe and Australia called Solitaire which uses a board and pegs, or marbles (see page 89).

CLOCK PATIENCE

Players: one
Age: children and adults
Equipment: regular pack of 52 cards, no Jokers

1 This is an intriguing game of chance. Do not feel defeated if often you cannot complete it. If you like games of patience, it is one of the most enjoyable.

2 Deal twelve cards face down in a circle representing the positions of the numbers on a clock face, (see illustration) then place one card in the centre of the circle face down.

3 Keep dealing three more rounds, placing a card in the centre of the circle after each round dealt. (Some people deal all four rounds and use the final four cards as the four cards for the centre, while others go further and check that none of the final four cards they have in their hand are Kings. If this happens they make one substitute anywhere on the clock 'face'.)

4 Pick up any of the four central cards and place it under the pile corresponding to its number, so that a six would be placed under the bottom card representing 6 o'clock on the dial. Then take the top card off that

pile and do the same again. If it is a Jack, Jacks go at 11 o'clock (Queens are 12 o'clock), and then the top card is taken from that pile and so on.

5 When a King is turned up, either from the four central cards or from a pile around the clock face, this is put face up in the centre and another central card is taken to begin again. You can see that if any of the four central cards are Kings from the deal, your chances of getting Clock Patience out are reduced.

6 You are only a winner if the last card turned up with all other piles correct is a King! Good luck – it does happen sometimes!

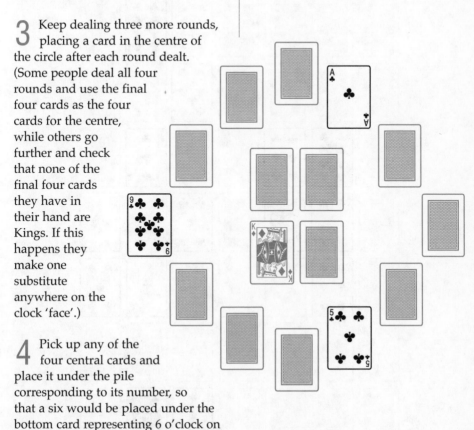

CROSSWORD

Players: one
Age: any age
Equipment: one standard pack with the twelve court or picture cards removed

1 Shuffle the cards and turn the top one onto a playing surface, keeping the rest of the pack in your hand.

2 Each card in turn is played to the board to touch a card already played, either at the top or bottom, either side or at a corner. The aim is to build a square of seven cards each way, in which the pips of the cards, in each row and column, add up to an even number. (See illustration.)

3 The court cards are only used as you would use a black square in a crossword – to serve as a stop. Use as many as you need to complete the game. The pips of the cards between two court cards, or between a court card and the outer edge of the square, must also add up to an even number.

4 When 48 cards have been played, there will be four cards left in your hand and only one square to fill. The player may look at all four remaining cards and choose which is the best to play.

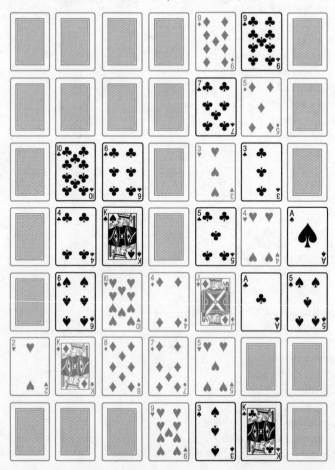

FLOWER GARDEN

Players: one
Age: older children and adults
Equipment: standard pack without Jokers

1 Deal the cards face up into six fans (or 'beds') of six cards each. These are known collectively as the 'garden'. The remaining cards (the 'bouquet') can be held in the hand or spread out in a fan shape on the table.

2 The aim is to build up each suit to king, from a foundation of four aces (as they become available). The exposed or top card in each garden fan is available for play as well as all sixteen bouquet cards.

3 To begin play, place any available ace that is exposed to one side to begin the foundation piles. Search the bouquet cards for any aces.

4 The play from now on is to place cards onto a foundation, or add to a 'bed' in a downward numerical sequence, regardless of suit. A sequence may then be transferred from one bed to another provided the numerical order is preserved. If these plays create the removal of an entire bed, it may be filled by any available card or by a sequence from another bed.

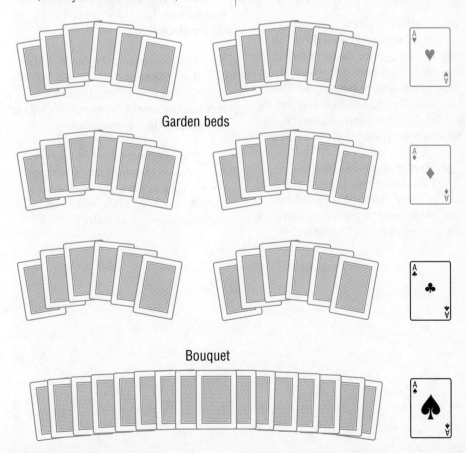

Garden beds

Bouquet

GRANDFATHER'S CLOCK

Players: one
Age: older children and adults
Equipment: a standard pack of cards with the Jokers removed

1 Remove twelve cards from a pack running from 2 to King which are in rotating suits, such as 2♥, 3♣, 4♦, 5♠, 6♥, 7♣, 8♦ and so on.

2 Place these cards in a circle resembling a clock face, with the 9 at 12 o'clock and the remainder following clockwise.

3 Shuffle the rest of the cards thoroughly and deal them out, face up, in eight columns of five cards each. It is from here that the clock foundation will be built upon. The last row dealt, or the exposed row, are the cards which are available for play (see illustration opposite).

4 To play and build on the foundation row is easy. Any card can be taken from the exposed row and placed on the preceding card in the same suit on the clock face.

Therefore, in the illustrations opposite, the 5♦ can be placed on the 4♦ on the clock face, and the 8♠ may be placed on the 9♠ on the clock face, and so on.

5 Once these cards have been moved up to the clock face, the card on the row above is exposed and the one available to play.

6 Additionally, within the tableau below the clock face there are some moves which can be made. Any card along the exposed row can be moved to another column as long as it forms a descending sequence with the exposed card in that column. It does not have to be the same suit, which means a 6♥ could be placed upon a seven of any other suit. This move can free up just the card you need to place on the clock face.

7 Another move to be made within the tableau of cards, is that when a column becomes empty, it can be replaced by any of the exposed cards in any of the other seven columns.

8 Play continues until each of the piles on the clock face has the correct card at the top – an Ace for 1 o'clock, a 2 at 2 o'clock and so on until a Queen reigns at 12 o'clock.

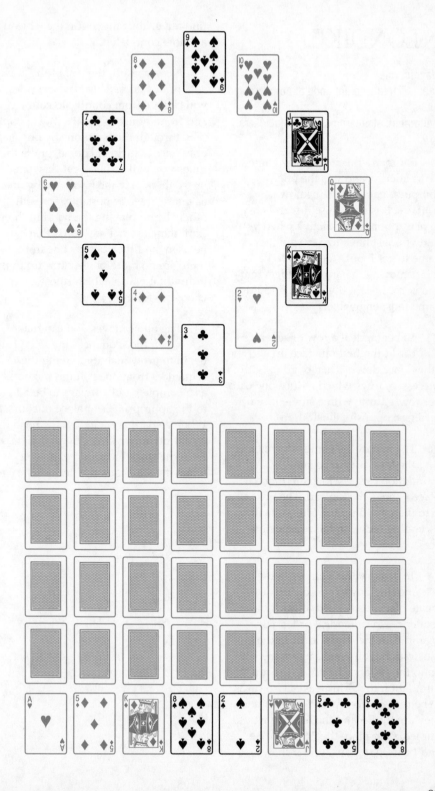

KLONDIKE

Players: one
Age: children who are good at numbers and adults
Equipment: standard pack with no Jokers

1 For many this is the only game of Patience, and it is the one computer game players know as Solitaire. It is easy to set up and easy to play, but most addictive when you find you just have to have another game to get it out. You need to keep it fast-moving, have good judgement and some luck and you will find this game most enjoyable.

2 To begin, deal a row of seven cards, the first one face up and the others face down. Then overlap with successive rows which reduce one card per row, ending with a single face up card (see opposite illustration).

3 The aim of the game is to release the four aces to become foundation cards, which are then placed above the tableau. The next step is to then build up the four suits in ascending order on their respective aces.

4 To achieve this you begin by moving any exposed cards to create black/red or red/black sequences in numerical order. For example, in the deal shown in the illustration, you would move the 10♦ on to the J♣, and the A♥ to the top foundation row. This leaves two cards to be turned face up. Let us presume they are the 7♠ and the 8♠. You would immediately place the 7♦ on the 8♠ and turn up the card under that, to

find a K♠. Your moves on the tableau are now completed.

5 Now you use the rest of the pack or the stock. This is where rules will change from country to country and from family to family. Most people play through the hand one by one and only once, which, of course, limits the times you will actually get this game out. Others play the hand one by one as many times as possible, and still others begin playing the hand in threes until there are not any cards that can be used, and then one by one until there are no more moves! It is up to the individual player which rules you choose to follow.

6 The other moves you can make when the sequences in the tableau begin to grow include moving these sequences from one column to another as a complete unit, always to be added to the appropriate sequence of course. When a space is created at the head of a column only a king can fill this, taken from the stock or from the tableau when it becomes available.

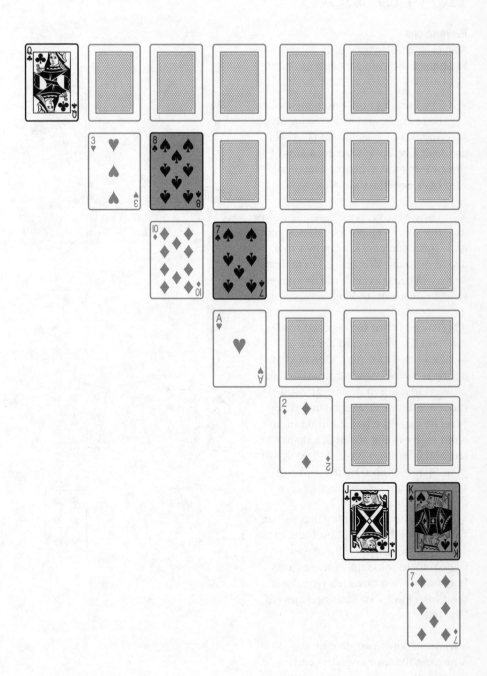

LOVELY LUCY

Players: one
Age: older children and adults
Equipment: standard pack with no Jokers

1 The French know this game as La Belle Lucie, and its attractive layout is certainly a plus as the cards to begin are dealt face up in seventeen fans of three cards each, with one remaining card over. See illustration facing.

2 The objective, once again, is to free the aces to create foundations of each suit which are set out in a row above or to the side of the fan tableau as they become available. The suits are built from ace up to king.

3 The end card (or exposed card) and the single card are the available cards for play. One card at a time is moved onto a foundation or built on to a fan in downward suit sequence. Some strategy is required here. Be careful when building on to a fan as, by doing so, any cards to the left of the built-on cards will be out of play. Spaces caused by the removal of a fan are left empty.

4 When no further play is possible, gather all cards not on foundation piles and thoroughly shuffle and re-deal them into fans of three cards (any one or two cards left over form their own fan). Two such re-deals are allowed.

Variation: Some people play by removing the four aces first and creating the foundation row, and then deal sixteen fans of three cards each.

MAZE

Players: one
Age: probably adults
Equipment: standard pack without Jokers

1 This is not the game to play when you only have 5 or 10 minutes spare. It takes much more time and quite a bit of thought to succeed, but many people believe it is worth the effort.

2 The entire deck is dealt out face up into two top rows of eight cards, followed by four more rows of nine cards each; this leaves two spaces at the right-hand side of the two top rows. Then the four kings are removed from wherever they may have fallen in the deal, leaving a total of six spaces. See illustration page 96.

3 The challenge is to rearrange the cards, one at a time, to get all four suits into correct ascending order from left to right, with one suit following the next, and the top left-hand card following the bottom right-hand card. This is probably much easier to read about than actually to achieve!

4 To play, a card can be moved into any of the six spaces, provided it is in the same suit as the card to the left or the right side of the space. Another rule is that it must be either lower than the card to the right of the space or higher than the card to the left of the space. (For example, a 2♥ can be moved to a space with either an A♥ to its left or a 3♥ to its right. In the example on page 96 the 2♥ could move to space 5.)

5 When a vacancy occurs to the right of a queen it may be filled with an ace as an alternative to the card one lower in suit sequence than the card on the right of the vacancy.

MONTE CARLO

Players: one
Age: probably appeals more to adults
Equipment: standard pack of cards with no Jokers

1 This is a game of luck where the player's decisions have little to do with the outcome of the game. However, it is an enjoyable way of passing some time.

2 Shuffle the cards thoroughly, then deal five rows of five cards (each face up) and put the remainder of the pack to one side. See illustration on facing page.

Maze

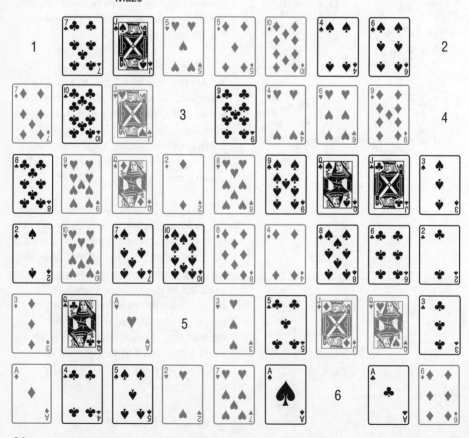

3 The aim of this game is to identify adjoining pairs. They may adjoin vertically, horizontally or diagonally and, therefore, any card has eight neighbouring cards to which it can be paired. This means the player should be extremely vigilant.

4 When all adjoining pairs have been removed, pair by pair, all the other cards are moved to the left to fill the gaps (including to the row above), so they are still in the order in which they are dealt, minus the pairings.

5 When this consolidation has taken place, the remaining cards are dealt face up to replace them to the maximum of 25 cards. After the pack is exhausted, continue to pair up cards until either you have 26 pairs or you are faced with a frustrating combination of cards such as 9-Q-9-Q.

6 There is only one instance where a player can influence this game, and that is when a card can be paired with more than one adjoining card to create a pair. In this case, first pair the cards which will create further pairs when the consolidation of the cards takes place.

Monte Carlo

NINETY-ONE

Players: one
Age: adults or children with good mental arithmetic skills
Equipment: standard pack of cards with no Jokers

1 Players of this game should be able to quickly add up to 91 without becoming too frustrated!

2 Shuffle the cards and deal all the cards face up into thirteen piles of four cards each. Each card has its pips as its value (aces are 1) and the jack is 11, queens are 12 and kings 13. The total of the top cards on all the piles is added to reach the required 91.

3 To manipulate the total, all that has to be done is to move the top card from any pile to another pile. Move each top card as much as is needed to achieve the magic 91 as a total, but at least one card has to be kept in each of the thirteen piles. (Here is a hint – the sequence from ace to king adds up to 91!)

4 The game is finished when the total of the tableau of thirteen piles adds up to 91, or your patience is exhausted!

Layout for Ninety-One

Example of cards adding up to 91

PYRAMID

Players: one
Age: adults and children
Equipment: standard pack of cards with no Jokers

1 This is another game where cards must be paired and, once again, luck plays more than a large part in whether it comes out or not.

2 Deal 28 cards face up in a pyramid shape beginning with one, then covering that with two on either edge, to a row of three and so on, finishing with a row of seven cards (see illustration).

3 Only the fully exposed cards in the last seven-card row are available for play. Begin by pairing off any two cards in this row which total thirteen regardless of which suit or colour they are. The kings are worth 13 and maybe discarded singly; queens are 12, jacks 11 and aces 1.

4 Cards in the stock are turned up one by one and the top card is always available to play. A pair may be made up of two tableau cards, one tableau card and one stock card or two stock cards turned up sequentially.

5 When the stock pile has been dealt once it may be re-dealt without shuffling. This is where the family rules come in again too. Some players do not allow any re-deals; others allow one or even two. You choose!

Layout

Waste-heap

THE FOUR CORNERS

Players: one
Age: usually adults
Equipment: two standard packs of cards
with the Jokers removed

1 Sometimes this game is known as
The Four Winds but, whatever its
name, it can be a frustrating game to
play as success really depends on the
luck of the cards and not decisive play.

2 Shuffle the two packs of cards
together. Lay out twelve cards,
face-up, as follows: one card at a
45 degree angle, then four down the
left-hand side of the playing area
ending with another card at 45 degrees
at the bottom of the column. Copy this
deal on the other side (see illustration
opposite). Space should be left in the
middle to allow for the aces and kings
of each suit to accumulate their suits.

3 Move any king or ace you have
just dealt into the central area and
replace these cards from the pack. The
kings occupy the two top rows and the
aces the next two rows. The idea is to
build up from any ace in the centre,
adding a 2, then a 3 and so on in the
same suit; and to build down from the
kings, a queen first, then a jack and a
10 and so on. At this stage you only
move aces and kings to the centre.

4 Each card in a column forms the
base of what is known as a depot
and the cards at each corner are known
as corner cards.

5 The catch now is that you can
only move any appropriate corner
card into the central piles, but you can
only move a card from a depot (that is
the outer columns to which you deal
cards) to a central pile if it is in the
same row.

6 Now repeat the layout sequence,
dealing the cards in exactly the
same order. Again, if an ace or a king
are revealed they are to be moved to
the central area and replaced from the
deck. Also, any appropriate corner
cards can be moved to the central piles.
If there are any newly appropriate
cards in the depots, they can be moved
if they are in the same row as the
central pile on to which they can be
built.

7 Continue dealing the cards and
moving them to appropriate
central piles until the stock is
exhausted. Now the rules change and
you can move a top card from any
depot onto any central pile in the
appropriate sequence. You can also
move any depot card or corner card to
another depot or corner as long as it is
in descending or ascending order in
the same suit. This is the only time the
player can influence the game – by
thinking about where it may be
appropriate to move certain cards. As
you play the game you will realise the
advantage this can give.

8 When it is felt nothing else can
move, you have another option.
Pick up the corner cards and depot
cards in the order in which they were
dealt and, without shuffling, form a
stock pack. These can then be dealt
around the layout to see if the situation
can be saved. This can be done twice.

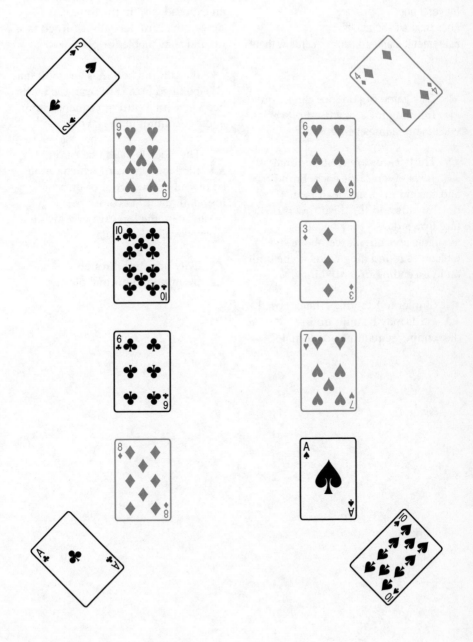

WESTCLIFF

Players: one
Age: children and adults
Equipment: standard pack of cards without Jokers

1 This game of patience can be quite fulfilling for a practised player, with many games being won.

2 Thirty cards are dealt in three rows of ten cards each. Both first and second rows are dealt face downwards and the third row is dealt face upwards. As they become available aces are placed above the tableau as foundation cards, to be built on in ascending order to kings.

3 Similar to Klondike, the exposed cards may be built up in descending sequences of alternate colour to any row, and sequences may be moved to build on others as long as the sequential order is retained. Once an exposed card in the third row is moved the card beneath is turned face up and is available for play.

4 If a column becomes vacant it may be filled by a card from the waste heap or with a card or sequence from another column in the layout.

5 The stock is dealt one card at a time and any card which cannot be placed in the layout or on a foundation card becomes part of a waste heap, the top card of which is always available for play.

6 Only one deal through is permitted in normal play.

Layout for Westcliff

Play in progress

CHILDREN'S GAMES

When children learn to play card games, the knowledge they gain is remembered and can be applied to adult card games many years later. Just learning the ranks and suits of cards, and having fun around the family room table playing these simple games, gives children social skills and heaps of fun that they will not derive from computer-generated games.

BEEHIVE

Players: one
Age: children who can recognise pairs, and adults
Equipment: standard pack of cards

1 Begin by dealing out ten cards face down. Then turn them over face-up on the table in front of you, keeping them in a pile, so you can only see the top card; this is the beehive.

2 Next, deal six cards from the pack face up and side-by-side; these are the flowers. Place the rest of the pack aside face down for the moment.

3 In the six cards making up the flowers, can you spot any pairs? If so, place one on top of the other. This leaves a gap in the flowers, so the card from the top of the beehive is taken and placed in the space left. However, if this card from the top of the beehive can make a pair with any flower card, it is then placed on top of that one and the next card taken from the beehive instead.

4 If all pairs have been made, pick up the rest of the pack and, holding it face down, count out three cards and place them on the playing surface with the top card face up. If it makes a pair with any of the flowers, place it on the matching flower. If this is not the case, continue counting out three cards at a time and looking at the third card to see if it will help.

5 Keep doing this, counting through the stock in threes and adding to the piles of cards in the flower garden – the aim is to get four of a kind – four Aces, four 3s, four 8s, etcetera.

6 When there are four of a kind in the flower garden, pick them up and place them to one side. Then take a card from the top of the beehive and put it down to begin another flower pile.

7 It sounds so simple, that this could just easily go on and you will get all thirteen piles of four cards. However, if the beehive runs out too quickly, that is, it is full of cards that make pairs with the ones already down, then you will run out of 'flowers to plant' and have big gaps. If that happens you know you will not be able to complete the game. Otherwise you may be blocked by having cards in the stock pile, but not being able to get at them because of the three cards at a time rule. That is just the game! Shuffle well and begin again! It can become addictive.

Hint: When you have been playing any card game in which pairs or four of a kind are collected, mere shuffling is usually not enough to separate the cards from their kind. Instead, 'deal' the cards to six or seven different piles in random order and then pick them up in a random way and, if you wish, shuffle them too. That should separate the pairs.

BEGGAR MY NEIGHBOUR

Players: two to six
Age: adults will enjoy this one too
Equipment: standard pack of cards or two packs if four or more players

1 Shuffle the cards thoroughly and then deal all the cards one at a time, beginning from the dealer's left. The players cannot look at their cards, but they may tidy them into a pile.

2 The player on the dealer's left turns up the top card in their pile and places it in the centre of the table. This play continues in a clockwise movement as long as the card revealed is between a 2 and a 10.

3 If one player turns up an honour or court card (jack, queen, king) or an ace, the next player must pay a forfeit. For a jack this is one card, for a queen it is two, for a king it is three and for an ace it is four cards. If one of the payment cards is an honour card, that player stops and it is the turn of the next player to pay the forfeit. This continues until a player paying out cards turns over the correct number of cards with no aces or court cards. When this happens that player collects all the cards on the table and places them to the bottom of their own pile of cards, and then continues play by putting down their top card.

4 As players run out of cards, they are out of the game. The winner is the one left, usually holding all the cards.

CARD DOMINOES

Players: two or more
Age: children need to be able to count well
Equipment: standard pack of cards

1 The aim of this game, often called Fan Tan, is to be the first to place all your cards onto a central pattern of cards in sequence.

2 Firstly, all the cards are dealt face down one at a time to the players. Each player looks at their cards and sorts them into suits and sequences without letting the other players see.

3 The player who has been dealt the 7♦ begins by putting that card face up in the centre. The player to the left continues by playing either the 6♦ or the 8♦ or any other 7. (If this player uses the 6♦ or the 8♦ it must be placed below or above the 7, but if they play another 7, it is placed beside the 7♦.) If any player cannot place a card they can 'pass' and the play goes to the next player on the left.

4 Play continues adding to the sequences, putting down a 7 or passing until the first player has put down all their cards. However, quite often, play continues to create four complete sequences.

CHEAT

Players: minimum of three, but more if possible
Age: old enough to know not telling the truth in a card game is acceptable, but unacceptable at any other time!
Equipment: standard pack of cards, or two packs shuffled together if more than five players

1 This game is also known as 'I Doubt It' for reasons which will become obvious.

2 Shuffle the pack and deal to all players face down until the pack is finished – it is not important if some players have more cards than others.

3 Players pick up their cards, keeping them covered from the prying eyes of their opponents, and sort them into high to low values, irrespective of suit.

4 The whole point of the game is to rid yourself of all your cards through bluffing or outrageous lying regarding their value. The player left of the dealer begins the play by placing one to four cards of the same rank, say all 9s, face down in the centre of the playing area. In fact, the cards do not need to be all 9s, but that is where the bluffing or outright cheating comes into the game. If only four people are playing and using only one pack, anyone else who has a 9 knows that the first player is cheating. They can then challenge by calling out 'I doubt it' or 'Cheat!' before the suspect player's cards are covered by the next player's cards.

5 The challenged player must turn over their cards and, if the challenger is correct, the cheating player must pick up all the cards in the central pile. The player who picks up these cards then begins the next round. If the challenged player did not cheat, the person who challenged must then pick up the central pile of cards.

6 Assuming everything is honest with the first player's call of four 9s, the next player has to place one to four cards down with the rank of 10, and the next must place Jacks, and so on, throughout the round. Of course it will come to be a player's turn who has none of the required rank of card and they will cheat. It is up to the other players to find out which of their opponents are cheating and when.

7 The aim is to be the first player to have no cards left.

DONKEY

Players: three or more
Age: young children like this game, as do older children and adults
Equipment: four cards of equal face value for each player, for instance, if four are playing, use four each of Jacks, Queens, Kings and Aces. Optional, non-breakable items such as buttons, matches or teaspoons can be included in the game – one item less than the number of players. (So if there are four players, only three items are needed per round.) Also a pad and pencil to jot down how close each player comes to being a donkey!

1 Four cards are dealt to each player from the limited cards chosen. Each player examines their cards and decides which are to be discarded. The aim is to accumulate a set of four cards, and to avoid becoming the 'donkey'. Hence, if one player had an ace, a jack and two queens dealt, that player would discard either the ace or the jack because it would seem a good idea to try to save queens.

2 Each player, when they have decided upon their discard, places it face down on the table and pushes it towards the person on their left. Everyone now picks up their new card and the same thing happens round after round as quickly as possible. This continues until one player quietly places four of a kind down in front of them and reaches for an object from the centre of the table.

3 When other players notice this, they too lay down their cards, whether or not they have achieved a set, and pick up an object from the centre.

4 The player who is last will fail to collect an object and gains a letter – D. The first player to be penalised with all the letters of the word 'donkey' loses the game.

ELEVEN UP

Players: one
Age: anyone who can add up to eleven!
Equipment: standard pack of cards

1 To begin, shuffle the pack well and deal three rows of three cards each face up, one below the other. Keep the rest of the pack in your hand or on the table with the cards face down.

2 The aim of Eleven Up is to add up two cards to total eleven (for instance, an 8 and a 3, a 6 and a 5, etcetera). Court cards do not count in this game so, if they are turned up, you immediately place another card on top until there is a number card.

3 The other aim is to keep going until the whole pack is used up, so after you have nine number cards, scrutinise them and work out if any add up to eleven. (See illustration.)

4 In the illustration below, firstly, new cards would be put on top of the J♠ and the Q♥. For example, say they were the 8♦ and the 8♥. Now it is time to look for cards adding up to eleven. There is the 9♠ and the 2♣ – place a new card on both of them, and also the 10♣ and the A♦ need two new cards. Depending upon what they were, you may be able to keep on going without using the cards in the stock pile for a while. Remember, if another court card (J, Q, K) comes up, another card is placed on top until there is a number card.

5 If you can keep on spotting two cards which add up to eleven and you use up the pile in your hand, you have won. If not, try again!

FISH

Players: two to five is best
Age: children and adults
Equipment: standard pack of cards

1 If only two or three players are playing, deal each seven cards, but if there are four or five players, they get only five cards each. The rest of the deck forms the 'fishpond' and is placed centrally, face down.

2 The aim is to collect a set of 4s. Each player sorts their hand accordingly and the player to the left of the dealer begins by asking the next player clockwise or to their left for a card. Say, for instance, the first player has a pair of 4s, that player would ask for a 4. If the next player has a 4 in their hand, it must be handed over but, if they do not have a 4, they can say 'Go fishing!', and the player making the request takes a card from the 'fishpond' and adds it to their hand. If it happens this is the card they requested, the player says, 'I fished upon my wish', and can request yet another card from the same player as previously. If the card is not the same, play moves to the next player.

3 As play continues and sets of four are formed, players place these cards on the table in front of them during their turn, and can ask for another card from the player on their left.

4 The winner is the first player to succeed in placing all their cards down on the table in sets of four. It is somewhat unusual to achieve this, so often the winner is the one with the most sets of four in front of them when the 'fishpond' is exhausted.

GO BOOM

Players: up to twelve, but it is a better game with three or four
Age: young children can enjoy this game
Equipment: standard pack of cards, or two packs if six or more players

1 The aim is to be the first to get rid of all your cards. The dealer deals seven cards to each player in a clockwise direction. Spare cards are placed face down in the centre of the playing area.

2 Each player takes up their cards and sorts according to rank (aces are high). Then the player on the dealer's left chooses a card and places it face up in the centre. Each player in turn then must follow on by playing either a card of the same suit, or a card of the same rank as the player before.

3 If any player is unable to play, they must take a card from the central pile until one card chosen is able to be played. All the other cards picked up go into that player's hand. If all the central pile of cards has been taken, a player says 'pass' and play moves to the next player. (Some people play that the central pile of cards can be re-used by shuffling them thoroughly and placing them face down to form a central pile once more.)

4 At the end of a round (each player has had one turn) the cards put down during the round are examined and the winner is the player who put down the highest card during the round. If two players have that honour, the first to place the card wins. The cards played during the round are put aside and the winner of the 'trick' leads off the next round with a card of their choice.

5 The winner of the game is the one who gets rid of all their cards, or the player with the fewest cards held. The winner usually shows off by shouting 'Boom!'

GOOD MORNING MADAM

Players: four or more
Age: easy game for children and adults
Equipment: standard pack of cards, or two packs if more than four players

1 All the cards are dealt out between the number of players taking part. From the player to the left of the dealer, each player places a card down, face up on a central pile one after the other.

2 If an ace, king, queen or jack appears, certain behaviour is required, and this is where the fun begins!

3 If an ace is turned up, everyone tries to be the first to slam down a palm of their hand on it; if it is a king, the first to salute wins; a jack requires players to shout 'Boo!' and, if a queen appears, everyone tries to be the first to say, 'Good morning Madam' as loudly as possible. Of course, with so much noise it is difficult to hear who wins each time, but that is most of the fun!

4 There is no score or penalty involved, just a lot of noise and fun.

GOOD RIDDANCE

Players: three to six or seven
Age: children who understand sequences and colours in cards
Equipment: standard pack of cards

1 The aim for each player is to get rid of their cards by seeing places their cards can go to build up a pattern of sequences and colours on the playing area.

2 Shuffle and deal all the cards out face down to everyone. It is a good idea for a couple of minutes being allowed for the players to sort their cards in their hands into suits (hearts, clubs, diamonds and spades) and sequences from Ace, 1, 2, 3, etcetera, up to King.

3 The player to the left of the dealer begins and puts out face up any one card they like.

4 The next person can put down three cards, one to the left of the first card, one to the right and one below, BUT the one on the left must be the same colour as the first card and one number lower. The one on the right must also be the same colour as the first card but this time must be one number higher. The card placed below the first card must be the same number as the first but a different colour. Because of these restraints, the player may only be able to play one card.

5 In the following illustration, the first player placed an 8♥ on the table. The next player had the 7♥ but not the 9♥, but also had an 8♠, so could play two cards, not three. The next player had the 9♥ and also a 6♦ and the 8♦ so could play all three cards. Unfortunately though, the next player had no cards that would fit the sequence in any way, so had to miss a turn. It is now the turn of the dealer, and this player was lucky with a 10♥, a 6♣ and a 7♣. Then the next player continues with 8♣.

6 The game continues until one player has put down all their cards – they are the winner.

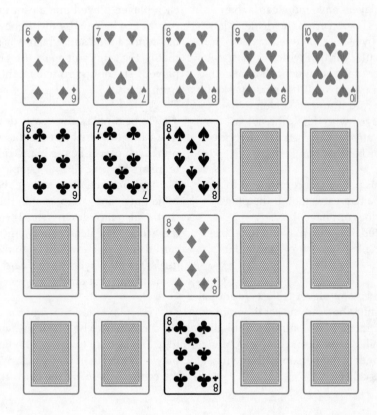

HAPPY FAMILIES

Players: three or more
Age: children love this game
Equipment: a special set of cards can be bought for this game, but it is often played with a standard pack of cards

1 The object is to collect as many complete 'families' as possible. With standard cards, the families are the sets of four. For instance, a player with 7♠ and 7♦ could ask for either 7♥ or 7♣ from any player in the game.

2 To begin, the dealer deals all cards to the players. It does not matter if some players have more cards than others. The player on the dealer's left begins by asking anyone, by name, for a particular card, of which at least one member of the set must be possessed by the first player. If the person asked has the card it must be given to the first player, who if holding at least one card in any set can then ask anybody for a card of that family.

3 This player can continue as long as a request is met. If the player asked does not have the card requested, it is that player's turn to ask someone, by name, for a particular card.

4 When any player collects four of a family they put the set down in front of them. Play continues until all the families have been completed and the winner is the person with the most families collected.

LINGER LONGER

Players: four to six is best, but three can play
Age: older children and adults
Equipment: standard pack of cards

1 This is an ideal game to introduce players to the concept of 'trump' play, in which players win 'tricks'.

2 Firstly, to explain those terms – a trump is a card belonging to the trump suit which is determined before each game is played. A trump card beats any card, even those of the suit led. A trick consists of one card from each player, played into a central pile. A trick can be won by the highest card belonging to the suit which was led, that is, the same suit as the first card played. The only card to beat this is a trump card.

3 To begin play, the dealer deals cards out one at a time, face down, until each player has as many cards as there are players. (If four people are playing each gets four cards.) The remaining cards are placed in the centre, also face down – this is called the 'stock'. The dealer shows the last card dealt (which would be to the dealer) to all players as this card's suit is the trump suit for the game.

4 The player to the left of the dealer commences by playing any card they like face up to the centre. Each player in turn then plays a card into the centre – these are the cards that

form the trick. If possible, players must play a card of the same suit as the one first played – this is called 'following suit'. If a player cannot follow suit, any card may be played, including a trump card.

5 A trick is won by the player who played the highest trump card, or if no trump card was played, by the player who played the highest card of the suit led. Aces rank high for this game.

6 When a player wins a trick these cards are placed face down in front of them and they then draw one card from the top of the stock to add to their hand. And then this player plays the first card of the next trick.

7 Play continues in this way. When a player does not have any cards left they must drop out of the game. The last player left in wins the game.

MY SHIP SAILS

Players: four to seven
Age: good for beginners to card games
Equipment: standard pack of cards

1 Each player aims to collect seven cards of the same suit, such as seven hearts.

2 Cut the cards for the deal – ace high wins. This means that the player who turns over a card which is an ace or closest wins the opportunity to deal. This player deals seven cards, one at a time and face down, to each player. The remaining cards are not used.

3 Each player sorts their cards into suits in their hand and decides which suit to collect. This is usually the suit for which they have most cards at the beginning of the round, but it can change while playing.

4 Now each player takes out an unwanted card and puts it face down on the table. When everyone is ready, they pass these cards to the next person on their right. Players pick up the card offered, sort their hands, decide on another discard and pass it along in the same way.

5 Play continues until one person collects seven cards of the same suit. They then calls out 'My ship sails' and win the game.

OLD MAID

Players: three or more
Age: young children love this game
Equipment: there are special decks of Old Maid cards, but use standard playing cards with one queen removed

1 A player deals all the cards face down, one at a time, to all players. It does not matter if some players have more cards than others. Each player's objective is to get rid of all their cards by matching and discarding pairs of equal face value and not being left with the 'old maid' or lone queen.

2 Once each player collects their cards, they sort out the pairs and place them face down in front of them. If a player has three 5s, they place only two, and keep the other in their hand. If a player has all four of a set, two pairs are laid down.

3 Play begins with the player to the left of the dealer who fans out their cards, not showing the faces, and offers them to the person on the left. This person takes one of the cards offered and, without showing or saying what it is, looks to see if it is of any use in their hand. If it pairs up with one of that person's cards, the pair can be laid face down in front. If not, the new card is added to that person's hand. These cards are then fanned out and offered to the player on the left.

4 Play continues in this way, until all pairs have been laid down and one person is holding the 'old maid' or queen. That player is the loser.

PELMANISM

Players: two or more
Age: an easy game which children can enjoy if they concentrate
Equipment: standard pack of cards

1 Shuffle the cards and spread them face down on a large table or the floor. Place them in rows, or at random in each and every position – the random positioning makes the game a little more difficult.

2 The first player turns over two cards of their choice, keeping them in the same position as they were. If they are a pair the player wins them and places them down in front on the table. If they weren't a pair – and only luck will give pairs in the early stages of the game – they are turned back face down exactly where they were at the start of the game. Everyone must try to concentrate and remember where the cards are when they are exposed.

3 The next player on the left has a turn, and so play continues in this way. More and more cards are revealed and those who concentrate will be able to gain pairs on their turn. If someone turns up a pair they get another go, and so on until they do not match.

4 The player who has the most pairs when the last card is gone is the winner and the dealer for the next game.

PLAY OR PAY

Players: three or more
Age: good for beginner card players
Equipment: standard pack of cards and 20 counters (or buttons or matchsticks) for each player

1 Players are aiming to be the first to get rid of all their cards in this game, which is good for beginners to cards as it concentrates on ranks and sequences of cards.

2 One player deals all the cards out face down in a clockwise direction, one at a time. It does not matter if some players have one card more than others.

3 The player to the left of the dealer chooses any of their cards and place it face up in the centre. The next player to the left then looks at their cards to see if they have the next card in sequence. It needs to be of the same suit and to be one up or one down – for instance, if the first player put down the 9♣ the next player is looking for either the 8♣ or 10♣. (The sequences run from Ace, 2, 3, 4, 5, 6, 7, 8, 9, 10, Jack, Queen, King in each suit.) If the first player had put down an Ace, the next player could play either a King or a 2 in the same suit. The second player places their card face up on top of the first card.

4 Now for the 'pay' part of the game. If any player cannot place the next card in sequence, they must pay a counter into a central pile.

5 Play continues with each player either paying a counter or playing a card next in sequence until all the cards of the suit have been played. The person who put down the last card has an extra turn and plays any card from their hand that they may choose. Play continues with this card.

6 The first player to get rid of all their cards is the winner of the round and takes all the counters from the central pile. All other players must pay the winner a counter for every card left in their hand too.

7 After an agreed number of rounds, the winner of the game is the player with the most counters.

SNAP

Players: two or more
Age: young children love it
Equipment: standard pack of cards, or two packs for four players or more

1 Everyone has probably played Snap at one time, so here is the refresher course.

2 The cards are shuffled thoroughly and dealt out one at a time, face down to all players. It does not matter if some players receive more cards than others.

3 From the player on the dealer's left, each player turns up the top card from their pile and places it next to that pile. If any two cards have the same value, that is they are both 2s for instance, the first person to say, or yell, 'Snap' takes both piles of cards and adds them to the bottom of their pile.

4 If a player runs out of face down cards they can still call 'Snap' when appropriate in an attempt to rejoin the game. But any player who has no face down pile or a face up card is out of the game. A player who yells 'Snap' when there is no match has to pay a forfeit of one card from their face down pile to every other player.

5 The game is won by the player who gains every card.

UNO®

Players: two to ten
Age: from seven up
Equipment: 102 card pack of special Uno cards

1 The cards are shuffled well and each player is dealt seven cards. The remainder of the pack is placed face down with the top card turned face up to begin a discard pile.

2 Apart from the number cards in Uno® there are several word cards too. If they are turned up at the top of the discard pile they have special meanings. The Wild Draw Card is returned to the deck and another chosen; Wild Card – the player next to the dealer on his left calls out a colour and then plays; Draw Two Card – the player to the left of the dealer must draw two cards and the following player begins play; Skip Card – the player to the left of the dealer skips a turn and the following player begins play; Reverse Card – reverses the direction of play.

3 Play begins with the player to the left of the dealer matching the card turned up on the discard pile either by colour, number or word. For instance if a 10♥ is turned up, the player must play either a red suited card or any colour 10. If this player cannot match these plays they draw a card from the face down pile. If they can play that card they do so, if not, play continues clockwise.

4 During play the word cards mentioned above have certain functions. When a player lays down the Draw Two Card the next player must take two cards from the draw pile and miss their turn. The Reverse Card reverses the direction of play. The Skip Card means that the next player to play loses their turn. The Wild Card can be played on any card as the person with the card calls any colour to continue play (they can even call the colour already being played). This Wild Card can be played even if the player has another playable card in their hand. The Wild Draw Four Card is a great card to get as the person playing it can call the next colour played, and the next player also has to pick up four cards and forfeit their turn. Unlike the Wild Card, this card cannot be played when a playable card is held which matches the colour of the previously played card.

5 When a player has only one card left they must yell 'Uno' (which means one) as they place their second to last card on the discard pile. Failure to do this and being caught means that player must pick up two cards from the draw pile. If they do not get caught and the next player has begun their turn, no one can challenge the player with only one card left.

6 If the last card played is a Draw Two or Wild Draw Four card the next player must pick up two or four cards which are counted in the scoring.

7 If the game is still going when the draw pile is finished, reshuffle them and continue playing.

8 Scoring in Uno – the first player to shout Uno and go out scores the points in all opponent's hands as follows: cards up to nine at face value, Draw Two, Reverse and Skip are 20 points, Wild Card and Wild Draw Four are 50 points. The winner is the first player to reach 500 points. (A variation keeps a running total of each player's score and when one player reaches 500 points the player with the lowest amount of points is the winner.)

NON-TRICK GAMES

These games have weathered the test of time and are played throughout the world. Most players would have been introduced to the games as children in a family situation and that is the best way to learn them all. Gin Rummy is probably the easiest to learn, but learn to play any of these games skilfully and they will provide you with hours of fun and entertainment, whether you are a child or an adult!

CANASTA

Players: two to six, but best with four, in two partnerships. If two or three are playing, they play as individuals, not in partnerships; if five play they play in two partnerships with one standing out; if six are playing there are three partnerships with partners sitting alternately at a table
Age: older children may enjoy this, but it is usually thought of as an adult game
Equipment: two standard packs of cards, including jokers, or a specially marked Canasta pack which has scoring values marked on the cards

1 There is quite a lot to learn to play Canasta, but when everyone is at the same stage, it is an enjoyable game. The aim of Canasta is to be the first partnership to score 5000 points. Although it is a part of the Rummy family, there is no advantage in being the first to 'go out', just who gets the most points. For those who are using a standard pack of cards, the cards are scored as follows:

jokers	50 points each
2s, aces	20 points each
K,Q,J,10,9,8	10 points each
7,6,5,4	5 points each
black 3s	5 points each
red 3s	either 100 points each, or 200 in special circumstances

2 All jokers and 2s are wild cards which can stand in for any card. Points are scored by forming 'melds' of cards which are combinations of three or more cards of the same rank, that is, 8, 8 and 8, or Q, Q, Q and Q. These are known as natural melds because they use only the cards of rank and no wild cards. If a meld was made up of 8, 8, joker or Q, Q, joker and 2 it would be known as a mixed meld, because of the mix of natural and wild cards. A meld must contain at least two natural cards and not more than three wild cards. Black 3s cannot be melded unless the player is going out in the same turn. Combinations held in the hand are not counted towards the scoring, only if they are placed on the table are they able to be part of the total scoring.

3 A meld containing seven cards is known as a canasta. If all seven cards are natural cards it is known as a natural canasta and scores much higher than a mixed canasta, which of course has wild cards represented. (There may not be more than three wild cards in any canasta.) Canastas are important as no side may go out unless it has at least one canasta (two for games with only two players).

4 Red 3s are important, too, as they are bonus cards which cannot be melded. Each red 3 has a bonus value at the end of a hand of 100 points, but if all four red 3s are held by the same partnership the value is doubled to 200 points each. However, beware! Only if a side holding a red 3 has made a meld can it claim the bonus points. If that side has not tabled a meld and is holding any red 3s, the bonus scores are applied as a minus when play ends!

5 If a player is dealt a red 3 it must be laid face up on the table and another card drawn from the stock to replace it. If a player draws a red 3 from the stock during the course of a game, it must be laid face up and another card drawn from the stock. If a red 3 is taken up from the discard pile it must be laid face up on the table without any extra card being drawn.

6 Partnerships can be arranged mutually or by cutting for partners. Aces are high, and the two who cut the highest cards play against the other two. Suits rank from spades (high), hearts, diamonds and clubs (low). If a player cuts a joker or there are two who cut equal cards, they may cut again. The player who cuts the highest card overall is chosen as dealer and can also have the choice of seats.

7 Cards are dealt one at a time, face down, in a clockwise direction until all players have eleven cards. (This is for four, five or six players; two players receive fifteen cards each and three players receive thirteen cards.) The remaining cards are placed face down as a stock and the top card turned over for the discard pile. Play continues with the player on the dealer's left taking the top card from the stock. That player makes any melds they can, or adds to those that the partnership have already laid out on the table before finally discarding, by placing one card face up on the top of the discard pile.

8 When melding initially, there is a minimum number of points this meld must accrue, according to the score made by a partnership as follows:

Once either partner has made this initial meld, both partners can make melds of any value and can add to melds they have already tabled, either their own or their partner's melds.

Score of partnership	Value required for initial meld
Minus	Nil
0–1495	50
1495–2995	90
3000 +	120

9 Instead of taking the top card from the stock, a player may wish to take the top card from the discard pile. This is only possible if they already hold two natural cards of the same denomination. The appropriate cards must be laid down first on the table and then the top card (or upcard) of the discard pile picked up to meld with them. The bonus is that the player can now take the rest of the discard pile and immediately add to any and all melds or make new ones. Any unused cards remain as part of their hand. The turn is ended by discarding one card to begin a new discard pile.

10 Other ways players may take the discard pile are if they can meld the upcard with one card of the same denomination and one wild card, or if the upcard matches an existing meld of a partnership.

11 The discard pile can be frozen in certain circumstances, as follows:

It is frozen for a partnership who has not made an initial meld;

It is frozen for a player if a black 3 is the upcard. (It is unfrozen after the player has drawn from the stock and discarded on top of the black three.);

It is frozen for all players if the discard pile contains a red 3 or a wild card. In this case further discards are placed crosswise on top of the freezing card. It can be unfrozen by a player melding the upcard or wild card with two natural cards from their hand.

12 If the stock pile becomes exhausted, play continues so long as each successive player can take the discard pile to meld the top card with the cards in their hand. It is compulsory at this stage for a player to take the upcard to meld with cards already melded and placed on the table.

13 Play ends when either the last card in the stock is a red 3, in which case the player drawing it must put it on the table and make whatever melds he can, but is not able to discard. Or, if a player cannot take the top card; does not wish to meld the top card with cards in his own hand; has no suitable melds on the table to use the

Add Bonuses	Points
For going out	100
For going out, concealed	100 extra
Red 3s (if side has melded)	100 each
Red 3s (if side has melded and holds all four)	100 extra each
Natural canasta	500 each
Mixed canasta	300 each
Minus Penalties	**Points**
Red 3s (if side has not melded)	100 each
Red 3s (if side has not melded and holds all four)	100 extra each
Keeping red 3s in hand	500
For obtaining permission to go out and not being able to	100
For taking a discard before laying down matching cards	50
For melding out of turn	100
For informing a partner of the minimum score required for an initial meld	100
Plus value of card on table (melded)	**Points**
See table page 125.	
Minus value of cards held in hand	**Points**
See table page 125.	

top card, or if the discard pile becomes frozen and it cannot be legally unfrozen.

14 There are several formalities about 'going out' too. No player can go out unless the partnership has laid out at least one canasta (or two canastas in the case of only two playing). A player can go out by melding all cards in their hand or by melding and discarding one card on to the discard pile. In partnerships, a player who is able to go out may, when it is their turn, ask 'May I go out?' The partner can only reply 'Yes' or 'No' and the querying player is bound by this reply. If it is 'No' play must continue on; if it is 'Yes' and it is then discovered he cannot go out, the partnership is fined 100 points.

15 When any player goes out, the game ends, and that player's side receives a bonus of 100 points in addition to the various hands being tallied and scored.

16 Scoring could be thought of as complicated but, if the game is played often enough, it will be remembered! The table on page 127 has all the possible bonuses and penalties which need to be tallied for each hand.

17 A game is won by the first side to reach 5000 points.

CASINO

Players: usually two, although three and four can play
Age: older children and adults, requires skill
Equipment: standard pack of cards, jokers removed

1 This is one of the older card games which can trace its origins back to 15th century France. It is still played in Europe and the eastern Mediterranean countries.

2 The aim is to capture certain cards while scoring the most points.

3 Cut the cards and the player with the lowest card (just for a change) becomes the first dealer. Cards are dealt two at a time, first face down to the non-dealer, then face-up to the centre of the table and then face down to the dealer. Repeat this sequence, so that each player has four cards which are not seen by the other player and there are four cards in the centre, which can be seen by both players. (If three or four are playing, the dealer deals two cards to each player including himself, then two face-up cards in the centre, two more cards to each player and two more cards to the centre.)

4 Cards score their face value from 2 to 10, Aces are 1 and court cards do not count at all. The player with the highest score at the end of the game is the winner.

5 Play begins with the non-dealer placing a card face-up on the table, which is used to capture, build or trail.

6 Firstly, cards can be captured if a table card has the same value as a player's card – this makes a pair of course. A player captures by placing their card face down on the face up card and taking possession of the pair. If two or more table cards match a single card in the player's hand, both may be captured at the same time. For instance, there are two 8s face up on the table and if a player has an 8, he may take both 8s away.

7 It is possible to capture groups too. If the combined value of two or more face-up cards is equal to the numerical value of a player's card, the player can capture all the face-up cards. For example, an 8 could capture an Ace, 3 and a 4 from the centre cards. If there is also an 8 in the centre cards (see illustration) the player can capture all the cards involved at the same time – this is known as a sweep and earns the player an extra point.

8 Court cards can also be used to capture other court cards. The most usual way is by pairing again, but this time if a player has one court card, say a Queen, they may capture either one Queen which is on the table, or three Queens. If there are two Queens on the table, only one can be paired.

9 Building is a skilful way of creating more cards and therefore more score, although the first rule is that the combined total of the cards is no more than ten. There are two ways of building – single and multiple.

10 A single build is when a player builds onto a central face-up card because they are holding another card that is of equal value to the build they are creating and, on their next turn, they would take that build. For instance, if a player holds a 5 and an 8, they can build the 5 onto a face-up 3, and say 'Building 8'. A build can be increased by either player with a card from their hand, provided that the total of all the cards in the build still does not exceed ten and that they hold a card equal in value to the build they are making.

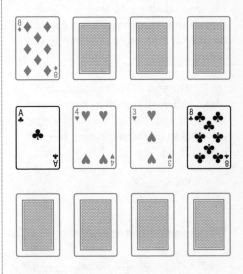

11 A multiple build happens when a single build is altered by duplicating the value, such as a player adding an Ace from their hand to a build of 7 to make a build of 8 (3+4+1), adds to that build another build of 8 (5+3) and says 'Building 8s'. A multiple build is captured by an equivalent value card (an 8 in the above example).

12 If a player makes or adds to a build, unless their opponent plays to the build in some way in their turn, on their next turn the building player must either capture it (by laying down the correct card) or make a new build or add to a build.

13 Sometimes it will happen that a player will not be able to capture or build on their turn, in which case a card from their hand is placed face up on the table in the centre – this is trailing.

14 Once both players have used up their cards, they are dealt a further four cards face down each (two by two) and no more are dealt to the centre.

15 The end of the round occurs when all the cards have been dealt out and the last player to capture cards takes all the remaining face-up cards for scoring.

16 Scoring:

For capturing most cards	3
For capturing most spades	1
For capturing 10♦ (Big Casino)	2
For capturing 2♠ (Little Casino)	1
For each ace captured	1
For each sweep	1

CRIBBAGE

Players: best for two
Age: probably adults, as this is a complicated game
Equipment: standard pack of cards, jokers removed; a cribbage board for scoring (or use pencil and paper)

1 This game is believed to have been devised in the early 17th century by an English poet. The winner is the first player to score 61 points. The method to get these winning points is described below.

2 First, the cribbage board. This was always a wooden board, provided with four small wooden pegs (two for each player), but nowadays all may be made of hard plastic. The board may be placed across or lengthways between the players and both players begin to score from the outside edge. Supposing the first player scores 2 points (for a pair, for instance), a peg is placed in the second hole along. Their next score is 3 points, and this is marked from the position of the first score and the second peg placed three along from the first peg. The next score is an 8, so the first peg is removed and the player leapfrogs the second peg by counting eight along, and so on. It sounds complicated when read, but actually playing the game makes it a lot easier to understand!

3 The game begins by the cards being shuffled and the cards cut to determine the dealer; the player with the lowest card deals. The cards count as their face value with aces low and court cards all valued at ten. All suits are equal.

4 Play starts with the non-dealer cutting the cards and, from the undercut, the dealer then deals six cards each, beginning with the non-dealer. (There are five-, six- and seven-card variations of the game, but only the six-card version is described here). The remaining cards are placed on top of the rest of the pack.

5 The crib, which is an extra hand scored by the dealer, is created by each of the players discarding two cards and placing them, face down, to the dealer's right. This means each player is left with a playing hand of four cards.

6 After these discards to form the crib, the pack is cut again by the non-dealer and the dealer turns up the top card which is laid down on the playing surface. This card is known as the 'start' or the 'starter'. If this card is a jack, the dealer immediately scores 'two for his heels'. The 'starter' card is used to make up the score of both players, and also the crib.

7 The non-dealer now plays a card, the value of which has to be called out, such as eight. The dealer then plays a card and calls out the cumulative total – in this case, if they had a 7 they would play it, call out fifteen and score 2 points for the 'fifteen'. The non-dealer, if holding another 7 or 8, would play it and score 2 points for a pair, as well as moving the total score to either 22 or 23 points. They could also play a 6 or a 9 and create a sequence (or run) with the two played cards – this scores 1 point for each card. The dealer now needs to bring the score to 31 points if possible with their next card – they need to

have an 8 or a 9. In this case they would also score either for a pair (two 8s), a pair royal (three of a kind) or a sequence (cards in a sequence do not have to be of the same suit).

8 However, if the player, at their turn, cannot play a card within the 31 point limit they say 'Go', and their opponent then plays any card which is low enough to keep under the 31 point limit. If 31 is scored, they score 2 points; if less than 31 they score 1 point and at their turn, say 'Go'. Play continues until all the cards are played or another 31 point limit is reached. The player who plays the last card of a hand scores 'one for last'.

9 Points are scored both during the playing of a hand (as mentioned in 7 point above) and when the hands are shown after play. Card combinations score as follows:

10 When scoring in The Show after play, if a player holds a jack of the same suit as the 'starter' card they score 'one for their nob', otherwise the scoring is as above. The dealer, after scoring their own hand, turns over the crib and scores it in the same way as above, except that the only flush allowed is a five card one.

11 Some players also initiate the Muggins rule which is loved in English public houses (pubs). This rule allows any player who sees that their opponent has missed points in their hand to declare them and take the score, while announcing 'Muggins' to their opponent!

12 While the luck of the deal is paramount in Cribbage, there

A jack as 'starter'	2 points
A pair, two cards of the same rank	2 points
A pair royal, three cards of the same rank	6 points (2 points for each of the possible pairs)
A double pair royal, four cards of the same rank	12 points
A sequence or run, cards do not have to be of the same suit	1 point for each card
A flush, four or five cards of the same suit (If a flush is also a run, points are scored for both features.)	1 point for each card
Fifteen, any combination of cards with a face value totalling that number	2 points

are some skills to learn to make the most of the hand dealt. Firstly, learn what combinations earn points and strive to earn them during play and in The Show after the round. The best thing to learn is that discards to the crib are important. Always keep 5s as they can be matched to any 10-point card (to score 15), and do not lead a 5 or any card which brings the total to 21. As around one-third of the pack is worth 10 points, odds are that an opponent will be able to make 31 points and so win the round.

13 As a dealer the score of the crib is gained. On average it is worth five points. As a non-dealer do not help the opposition by not discarding 5s or Jacks or cards in sequence (such as a 7 and an 8) – of course, as dealer this does not apply as the crib and its points are inherited.

14 By the way, the best hand for The Show scores 29 points and it is rare to achieve. It would be a hand comprising three 5s and the Jack of the starter suit, with the fourth 5 as the starter.

Pair, 2 points   Pair royal, 6 points   Double pair royal, 12 points

Sequence, 4 points   Flush, 4 points   Fifteen, 2 points

GIN RUMMY

Players: two
Age: adults, but older children love it too
Equipment: standard pack of cards, jokers removed

1 For play, the cards rank normally, with aces low. For scoring, each card is valued at its face value and the court cards (Jack, Queen and King) are worth 10 points each.

2 The player who cuts the highest card wins the deal and deals ten cards face down to each player, one at a time, beginning with their opponent. The next card is dealt face up and placed on the table as the first card in the discard pile. This is known as the upcard. The rest of the deck is placed face down next to it as the stock.

3 As the objective of play is to create melds of groups or sequences, players begin by sorting their cards into pairs, and sequences or three of a kind if they are lucky enough to have been dealt this type of hand. In Gin Rummy the aim is to achieve the melds in your hand. Players do not lay melds on the table as play progresses, only when one player ends the hand by 'going gin' or 'knocking'.

4 The non-dealer begins play by deciding if they want the upcard. If they decide it is needed, it is offered to the dealer. If the dealer does not want it, the non-dealer takes a card from the top of the stock and places it in their hand. The player who takes a card must then discard one.

5 In subsequent turns each player takes either the top card from the discard pile (face up) or the top card from the stock (face down), adds it to their hand and then discards one card. Keeping a straight face when making a meld is a good way to practise playing Gin Rummy.

6 There are two ways to go out in Gin Rummy, as mentioned in point 3 – 'going gin' or 'knocking'. Going gin usually gains more points than knocking but if a player has a nearly melded hand early on in the game, it is worth knocking as it is then hoped the opponent has plenty of unmatched cards (or deadwood), in their hand.

7 To 'go gin' a player has to meld all ten cards in matched sets. The time to declare this is when it is their turn and all their cards are laid face up on the table. The opponent may lay down their own melds, but may not lay off any cards to the winner's melds.

8 Knocking is an alternative, slightly risky, way of going out. It can only be contemplated if the deadwood in a player's hand add up to 10 points or less (for instance, the player is holding an A♥, 2♠ and 5♣), which add up to 8 points. A player can only knock at their turn. They draw a card in the usual way, knock on the table and discard a card face down. Then they lay out their hand face up, grouped into melds and unmatched cards. Their opponent must immediately lay out their cards on the table, also grouped into melds and unmatched cards, but this player can lay off unmatched cards to the knocking player's melds if possible. Each player's deadwood cards are then totalled for comparison. The

Player A

Player B

illustration shows Player B's knocking hand – three threes-of-a-kind and one card which was 10 or less points. Player A was left holding three Kings which could be laid down, but the two Jacks, two Queens, two 6s and a 2 could not and created a deadwood total of 54. Taking away Player B's deadwood total of 6, this player scored 48 from this hand, which was much more than the 25 they would have achieved from waiting and going gin.

9 Scoring is as follows:
- For going gin a player receives 25 points bonus in addition to the value of their opponent's deadwood cards.

- If a player knocks and their deadwood count is less than that of their opponent, the knocker wins the hand and scores the difference between the two deadwood counts.

- If a player knocks and their opponent's deadwood count is lower than or the same as his, the opponent has undercut the

knocker and wins the hand. (There is a risk involved as mentioned above.) For this the opponent scores a 25 point bonus and the difference between the deadwood count.

10 If neither player goes out in either way and there are only two cards left in the stock, the game is declared a no game and no points are scored. The same dealer would deal the next hand.

11 A running total is kept on paper of each player's score. When a player wins a hand a line is drawn under their score (this is called a box). The first player to reach 100 or more points wins the game and has 100 points added to their score. If their opponent has failed to win a hand, the winner receives double the score. For every hand won both players receive an additional 25 points.

RACING DEMON

Players: two to eight
Age: all the family
Equipment: standard pack of cards with jokers removed for each player; pencil and paper for scoring

1 With more than four players, this game can become hectic, but is always fun. Each player needs good observation skills, quick card skills and probably a little luck to win and beat the Demon!

2 You will need a large table or even a cleared floor space with lots of room in the middle. Each player has their own pack of cards which needs to have a different design on the back. It is possible for a game including more than four players to use a non-playing referee if it is thought that tempers could become frayed. This job can rotate, with one player standing out each round.

3 Each player shuffles their pack and the referee (or one nominated player) shouts 'Go!'. Each player deals thirteen cards face down in front of them in one pile. They are turned over so the top card is now face up and placed on the playing area. Four cards are now dealt face up next to this pile as the layout below shows.

The K♦ is the top card of the pile of thirteen cards, while the other four cards are the next deal.

4 The remaining cards are held face down in the players' hands. The aim now is to get rid of the thirteen cards on the left as quickly as possible. Cards can be unloaded into an ascending sequence of A, 2, 3, 4, 5 etc to J, Q and K, so the first thing is that everyone is looking for Aces to create the foundations for the sequences. In addition, the rules state that sequences must be used in suits – in other words, a 7♦ cannot be placed on top of a 6♥, and only one of each number can be used in the sequence. Those are the little things that a referee will need to watch!

5 Players begin to look for Aces (unless they are lucky enough to have one showing either as the top card of the left-hand pile or in the row of four already dealt) by going through the stock in their hands three-by-three. While this is being done, players also need to keep an eye out for others finding Aces in their hands – these are placed in the middle of the playing area and then everyone can build on these Aces. For example, a player is looking for Aces in their hand but notices that another player has placed an A♥ in the centre. As soon as this is seen, they pick up their 2♥ and slap it down on top. It should be remembered that every other player has a 2♥ and they want to get rid of their cards too!

6 If it is thought everything is already happening at once, there is still more to do. To help decrease that pile of thirteen cards to the left, spaces can be filled in the line of four

with the top one at any time, and a player can also begin to build their own sequences from their hand and the pile to the left of these cards in the line of four (see above). These sequences must be consecutive cards which run downwards and they must be alternate colours as seen in the example. Only the bottom cards in each sequence are available to play into the middle sequences. But once the 3♣, for instance, had gone to the middle, the 4♥ would be available to play.

7 There are endless possibilities from using this system. In the example above, if a red Jack appears in a player's hand stock, it can be placed on the Q♠, and the 10♠ can be placed on it from the pile of cards, so reducing it by one again. Remember, the aim of this game is to get rid of all the cards from the left hand pile of thirteen while getting as many cards in the middle as well, and then shouting 'Out!'. The game then stops. It should

be noted, however, that the winner of the game is not necessarily the person who disposed of their pile of thirteen most quickly.

8 First score comes from the sequences in the middle. Each is broken up and the cards returned to the owners (that is why the different design on the back of each pack is so important). The number of cards left in the main pile of thirteen is added up and that number is subtracted from the number of cards placed in the middle. For instance, if there were 21 cards in the middle, but still nine cards left in the pile for one player, that player's score would be 12.

9 The winner of the round (the person who shouted out) adds three points to the total number of cards they had in the middle. Using the example above, there were 21 cards in the middle, so they scored 24 points as a bonus for being the first out.

TRICK GAMES

Many people would argue that the following games are not family games, but if these complicated and thoroughly enjoyable games are learnt in the family environment, they will be a social asset forever! Taking on Bridge when retirement is close means that you will be learning strategies for years but, on the other hand, people who learnt Bridge as children say that they are still learning at retirement! Of the following games, Bridge would be the most popular (and the most complicated) and there are hundreds of books written on plays and strategies. There are also a great many Bridge clubs around the world, who enthusiastically welcome new players. Enjoy!

BÉZIQUE

Players: two
Age: adults
Equipment: two standard packs of cards, with identical back designs

1 This card game originated in France and is based on games played nearly 400 years ago. A German game, Penuchle, is similar and it is that version which travelled to America and is now known as Pinochle there.

2 Bézique uses the packs of cards with the 2s to the 6s removed, and the cards rank Ace (high), 10, K, Q, J, 9, 8, 7.

3 The objective of the game is to make winning melds or declarations, and to take tricks containing scoring cards known as brisques.

4 The dealer gives eight cards to the players face down, dealing three, two and three cards at a time. The next card is placed face up on the table to indicate the trump suit for the hand. If this card is a 7, the dealer immediately

scores 10 points. The remaining cards are turned face down in a pile to form the stock.

5 There are two stages of play. To begin, the first stage lasts as long as there are cards in the stock. The non-dealer leads first, and afterwards the winner of each trick leads. After each trick the winner may make any declaration (see point 7) and then both players draw cards from the stock to replenish their hands, with the winner of the trick drawing first. During this first stage players do not have to follow suit. A trick is taken by the higher card of the suit led or by a trump card. If cards of equal value are played, the card that led takes the trick.

6 The second stage of play begins when the stock is gone. For this stage, the final eight tricks, the players must follow suit, although they may trump if they cannot follow suit. The winner of the last trick scores 10 points.

7 Declarations can be made after winning a trick. These include:

Common Marriage (King and Queen of non-trump suit)	20
Royal Marriage (King and Queen of trump suit)	40
Any four Jacks	40
Any four Queens	60
Any four Kings	80
Any four Aces	100
Sequence A, 10, K, Q, J of trump suit	250
Single Bézique (Q♠, J♦)	40
Double Bézique (both Qs♠ and both Js♦)	500
7 of trump suit	10

Only one declaration combination can be made at a time after winning a trick, but if a player's exposed cards show a second possible declaration, they can announce that they will declare it when they next take a trick. No card may form part of a second similar declaration, for example, a J♦ in four Jacks cannot form part of a second declaration of four Jacks, but could form part of a single Bézique.

8 At the end of the game, brisques, which are every ace and every 10 taken in a trick, count 10 points each. The game is usually 1000 or 2000 points up.

CONTRACT BRIDGE

Players: four, in two partnerships
Age: usually adults
Equipment: one/two standard packs of cards

1 Thought of as the most sophisticated, intellectual card game, Contract Bridge, or Bridge as it is usually known today, is part of the Whist family which had its origins at least back in 17th century Europe. It is said that Bridge was invented in the 1930s by an American billionaire.

2 Basically, the object of Bridge is to win tricks, and thereby a partnership wins a rubber, by winning the most points in the best of three games. A game is won by scoring 100 points, earned by taking tricks. It should be noted this simple summary gives away nothing about the complexity of the bidding, the contract and the scoring involved in the game. There have been a great many books written on specific topics in bridge, such as open bids or bidding in general, as well as hundreds on the whole game. Most towns, and certainly suburbs in cities world-wide, have Bridge Clubs which welcome players of all standards. These following instructions are only the very minimum to assist a beginner wishing to play.

3 The four players are seated in pairs across a table from each other. They are conventionally known as North, South, East and West.

It is usual to have two standard packs of cards, jokers removed, in different designs which are used for alternate hands. One pack is used by the partnership, North-South, the other pack by East-West. Each player needs a score pad, although in some social bridge games only one player keeps score.

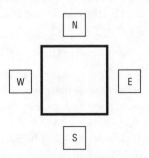

4 The cards are ranked as normal, Ace high and 2s are low, but in this game suits are ranked also: spades (high), hearts, diamonds and clubs (low). When players have drawn for, or agreed, partnerships, they then draw for deal – highest card wins. If cards are tied in value, the highest suit takes the deal.

5 Dealer selects a pack and offers it to the player on their left to shuffle, who in turn offers it to their partner to cut. The dealer then deals out all the cards, one at a time face down, beginning with the player on the left. Players pick up their cards and sort them into suits, colours alternating, with a descending rank. A sample sorted hand is shown below.

6 Bidding is probably the most difficult part of bridge to learn and implement. Bidding – it is also known as the auction – begins with the dealer. Players bid individually, with partnerships competing for the right to nominate the trump suit or play no trumps. Bidders declare the number of tricks they will attempt to make with their chosen suit, such as 2♠. This is known as the contract. If it is accepted and then the partnership fulfils it, they are rewarded with points. If the contract is not fulfilled of course they are penalised. To make things even trickier, a bid such as Two Spades above actually means that the partnership believes it can achieve eight tricks. The convention of bidding in bridge only takes into account the additional tricks a bidder believes the partnership can make over six tricks. Hence, a bid of 'four no trumps' offers that the partnership will make ten tricks in all, if no suit is trumps. A player can also call pass, double or redouble. (These terms are explained further on.)

7 As the auction continues, each successive bid must be higher than the previous bid. This can be by calling a greater number of tricks or by naming a higher ranking suit. For example, if someone has just called 2♦, a call of 2♠ is higher, because

spades is the highest ranking suit. A no trumps call rates higher than any suit.

8 To evaluate one's hand before bidding, there are ways of estimating how many tricks could be made from the hand. High cards, trump cards and low cards in long suits usually take the tricks, so firstly give yourself points for your highest cards as follows: Ace (4 points), King (3 points), Queen (2 points) and Jack (1 point). If the hand totals 11 points or more it is an above-average holding of high cards. With trumps, if you are short in a suit (that is, you only have one, two or no cards in that suit) you will be able to trump your opponent's high cards. Therefore, add more points as follows: void, or no cards in a suit (3 points), singleton, one card in a suit (2 points), doubleton, two cards in a suit (1 point). Make allowances for long suits too: five-card suit (1 point) or six-card suit (2 points), and so on.

9 Bidding takes time to learn well, as does playing in partnerships. Beginners are advised to bid as naturally as possible, always bidding to the full strength of your hand. Under-bidding usually is not rewarded because if more tricks are scored than contracted for, they are only entered 'above the line' (see scoring) and score little extra. Overbidding can sometimes be justified but only if you will end up scoring more than the penalties which will be imposed. Bidding systems proliferate in bridge. Your partner will have one and your bridge club will promote one. In addition you will borrow or buy a book to improve your game and there will be another. Whichever system you learn, ensure your partner knows it too, because deviations from

conventions are more likely to deceive your partner than anyone else.

10 Some terms you need to know: *'pass'* – the player places no bid;

'making the book' – refers to the first six tricks taken by the contracted bidders;

'grand slam' – when a side bids and wins the maximum 13 tricks in a hand;

'doubling' – when a player says 'double' after any of their opponent's bids because they believe they could prevent them making their bid if it became the contract. A bid that has been doubled can be overbid in the usual way by either partnership. If, however, it does become the contract and succeeds, the contracting players' score is doubled. Should the bidders fail or not make their contract, the side that doubled gets twice the score than it would otherwise have had.

'redoubling' – refers to when either player of the bidding partnership of a bid which has been doubled, confirms their confidence that the bid can be made. A bid that has been redoubled can be overbid in the normal way. A redoubled bid affects the scoring and, if successful, redoubling doubles the doubled score!

'the declarer' – refers to the player in the contracting side who first made a bid in the trump suit of the contract. They play both hands of the contracting partnership's game.

11 The opening lead is held by the player to the dealer's left, who plays the first card after the bidding ends. From then on the winner of each trick makes the next lead. A player may lead any card, and the other three players must follow suit if possible. If a player cannot follow suit, they may play any other card in their hand.

12 As soon as the opening lead has been made, the declarer's partner lays down their cards face up on the table, sorted by suit, with trumps to their right. The exposed cards and the declarer's partner are now referred to as 'dummy' for the hand. Only the declarer can choose the cards to play for the dummy hand – the dummy partner only participates to place the specified card on the table.

13 If none of the four cards is a trump, the trick is won by the highest card played, in the suit led. If one or more of the four cards is a trump, the trick is won by the highest trump. But when a 'no-trump' bid becomes the contract, all suits have equal rank and the highest card in the suit led always wins the trick.

14 The declarer for their side, and either opponent, gather tricks won and place them face down on the table in a convenient place where they are easily seen and counted. Usually the first six of the declarer's tricks are placed in one group so that it is clear how many extra tricks have been made.

15 Over the page is a scoring table for bridge. Learn the bonuses and penalties as it will stand you in good stead as a team person!

Some explanations of the above sections follow. The scoring pad is divided into We and They on the left and right hand side respectively, with a line drawn across both columns about half way down.

This last line gives rise to the phrases 'above the line' or 'below the line' in scoring.

16 Firstly, trick points are entered below the line. Only the declarer's side can score trick points on a hand, and only if the contract is made. Thus, only the odd or extra tricks contracted for are scored below the line. Premium points are scored above the line, by both sides in any

WE	THEY

hand. Undertricks are scored if the declarer's side fails to make the contract. The number of tricks by which the partnership has failed are known as undertricks and are credited to the opponent's side above the line.

17 A partnership is 'vulnerable' if it has won its first game toward the rubber, so it is possible for both partnerships to be vulnerable at the same time.

18 The first side to reach a score of 100 or more, either in one or more hands, wins the game. A horizontal line is drawn below the trick scores of both sides and the trick scores for the next game are entered below this line.

19 When one side has won two games, the rubber ends. Look at the table to see how many points this winning side can add to their total. All trick and premium points are totalled and the side with the higher total wins the rubber.

Trick score: below the line	♣	♦	♥	♠	NT
First trick over six bid and made	20	20	30	30	40
Subsequent tricks bid and made	20	20	30	30	40
Doubling doubles trick score					
Redoubling doubles doubled score					

Premium points: above the line	Not Vulnerable	Vulnerable
Small slam	500	750
Grand slam	1000	1500
Each overtrick undoubled	trick value	trick value
Each overtrick doubled	100	200
Each overtrick redoubled	200	400
Making a doubled or redoubled contract	50	50

Rubber, game and partscore: above the line	
For winning rubber, if opponents have won no game	700
For winning rubber, if opponents have won one game	500
For having won one game in an unfinished rubber	300
For having the only partscore in an unfinished rubber	50

Honours: scored by either side above the line	
Four trump honours in one hand	100
Five trump honours in one hand	150
Four aces in one hand, no trump contract	150

Undertricks: scored by opponents above the line	Undoubled	Doubled	Redoubled
Frist trick, not vulnerable	50	100	200
Subsequent tricks	50	200	400
First trick, vulnerable	100	200	400
Subsequent tricks	100	300	600

EUCHRE

Players: four in two partnerships
(although there are versions for two-
and three-handed euchre)
Age: usually thought of as an adult game
Equipment: 32 cards, made up from a
standard deck with the 6s, 5s, 4s, 3s and 2s
removed

1 This game is derived from an old
French game and dates from the
1800s, possibly even the late 1700s. For
a time in the mid-18th century it
became the national game of the
United States, until overtaken by Whist
and Bridge.

2 Aces rank high, and 7 low. The
jack of trumps (called the right
bower) ranks as the highest trump and
the jack of the same colour (known as
the left bower), ranks second.
Therefore, if hearts are trumps, the
ranking would look like the illustration
below:

3 The objective of the game is
simple – each partnership tries to
win the most tricks.

4 Players draw for the deal and the
lowest card deals. Each player is
dealt five face down cards, either two
and then three, or three and then two.
The dealer then turns up the next card,
which indicates trumps. (The deal
passes clockwise around the table.)

5 Each player can either accept or
reject the trumps suit, beginning
with the player on the dealer's left. To
accept, the player only has to say 'I
order it up' and the dealer discards one
of the cards from their hand and adds
the face-up card to it. To refuse, the
non-dealer says 'I pass' and the dealer
puts the face up card at the bottom of
the stock. When one player has
accepted the trumps, play begins. If all
players reject the trump suit, the
'eldest' player (the player to the
dealer's left) is entitled to name a suit
for the trumps (not the one already
rejected) or pass. Each other player has
the same entitlement. If no one names
a suit in this round, the hand is thrown
in and the deal passes to the next
player on the left.

6 The player who accepts trumps is
called the 'maker' and has the
opportunity to play without their
partner, in which case they say, 'I play
alone'. The partner then lays their
hand face down on the table.

7 The opening lead is made by the
player to the left of the dealer,
unless the maker plays alone, when the
opening lead is made by the player to
his left. Players must follow suit to the
card led but, if unable to, they may
play any card. Although there is no
obligation to trump or win the trick,
the object of play is to win the majority
of tricks – at least three. The trick is
won by the highest trump or the
highest card in the suit led. The winner
of the trick leads the next.

Right   Left
bower   bower

8 If a partnership makes (wins) all five tricks it wins the 'march' and scores two points for the side. If the maker is playing alone and achieves a march, they score 4 points. If a making side wins four or three tricks, they score 1 point, but if they fail to win three tricks they are said to be 'euchred'. In this case, the opponents score 2 points.

9 A game is generally 5 points and, while counters can be used to keep score, the more usual way is to use one of the 3s and a 4, which have been discarded. One card is used face up and the other face down for each scoring position as follows:

Euchre scoring

Five Hundred

Players: three (although there are four-, five- and even six-handed variations)
Age: usually adults
Equipment: as for Euchre – 32 cards, made up from a standard deck and one Joker, and with the 6s, 5s, 4s, 3s and 2s removed

1 Five Hundred is part of the Euchre family of card games and was invented in the early 1900s in America, where it is very popular. It is also popular in Australia.

2 The aim of the game is to be the first player to score 500 points, by winning tricks by bidding and establishing a contract.

3 In the trump suit cards rank as follows: joker, right bower (jack of the trump suit), left bower (other jack of the same colour), A, K, Q, 10, 9, 8, 7. In no-trump hands there are no right and left bowers. The holder of the joker may use it to represent any suit they prefer, and the joker then automatically ranks as the highest card of that suit and takes any trick to which it is led or played.

4 Players cut to deal and the lowest ranked card wins (kings are high, ace low and joker lowest). Ten face down cards are dealt to each player in 'packets' of three, then two, then three and finally two. The remaining three cards are placed face up on the table and called the 'widow'.

5 Now the bidding begins. Each player studies their ten cards and then makes a bid specifying the number of tricks they intend to take and their choice of trumps. The lowest number of tricks that can be bid is six, with the highest being ten, or a player can pass A player who passes cannot make another bid in that round of play. For bidding the calls are ranked: no trumps (highest), hearts, diamonds, clubs and spades (lowest). Each bid carries a points value that is awarded to the player whose bid is successful, or is deducted from their score if they are not successful in reaching their bid, as seen below:

Tricks	6	7	8	9	10
No trumps	120	220	320	420	520
Hearts	100	200	300	400	500
Diamonds	80	180	280	380	480
Clubs	60	160	260	360	460
Spades	40	140	240	340	440

Two other bids are possible – a misère (250 points) or an open misère (520 points). The first means that the player thinks they will not win any tricks in a no-trump game. If this bid fails, the opponents score 10 points each for every trick the bidder wins. An open misère is the same bid as a misère but the bidder must lay their hand face up before play begins so the other players can see the hand as it is being played.

6 The player who made the highest bid now must try to carry out their contract. Before play begins the highest bidder has the option of picking up the 'widow' and discarding three cards from their original hand face down on the table. They then play the opening lead. Play continues to the player's left with players responding by following suit where possible, otherwise they can play any card. A trick is won by the highest trump or the highest card in the suit that was led. The winner of one trick leads the next. The joker can be played at any time except, when a no-trumps was bid, the joker can only be played if the player has no card in the suit that was led. The player then must declare the suit it represents, but it cannot be a suit in which they had no cards at the beginning of the hand.

7 Each player keeps the tricks they win and at the end of the hand they are counted up and 10 points awarded for each trick won. If the highest bidder makes the contract, points are awarded as shown in the table above. If the bidder wins all ten tricks the score is either 250 points or the score in the table, whichever is the greater. If the bidder fails to make the contract the number of points is deducted from their score. This makes it possible for the bidder to end up with a minus score. It is marked on the scoring sheet by circling it.

Variation: The most popular version of this game in Australia is the four-handed version. Four players play in two partnerships using 43 cards, with the 2s, 3s and black 4s taken out and a Joker added. The dealer is chosen at random. If misère or open misère is bid the bidder's partner drops out and the bidder plays alone. Misère can only be bid if someone else has bid 7 of a suit, but an open misère bid can follow any other bid. The highest bidder can pick up the three widow cards without showing them to anyone and making three anonymous discards. The difference in scoring in the four-handed game is that partners keep their scores together, in which case it is the first partnership to reach 500 that wins. The game is lost by a partnership that reaches a score of minus 500, which is called 'going out the back door'.

HEARTS

Players: three to seven
Age: all the family, and particularly all adults enjoy this game
Equipment: standard pack of cards, with the 2s discarded as follows to balance the number of Players: one 2 if three play; none with four; two 2s with five; none with six; three 2s with seven (but leave the 2♥)

1 Hearts is known as an avoidance game, meaning it is based on the principle of not taking penalty cards (which are all the hearts) rather than winning tricks. It is particularly important not to win any tricks containing hearts. This game has been entertaining families since the nineteenth century.

2 The cards rank with Ace high and there are no trumps.

3 Choice of first dealer is by low cut and the dealer deals all cards out one at a time, face down, beginning with the player to their left and continuing clockwise.

4 This same player to the dealer's left is the one to lead the first trick. Each successive player follows suit if possible, but if they do not have any of a particular suit they may discard any card. Obviously it is a good idea to play a heart; in fact, a player's highest heart should go in this situation.

5 Hearts can be a simple game, but there are a few tactics to learn and observe which will make it far more skilful and mean that you win more – by taking fewer and fewer tricks containing hearts. For instance, if you

are first or second to play, play a low card whatever the suit because you are unlikely to win the trick and take an unwanted heart with it. Conversely, if you are playing third (with four playing) you may risk your highest card, hoping that the fourth player will not have a void and play a heart. If you are fourth to play and there are no hearts in the trick, win it with your highest card, and lead the next trick with your lowest.

6 Play continues with the winner of the trick leading for the next trick. Always follow suit as there are penalties for 'revoking', that is, if not following suit when you have a suitable card in your hand, you are fined 10 points.

7 Once the hand is played out (all cards are used) the scoring begins. For every heart taken in a trick a player scores a penalty point. If you have no hearts at all, no penalty points are scored.

8 The winner is either the player with the fewest points after an agreed number of hands, or the player with the fewest points when one player reaches a set number of points, say 50.

Variations: Black Lady or Black Maria are both popular variations of Hearts. In Black Lady the Queen of spades is an extra penalty card, scoring 13 penalty points. Each heart still counts as one penalty point.

In Black Maria, as well as all the hearts (one point for each card), there are three more penalty cards, the Ace of spades (7 points), the King of spades (10 points) and the Queen of spades or Black Maria (13 points). Also in Black Maria, there is the custom of exchanging. This means that after the deal, players study their cards and then pass three cards on to the player on their right. A player may not look at their cards until they have passed on their own cards.

KNAVES

Players: three
Age: families and adults
Equipment: standard pack of cards, jokers removed

1 This is an interesting and fairly quick game combining skill and chance. The cards rank from Ace (high) to 2 (low), the suits are equal but the Jacks, or Knaves, are cards to watch out for!

2 Deal the cards singly clockwise, starting with the player on the dealer's left, until players have seventeen cards each. The last card determines the trump suit but is otherwise not used.

3 The objective of the game is to take as many tricks as possible, with each trick scoring one point. However, avoid the Jacks! Penalty points for picking up Jacks in tricks are

Knave of hearts	4 points
Knave of diamonds	3 points
Knave of clubs	2 points
Knave of spades	1 point

as follows:

As each trick is only worth one point, it is easy to see that minus scores are possible!

4 Play begins with the player to the left of the dealer playing any card to the centre. The other two players contribute a card to the trick in turn, with players following suit if possible. If this is not possible, they may trump or discard. Highest trump wins the trick. If no trump is played, then the highest card of the led suit wins. The winner of the trick leads the next trick.

5 Players agree before play to the game total, which is usually 20 points up, and a game is completed in six or so hands more often than not.

6 Just a couple of hints . . . high cards are both good and bad, because on one hand they ensure winning tricks. However, they also encourage the Knaves, as players holding Knaves naturally try to discard them or play them under high cards.

7 If one player is ahead on points, the other two players can conspire to reduce that player's lead, but if two players were together in the lead they would rather concede tricks to the back player than to each other. This means that runaway victories are rare.

WHIST

Players: four, in two partnerships
Age: all the family
Equipment: standard pack of cards, jokers removed

1 Whist has been a popular game since the early 18th century throughout the English-speaking world, especially gaining popularity through the work of card guru, Edmund Hoyle. It is a simpler game than Bridge, and so is perfect for family fun. It is also thought that Whist provides an excellent training for good Bridge players.

2 The cards rank from Ace (high) to 2 (low), and the aim of the game is to take as many tricks as possible, and thereby score points towards winning a 'rubber'. The first side to win two games wins the rubber.

3 Cards are dealt one at a time, face down, clockwise beginning with the player to the dealer's left, until each player has thirteen cards. The last card (which is part of the dealer's hand) is turned up for all to see as this is the trump suit for the deal.

4 The eldest hand (the player to the left of the dealer) leads the first trick, leading any card. Each player plays a card in turn, if possible of the suit led, but a player without a card in this suit may play a card of any other suit. The four cards played form a trick, which is won by the player who played the highest card in the suit led, or, if the trick contained a trump, by the highest trump. The winner of the trick leads the next trick. One player from each side collects the tricks for the partnership.

5 When all thirteen tricks from the hand have been played and won, the result is scored and the deal passes to the player to the left of the dealer.

6 Various systems of scoring have developed throughout the world. Most players of Whist have adopted the somewhat simpler American system, over the British system. Both share the basic feature that the side taking most tricks scores one point for each trick taken over six. So, if one partnership takes nine tricks and the other side only manages two tricks, the first partnership scores 3 points (the difference between nine and six) while the other side does not score any points.

After this, the American system dictates the first side reaching 7 points to be the winners of the game, whereas the British system says only five points are required to win. Also, in the British game, points are scored for honours, so if a side has been dealt all four honour cards – the Ace, King, Queen and Jack – of the trump suit, they score 4 points. If they have three cards, they score 2 points. The only exception is that if their score is already 4 points they cannot score anything for honours. Many players dislike this system of scoring favours just for being lucky enough to be dealt a good hand.

The other difference in the systems is when a player 'revokes' or does not follow suit when they can. In the American system 2 points are transferred from the revoking side to their opponents, but in the British system, 3 points are deducted from the offending side's score, or, if this gives them a negative score, 3 points are added to their opponent's score.

7 The skill of Whist (as with Bridge) is the ability to learn to play within a partnership. The other skill is to notice and remember which cards have been played throughout the hand, which means a player has some idea of what is left. This can be particularly useful for the trump suit. There are complicated conventions involved with indicating to a partner the cards actually held but, as a general rule, players should lead the fourth highest card of their longest and strongest suit.

GAMBLING GAMES

There are many gambling stories from all around the world associated with cards – usually bad. However, the truth is that people can gamble on anything, and perhaps cards have just been highlighted. Equally, these following games can be played without money changing hands – use coloured counters and play for the 'kitty' which will easily show the winner by the stack of counters or chips they have in front of them! Most importantly, enjoy the play, the social aspect and the fun involved in winning occasionally – then you will be able to play for money in a sensible manner if a visit to a casino is made at some time.

BRAG

Players: three to nine
Age: adults usually
Equipment: standard pack of cards, betting chips, counters or cash

1 Brag developed around the time of the Tudor Kings and Queens in England from a Spanish game called Primero. Since then, Brag itself has spawned Poker in its various forms, but the original game is still popular, especially in Britain.

2 In its most traditional form, Brag is a three-card game, with the objective for each deal to win the pot (or kitty, or pool) by holding the best ranking hand or having all the other players drop out of the betting.

3 Betting limits can be agreed by players before the game begins. Typical limits could be: a maximum one unit bet, or maybe somewhere between one to five units to bet or raise. The way some people play is before each deal one unit must be contributed to the pool by each player – this is known as the ante.

4 A dealer can be chosen by cutting high or low, as agreed. One card at a time face down to each player is dealt, beginning to the dealer's left and continuing clockwise, until each player, including the dealer has three cards.

5 Players look at their hands and bet accordingly. Bets are placed in a central pool (or added to the ante if that is being played) and bluffing (or bragging!) is unrestricted – any hand can be bet upon.

6 Originally only three of a kind and pairs scored in Brag, but today there are six hands which are winners, as follows, the highest ranked is first:

(a) Three of a Kind – this is still the highest ranked hand in Brag. It can be any three cards of the same value, such as the three Js pictured, but the best is three 3s – nothing can beat it. Next best is three Aces, then three Kings and so on down to three 2s.

(b) A Running Flush – needs to be three cards of the same suit, running in sequence as the 8-9-10 of clubs are pictured. The best Running Flush is the Ace-2-3 (Ace can rank high or low in Brag) with the next best being Ace-King-Queen, then, King-Queen-Jack and so on to 4-3-2, which ranks lowest.

(c) A Run – similar to a running flush, though in an ordinary run the three cards may be of different suits, such as the 5-6-7 pictured. Ace-2-3 is also the best run, and the ranking is as described above.

(d) A Flush – this is three assorted cards of the same suit as pictured in (d) The value of the flush is determined first by the highest of the three cards. The best flush is an Ace flush, such as Ace-4-8 spades. If competing flushes have the same high card, the next highest card is taken into account, and if necessary the third card is considered too.

(e) A Pair – two cards of the same value, with one useless card. The best pair is again Aces, then Kings, etcetera, down to 2s. If two players have the same pair, the third card determines who is the winner – for example, two 8s with a Queen beats two 8s with a Jack.

(f) A high card – if none of the above hands have been dealt, a high card can still win, although it may need all your bragging skill! So King-8-6 will beat a Queen-Jack-5. Again, if the high card is the same with two players, the next card needs to be taken into consideration.

The following hands illustrate the previous points (a) to (f):

(a)

(b)

(c)

(d)

(e)

(f)

7 Now that the players' hands have been scrutinised, players begin the betting round. There are usually only two ways people bet in Brag (although Poker betting is sometimes used, but will not be covered here), and they are 'round the table' or 'bet or raise'. Round the table is the simplest where, every time it is a player's turn to bet, one unit must be bet or they drop out – this is known as 'stacking'. Betting continues even when there are only two players left, although either player in this scenario can pay double to see their opponent. Both players then show their cards without any further betting.

8 In 'bet or raise' style of betting, limits are agreed to prior to play (mentioned in point 3 above) so no one may bet or raise the pool by more than the agreed units, say two. To stay in the game, players must bet the minimum limit although, if they feel their hand is particularly strong, they can raise the bet to the highest limit, after which all players must bet this higher limit to stay in the game.

9 Play continues around the table in the chosen manner and one by one the weaker hands, or the hands held by players with weak nerves, are stacked, until only two remain. Then one player chooses to see the other, who must place their cards on the table immediately. The 'see-er' then shows their hand if it is better and scoops the pool but, if it is not a winner, they stack their hand without showing it and the seen player takes the kitty.

CHEMIN DE FER

Players: at least ten
Age: usually adults
Equipment: one or more identical standard packs of cards, jokers removed; gambling chips or counters

1 Popular in casinos, Chemin de Fer can be played with a group of friends at home, with a game taking an hour, through to a whole evening to play several games.

2 The object is to gain a hand of two or three cards whose face values total nine, or as near to nine as possible, and to win a bet against the bank by having a higher total than the dealer. To arrive at a hand's total, cards score as follows:

aces	1
twos to nines	2 to 9 as per face value
tens, Jacks, Queens and Kings	zero

Also, when adding up the scores, 10s are ignored, so 9 + 2 = 11 = 1.

3 When using two or more packs of cards, it is best to split them into smaller packs for shuffling, and then play begins with an auction to determine who will be the first banker. The player willing to put up the highest amount wins the right to be banker and then betting begins.

4 Yes, betting begins before any cards are dealt in Chemin de Fer! Players only bet against the bank, and the total of bets on a single play is limited to the amount of the bank – no excess payments are made by the banker.

5 The first to bet is the player to the banker's right and betting passes around the table until the entire bank is covered by several bets, or all players who wish to bet have done so, or a player has called 'Banco' which means they are betting against the entire bank.

6 The banker deals two hands of two cards each. The cards are dealt one at a time and face down, one to the player who holds the highest bet against the bank and one to the banker.

7 The players examine their cards and if the bank's opponent (the player) has a natural eight or nine it must be shown immediately. If the total is less than five, a third card must be requested, but if the total is five the player has the option of asking for a third card, but is not forced to do so. If the total is six or seven the player stands. The additional card is dealt face up.

8 Now the banker must decide whether to take a third card, based on what is being held and what may have been learnt from the opponent's subsequent third card if dealt If the hand is a natural eight or nine the banker will always stand, as it would to a seven. The banker will always draw another card to a zero, one, two or three. With another total, the banker's choice is based on

whether the opponent took a third card and what it was. The tables below help both players and bankers:

Player holding	Action
0, 1, 2, 3 or 4	draw
5	optional
6 or 7	stay

9 If both hands are naturals, a nine beats an eight, but if both hands are naturals of the same number, it is known as a 'stand-off' and all bets are returned. If the player's hand does not contain a natural they say 'pass', and the banker examines their own hand. If it contains a natural, it is declared and wins all bets.

10 The hand totalling nine or nearest to nine wins. So, to summarise, if the totals are the same, all bets are returned. If the banker has won, that person collects all bets; if the banker has lost, each player collects the amount of the bank they had covered.

11 If the banker wins they may keep the bank for the next hand. In this case, the new bank comprises the original bank plus the winnings. If the banker wins the hand but chooses not to keep the bank, they may take their winnings and pass the bank. The bank is offered to the players in turn until one accepts it and decides the amount of the new bank.

12 If the banker loses a hand, the bank is offered to the players in turn.

After giving	Banker stays on	Banker draws on
0 or 1	4, 5, 6 or 7	3, 2, 1 or 0
9	4, 5, 6, 7 (or 3)	2, 1, or 0
8	3, 4, 5, 6 or 7	2, 1 or 0
7 or 6	7	6, 5, 4, 3, 2, 1 or
5 or 4	6 or 7	5, 4, 3, 2, 1 or 0
3 or 2	5, 6 or 7	4, 3, 2, 1 or 0
Player has stood	6 or 7	5, 4, 3, 2, 1 or 0

FARO

Players: up to ten
Age: usually adults
Equipment: standard pack of cards, jokers removed; a suit of spades from another pack of cards; betting chips or counters; extra counters or coins for betting

1 Faro was known as Pharaon in the French court of Louis XIV, and in the 1700s it was the most popular gambling house game in England. It travelled to America in the 1800s and gained popularity there also.

2 The game needed much in the way of equipment in those days – a table covered with a green baize Faro layout, a dealing box, a casekeeper (a frame used to show which cards have been played), cards, betting chips, coppers (chips of either red or black used for betting), and bet markers (used to make bets over the bettor's funds). These days it is possible to play this game at home with nothing more than two standard packs of cards and some betting chips or counters.

3 Firstly, lay out the extra suit of spades on a table, face up as shown below.

4 Players can now wager on individual cards and on card combinations. Stakes are placed in certain positions to indicate the bets – placings for bets are also shown in the illustration below. Players can bet that a card or combination will lose.

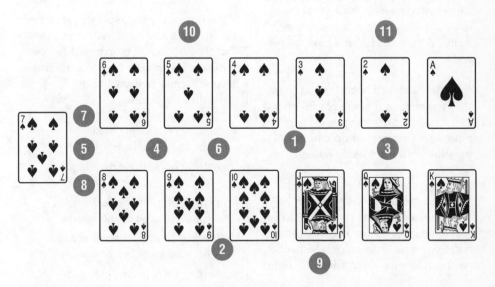

BETS:

1 single card
2 adjacent pair (9,10)
3 vertical pair (2, Q)
4 diagonal pair (8, 5)
5 corner three (6, 7, 8)
6 four (4, 5, 9, 10)
7 bets 6, 7
8 bets 7, 8
9 bets three denominations horizontally adjacent (10, J, Q)
10 bets the odd denomination in each turn
11 bets the even denomination in each turn

This is done by 'coppering' – placing a coin or token on top of the stake. Or bet on odd or even denominations.

5 The banker puts the shuffled and cut pack in front and turns up the first card – this is called the 'soda' and is not used, except to begin a discard pile. Cards are then turned up into play two at a time with the first card always being the losing card (the banker wins), followed by the winning card (players win). Only the denomination of the card is counted; suits are irrelevant. If a turn is 'split', that is both cards have the same rank, the banker takes half the stakes on that denomination.

6 Any bets are now settled. Other bets can be changed and new bets made. (If a casekeeper is used it now shows which denominations of cards have already appeared, or someone writes down which cards have been used.)

7 The next turn begins with the last winning card being placed on top of the soda, or discard pile first. Two more cards are turned up and this is the play until three cards remain.

8 Now players have one more bet they can place. They can bet on the sequence that the last three cards will appear. Everyone knows the cards if there is a casekeeper, or if someone has been logging the cards used, but if no one has been doing this the banker can first look at the cards and name them. If all the cards are different numbers the odds are 4-1, but if there is a pair amongst them the odds reduce to 2-1. The last card is not used, except for this extra betting purpose.

HOGGENHEIMER

Players: for two or more, but probably best for around ten
Age: adults
Equipment: standard pack of cards, from which the 2s, 3s, 4s, 5s and 6s have been removed; one joker; betting chips or counters

1 Each player is banker in turn and, after the cards are shuffled and cut, the banker deals four rows of eight cards face down on the playing surface. The last card is dealt face down separately to one side. This grid represents the four suits from the top spades, hearts, diamonds and clubs, and the cards across from A, K, Q, J, 10, 9, 8 and 7.

2 The object for the players is to bet on a card or combination of cards that they hope will be exposed before the joker is exposed. Betting can take several forms, as shown in the illustration opposite:

(a) betting on a single card
– the Queen of hearts

(b) betting on a single card
– the Ace of clubs

(c) betting on two adjacent cards
– the 7s of spades and hearts

(d) betting on two adjacent cards
– the Ace and King of spades

(e) betting on four cards in a square
– the 8s and 9s of hearts and diamonds

(f) betting on a column of cards
– all the Jacks

(g) betting on a row of cards of the same suit – all the clubs

3 The banker begins play by turning up the last card dealt. If it is the joker, the deal ends and the banker collects all bets. If it is not the joker, the banker places it in its correct place on the layout and any bet on that position is replaced on top of the new card. The face down card which was in that position is turned face up and, in turn, placed in its correct position in the layout. Play continues in this way until the joker is turned up.

4 As soon as the joker is turned up, play stops and settlement of the bets takes place. A player's bet wins if all the cards bet on, for instance in the illustration below, if all the Jacks in bet (f) are turned over the player who bet on that would win.

5 Bets on single cards are paid even money (1-1); bets on two cards are paid 2-1; bets on four cards in a square or column are paid 4-1; and bets on eight cards in a row are paid 8-1.

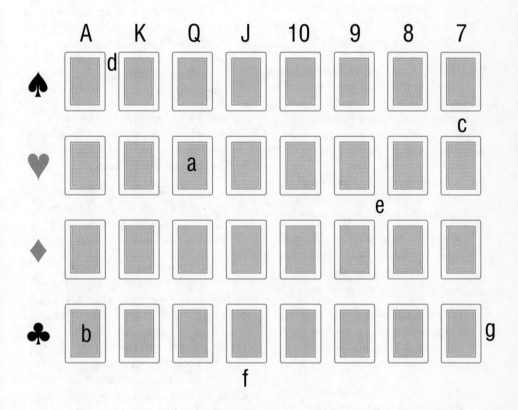

POKER

Players: five, six or seven is generally considered best
Age: adults
Equipment: standard pack of cards, jokers removed

1 There are several versions of Poker, but most people play Draw Poker, so the rules for that game are described here. It is probably the simplest form of Poker and if you have tried Brag you will see the similarities. The other popular Poker game is Stud Poker.

2 In any form of Poker, the object is to bet against the other players that your hand is the best hand. All bets are placed in a central pool, or pot, and the object is to win that pot.

3 Firstly, though, every player needs to learn the hands which will help to win that pot. Every person contemplating playing Poker should commit to memory the ten following winning hands:

(a) A Royal Flush – this hand will beat anything else! Five cards of the same suit in sequence, Ace high.

(b) A Straight Flush – five cards of the same suit in sequence but any denomination. The lowest is Ace-2-3-4-5 and the best 9-10-J-Q-K.

(c) Four of a Kind – four cards of the same denomination, such as the 5s above and one useless card. The best is four Aces, the lowest 2s.

(d) A Full House – three cards of one denomination, plus a pair of another. The value of the three of a

kind is how a full house is determined, so if you have one with three Aces, that is best.

(e) A Flush – five cards of one suit, but not necessarily in sequence. The value of a flush depends upon the top card.

(f) A Run – five cards of mixed suits that do run in sequence. The value of a run also depends upon the highest card, but if two players have the same run, they share the pot.

(g) Three of a Kind – three cards of one denomination, plus two indifferent cards. Three Aces are best, down to three 2s.

(h) Two Pairs – two different pairs and one indifferent card. Again, the highest pair wins, so Aces and 4s would beat Kings and Queens. Only if two players have identical pairs does the fifth card come into play – the highest wins.

(i) One Pair – two cards of the same denomination, such as the 8s above, and three useless cards. Again, the best pair would be Aces.

(j) A High Card – no matched cards at all, but the highest card (preferably an ace) is taken as a winner if no one else has anything better.

4 And now to play. Poker has a reputation for sordid all-night affairs, with men 'losing the shirts off their backs'. For an after-dinner game with friends it is probably a good idea to use counters, not money, and place a limit on both the ante and a maximum bet. Say the maximum bet is twenty chips, and the ante (or entry bet) is just the one chip (or counter).

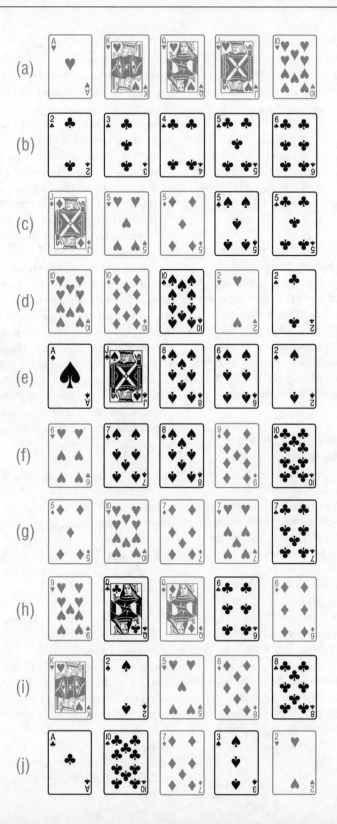

5 The first dealer is chosen by turning up the cards round the table until a Jack appears. The player who gets the Jack is the first dealer and then the deal moves around the table clockwise.

6 Each player now places an ante into the pot. Cards are dealt one at a time and face down until each player has five, and everyone looks at their hand and evaluates it.

7 One player has to open, that is open the betting by throwing in, say, five chips and saying 'Open for five'. However, a player can only open if they have a pair of Jacks or better in their hand. This is good as it ensures there is one good hand and also, as there will be times no one can open, it helps build up the pot, as the ante stays where it is for the next game.

8 If the player to the left of the dealer (always known as the elder) cannot open, they say 'Pass' and play moves to the player on the left. Play goes on until someone opens, or everyone passes. If everyone passes there is another deal and the ante must be added to by the minimum.

9 On the second deal a pair of Queens or better is required to open. If no one can open, another chip goes into the pot from each player and another deal occurs. This time it is Kings required, then Aces if another deal is required. It would be unusual to go on this long without a game happening, but if it does, the deal requirements go backwards again now. After Aces, it reverts to Kings, then Queens and Jacks.

10 Once one player has opened, betting begins in earnest. It is easier to follow the betting with illustrated hands, so read on looking at the hands on the facing page at the same time. Player A has dealt so B is the first player able to open and does so for five, because he has two fairly good pairs. Player C hopes to gain a flush as he already has a good start with four cards, so he also bets five. D has two low pairs and also calls for five. Player E with three 9s in his hand is happy to raise to ten. F with a lowly pair of 3s rightly decides to stack and save the counters (money) for a better hand. Player A, sitting on four to a Straight Flush raises to twenty. B calls, putting in another fifteen to make up the twenty now needed. C also comes in, putting in fifteen to make up the twenty required. D probably knows he is outclassed with two low pairs, but comes in anyway, putting in another fifteen too. E is happy to add another ten to stay, of course.

11 After the opening betting is concluded as above, everyone remaining may now change cards, with the only object being to improve the hand they were just betting on! Occasionally, a player will not want to change any cards and keeps the ones in their hand.

12 The dealer asks everyone in turn, from the player on the left, how many cards they want. Players who want one, two or three cards get them immediately, but a player who wants four cards will get three in this round, and then the extra one after everyone else. If the person who opened wants to throw away one of the opening cards they must show the card they are discarding and say to the

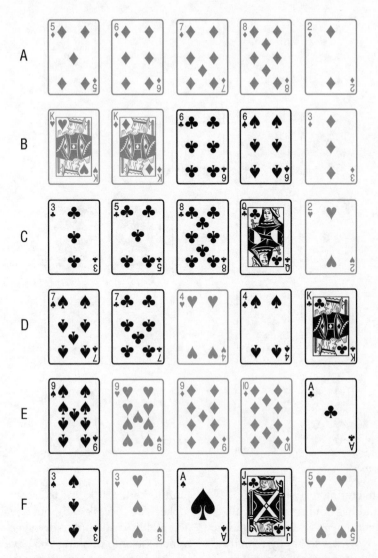

other players 'opener away'. They will know exactly what is happening, but also that the player did have the openers to begin with.

13 When everyone has received their final hand (see illustration on page 166 – Player A took one for 2♣, B one for 3♦, C one for 2♥, D one for ♣ and E tried two for 10♦ and A♣), betting recommences with the last player to raise, which was Player A.

14 Player A has not made the Straight Flush hoped for and has a good run instead, but this is a cautious player so checks (this means they will not bet but retain the right to do so and remain in the game if anyone else bets in this round). B's hand has not improved at all, and also checks. C has made the wanted Flush and bets twenty. D's gamble paid off and that player is in the happy position of possessing a Full House so has decided to see twenty and raise twenty.

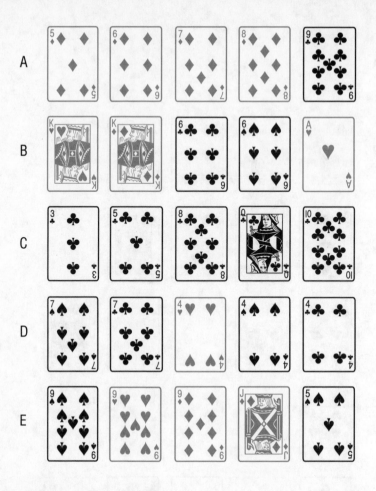

Faced with betting forty to call, E, whose hand has not improved at all, has to admit defeat, and stacks. Back to Player A. Now not so happy with the run, A still feels compelled to call so puts in the forty required to do so. B stacks and C decides to call by matching the twenty put in already and not raising. Thus, the hand is called now as everyone who remains in the game has put in forty. The three hands left (A, C and D) are shown and Player D scoops the pool, which is now quite large, with his Full House.

15 A few hints, especially useful if you are playing with the same group often! Be inconsistent – do not bluff too often. It is fine to use a 'poker' face occasionally, but equally acceptable to attempt to deceive opponents into thinking you have a terrible hand when you have a good hand by facial expressions of disgust – just do not overdo it. If you have a good hand, do not over-bet. This may mean that nervous players will immediately stack, thinking they cannot win, and that means the pot is smaller for your win!

PONTOON

Players: any number can play
Age: adults
Equipment: standard pack of cards, with one joker used as an indicator card

1 Pontoon is also known as Blackjack, Vingt-et-Un, Twentyone and Vanjohn, with slightly differing rules. Whatever its name, there are two main forms: the changing bank version which is mainly played at home, or the permanent bank version which is found in casinos.

2 The object of the game is to gain a total of 21 points or as near to as possible without 'busting' – going over 21 – with two or more cards. A two card hand with a value of exactly 21 (made up of a face or honour card, or ten and an Ace) is known as a 'natural' or a 'blackjack'. The value of cards is as follows: an Ace can count as 1 or 11, at the player's option; a face or court card is valued at 10; all other cards count for their pip value.

3 At home, the game is played with a changing dealer/banker and the deal is chosen by deal, usually the first Ace decides who is the first dealer/banker. There is a choice of triggers for a change of dealer; either after five deals or when a natural is dealt within a hand.

4 Once the deal has been settled, the dealer shuffles the cards and offers them for cut to any player who wants to cut the pack. The pack is placed face down on the playing surface on top of the joker which is used as an indicator card. The dealer at this stage decides the minimum and maximum bets, which, for home games especially, can be placed by using counters or matchsticks rather than cash!

5 Only bets against the dealer are allowed and all players bet after receiving their first card which is dealt face down, except the dealer's card which is placed face up. Once these cards have been viewed, a second card is dealt face down to each player in turn, with the dealer last.

6 If the dealer's face-up card is an Ace or a card worth 10 points, the dealer looks at their face down card to see if they have a natural. If so, they immediately announce this and turn both cards face up. The other players show their cards and, if any have a natural, they have their bets returned. while others have their bets collected.

7 If the dealer's face-up card isn't an Ace or a 10-point card, or they find they do not have a natural, the player to the dealer's left commences play.

8 All players have three options when it is their turn to play. They can 'stick' with the cards they have, declining further cards, provided the total pip count is not less than sixteen; they can buy a card face down by adding to their original stake; or they can 'twist' when no addition is made to their stake, and the dealer provides a card face-up. If a player buys a card, a choice can be made to either buy or twist again if necessary, but if the player twists, this must be continued until the player sticks or busts.

9 Each player continues until they are satisfied with the count (that is, their hand is on or below 21) or they bust when the cards exceed 21 and lose their stake to the dealer. If a player gets pontoon (or blackjack) they disclose this by turning over one of the cards, and are paid at two to one instead of the more usual evens.

10 When all players have finished, the dealer's cards are turned over. If there is less than 16 points, the dealer (like the other players) cannot stick. They take the next card off the top of the pack and show it. If they go bust, they pay all the players still in the amount equal to their stake. Otherwise they announce they will pay players with a card count one higher than their own card count. Hence, if the dealer's

card count is 19, they will say 'Pay 20s'. Players now reveal their hands and those with 20 or 21 are paid by the dealer an equal amount to that of their stake. (Some rules allow the player's bet to be returned for 19, the same as the dealer, others take the stake.)

11 Other ways to beat the dealer include five-hand cards and three 7s. A hand of five cards totalling 21 or under – even if under 16 – is only beaten by pontoon or by three 7s, and a hand of three 7s beats everything. It is often paid double or triple stakes – your dealer will decide.

12 If a player has a pair they may be split into two hands, and played and bet upon as if they were two hands or if they were two players.

BOARD
GAMES

Board games have been around since ancient times, and most of the world has some form of board game ready for play in the family home. However, board games really reached their heyday in the 18th and 19th centuries in Europe and America when more and more were invented, principally for educative purposes. At the same time, they were also found to be very entertaining and great to while away long, cold winter's evenings. Many are played in one form or another today.

Some of the most popular modern board games include Monopoly®, Trivial Pursuit® (which should be held accountable for the spawning of so many fund-raising trivia nights which we have all suffered or enjoyed!), Risk® and Cluedo®. Along with Scrabble® and Othello®, they probably account for the most popular family games. Any good toy or games shop will be able to introduce you to these fabulous board games – Scrabble® and Othello® are described further on.

RACING BOARD GAMES

Most of the board games under this category are old-fashioned racing board games, where to win a player must beat the rest of his opponents to do something – usually get counters or men safely 'home'. Others are races in that they need the players to answer questions or create words and beat the other players in one way or another.

ALLEYWAY

Players: any number can play
Age: children and adults
Equipment: semi-circle drawn on a board, marked with 25 numbered spaces, with the 13th space or alleyway left open; a different coloured counter for each player; one dice

1 This is a simple family game which younger children will enjoy too. To begin, each player throws the dice and sets a counter on the space with the corresponding number.

2 Players then take it in turns to throw the dice and move their counter around the semi-circle to match the number indicated on the dice. If a player's counter lands on a space that is already occupied by an opponent's counter, the opponent's counter must be moved back as follows:

a) if the counter was on a space from 1–12 or in the alleyway, it must go back to the beginning;

b) if the counter was past the alleyway, it must be moved back two spaces. Should that space also be occupied, that counter must move back two spaces as well;

c) if the counter was on space 14 or 15 and so has to retreat two spaces, it then has to go right back to the start, as does any opponent it encounters in the alleyway or on space 12.

3 To end the game is slightly tricky too. If a player's counter lands on space 25, it has to retreat to space 14, so the winner is the first player whose throw gets them past space 25.

BACKGAMMON

Players: two
Age: usually adults
Equipment: marked backgammon board, two dice and a cup for each player, 15 counters each, usually in black and white or black and red, and a doubling cube if players are to bet on the game

1 Backgammon, or something similar, has been played since pre-Roman times and for centuries it has been the favourite café game of the eastern Mediterranean countries, where it is still extremely popular.

2 In this simple race game, the objective is to be the first player to move the 15 counters (men) around the board, according to numbers thrown on the dice, to your own inner table, and then remove them (called 'bearing off'). The first player to 'bear off' all fifteen of their pieces wins the game.

3 Backgammon is played on a rectangular board marked with twelve triangles along each side, alternately light and dark coloured; each triangle is called a 'point'. The board is also divided into two halves by a bar. The two halves are known as the inner or home table, and the outer table. The illustration below shows how to set up a game of backgammon. The numbers are not shown on any backgammon board, they are merely for notation in this book.

4 Players draw for colour and then place their men as above. Each player now throws a single dice to determine who begins play; the higher number has first turn (if equal they throw again). The player throwing the higher number moves a man or men of their choice the total shown on both dice. So, for example, White threw a 3 and Black a 4, Black starts and may either move one man 3 points and another man 4 points, or a single man seven points. Counting begins from the next point to where a man is located,

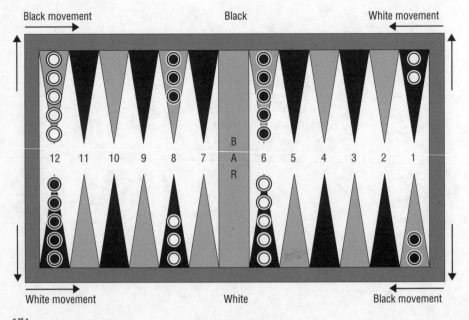

so for example Black could move a single man from B6 to W2 using their throw of 7.

5 After this first roll, players throw two dice alternately into the inner table and move accordingly. If a doublet is rolled (say 4:4) a player moves four times the number in any legal combination possible (4, 4, 4, 4; or 8, 4, 4; or 8, 8).

6 A man may be moved to any vacant point, to a point where a number of his own men sit, or to a point occupied by only one man of the other team. For a multiple move of one man as above, the intermediate point and the end point of the throw must be available – which they were as Black could use a count of 4 first and B2 would be the intermediate point, which is vacant, and then the 3 sees that player land on W2.

7 A point with only one man on it is known as a 'blot'. If an opposing man lands there (even in an

intermediate stage of a combined move), the blot is hit and the man is moved to the bar. A player with one (or more) men on the bar must bring their man or men back into play before being allowed to make any other moves. Entry is through the opponent's inner table – B1-B6 for White and W1-W6 for Black. If the player cannot enter a man because the points indicated by the roll of the dice are occupied by two or more of the opponent's men, that player loses a turn.

8 A player cannot bear off until all their men are in their inner table. If one of their men is sent to the bar during this bearing off, the player cannot bear off any more men but must throw to re-enter their man and bring him around the board to the inner table again. A man is borne off by a throw which takes him at least one point past the first point. For example, if White had a man on W5, a 6 would have to be thrown to bear him off.

Black

White

9 Although the point of the game is to bear off all men, bearing off is optional. Strategically it may be much better to use a low scoring throw, say 1:2, to consolidate what is known as a 'prime'. A prime is where six consecutive points are controlled by one side, so if Black had two men on B1, B2, B4 and B5 and three men on B6 but only one on B3, that player could use a low 1:2 throw to create a prime by moving one of the three men from B6 to B3. There would then be two Black men on each of the B1-B6 points. This would mean that White would not be able to re-enter if a man got hit and put on the bar until Black freed up the prime by bearing off men.

10 Scoring is an uncomplicated area. A player who bears off all their men and their opponent has borne off at least one counter wins a single game. If the opponent has not been able to bear off any counters, the player wins a double game or Gammon. And, if the opponent has not borne off any men and one or more men are still in the winner's inner table or on the bar, the player wins a triple game or Backgammon. Strategy has been touched on above, but as you get to know the game better you will see certain patterns of play emerging and you will get to know the way your usual companions play – as they will your play! However, if the dice favours you with large scores, quickly establish a running game. This is where you race all your men to your inner (home) table as quickly as possible, trying to avoid leaving blots (lone men) and being ready to bear off men as soon as you can. You give little thought to what your opponent is doing in this process.

BEES TO THE HONEYPOT

Players: two to four
Age: children old enough to count and use dice
Equipment: drawn board; four coloured counters of four different colours to act as hives (16 counters in all) and one matching coloured counter to move around the board; two dice

1 Bees to the Honeypot is adapted from a game first seen in England in the 1920s and, with a little effort to draw the board, it is a great game to entertain most children. However, you do first need to draw up a board which has eleven six-sided shapes across the middle and narrows at both ends to six shapes, as in the illustration on the facing page, and then you need to add the numbers between the honeycombs as shown.

Each player takes a counter of a different colour, which preferably matches one of the colours of the four stars on the edge of the board. The four different coloured hive counters are set out four at each star in the batches of the same colour, again preferably matching the colours on the board.

2 The object of the game is for each player (the bees) to visit each star (representing a flower) and collect four hives of a different colour each.

3 Players throw the dice to determine who begins, with the highest score going first. This first player places a counter on the central

spot and throws the dice. Both dice count and the bee counter is moved through two 'cells' at the numbered openings corresponding to the two numbers turned up by the dice. The player can choose in which order to use the numbers, which gives some measure of control.

4 Once the first bee begins, the second moves on to the centre spot and moves off according to the dice. Other players follow suit. However, a bee may not enter a cell already occupied by another bee and, if this means a bee is unable to move in either of its two possible directions, it must miss a turn.

5 To visit a flower (represented by the stars) and claim a coloured hive, the bee enters from one of the adjacent cells. At the centre line, either cell can be entered according to the bee's wish. Once a player collects a hive, it returns to the centre spot to resume flying to the other hives. If one of the dice scores will enable the bee to collect a hive, the other dice score can be used to begin from the centre spot.

6 The winner is the quickest bee to collect all four different coloured hives.

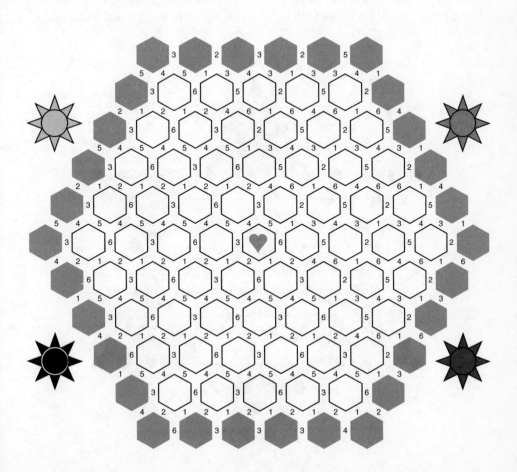

CHINESE CHECKERS

Players: two to six
Age: children and adults
Equipment: checkers board which is in the shape of a six-pointed star and has indentations to hold the pieces; six sets of 15 pieces – either pegs or marbles – with each colour being the same as one of the six-pointed stars on the board

1 The objective of this game is to be the first to move pieces from one coloured star to the opposite star. With two players, each player plays from the opposite side to the other, with three or more players, each takes any

point. With four or six players, players can play in two or three partnerships if preferred.

2 Each player moves one piece in turn, and the moves may be along any of the lines on the board, that is, in six directions. Moves are known as steps or hops, and while multiple hops can be made in one move, steps and hops are not combined in a move.

3 A player may hop over their own or another player's pieces but these are not removed from the board, as in other games.

4 The winner is simply the first player, or partnership, to move all their pieces to the opposite point of the star.

COWS AND LEOPARDS

Players: two
Age: older children and adults
Equipment: board (a draughts board is fine) and 5 counters, 4 of one colour and 1 another

1 A similar game to Fox and Geese, but Cows and Leopards comes from Sri Lanka, whereas Fox and Geese is thought to be Scandinavian in origin. Simple to learn, it can be harder to win and it is best if the two people playing take turns in being both the cow and then the leopard.

2 Using a standard 64-square board, place four counters along the back row on the black squares – these are the cows. The leopard can be placed on any black square on the board.

3 Cows can move one square forward on a diagonal at any turn but, on the other hand, the leopard can move two squares both diagonally forward and backward. Neither piece jumps or captures.

4 The cows win the game if they are able to crowd in the leopard, leaving it without a legal move. The leopard wins if it breaks through the line of cows and reaches the cows' end of the board.

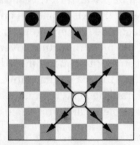

FOX AND GEESE

Players: two
Age: children and adults
Equipment: board and 14 counters, with preferably 1 of a different colour

1 This game has many similarities to Draughts, except that it is played on a board which is similar to Solitaire. The 13 'geese' are laid out as shown below, with the fox hovering very close!

2 For each game, players draw lots to determine who will be the fox and who will be the geese. Both the fox and geese move in identical fashion, one square forwards, backwards or sideways on each turn.

3 However, only the fox is allowed to capture, which it does by leaping over an adjacent goose and landing on a vacant square beyond. The fox can also capture more than one goose in a series of leaps in one turn, as long as the spaces are there. Geese do not leap, but try to crowd the fox into a corner.

4 The fox wins if it manages to capture so many geese that there are not enough left to trap it, or if it reaches the geese's end of the board. The geese win if they can immobilise the fox by surrounding it.

FOX AND GEESE SOLITAIRE

Players: one
Age: any age
Equipment: board and 32 pieces

1 It is said that the game of Solitaire was invented by a French prisoner in the Bastille during the French Revolution. The French version uses a round board which has 37 holes but this English version makes use of the Fox and Geese board and has 33 holes and 32 pieces used.

2 The layout for this Solitaire is shown below, with every point occupied except for the central point.

3 There is only one move allowed and that is a jump over the adjacent peg or piece into a vacant spot, removing that piece from the board. These jumps can only be horizontal or vertical, not diagonal.

4 The object of the game is to remove all the pieces from the board except one, and that one piece should be in a pre-designated place, usually the central hole.

HALMA

Players: two to four
Age: adults
Equipment: a 16x16 chequered board; 52 pieces (13 each for three or four players), or 38 pieces, 19 pieces each for two-player games

1 Halma takes its name from the Greek word for 'jump'. This is appropriate as the players' pieces do just that to reach the other side of the board and a safe 'camp'.

2 The board has 'camps' or 'yards' marked off in each corner as seen in the illustration below on page 181.

3 In the two player version, each player has 19 pieces arranged as in the above diagram, using the top left and bottom right 'camps' to begin. For three players, reduce the pieces to 13 each and also use the bottom left camp. Keep the pieces at 13 each for four players and use all four corners.

4 The players decide who goes first and then take alternate turns. In any turn only 1 piece may be moved, but there are two ways they are able to be moved – the step or the jump.

5 With a step, the piece can move to an adjacent square in any direction – vertical, horizontal, diagonal, backwards or forwards. However, if there is a piece in an adjacent square (either an opponent or fellow), the piece may jump over that piece to an empty square immediately beyond it. This is a similar move to that in Draughts. Having made one jump, that piece can jump again and

again until no more jumps remain.

6 The idea in Halma is to construct 'ladders' across the board so your rear pieces can travel rapidly across to the other side. Remember, with these ladders it means your opponents are able to use them, too.

7 The winner is the first player to occupy the opposite camp to your own side.

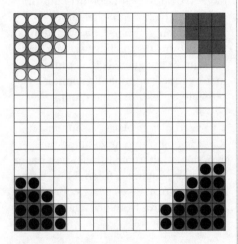

Top left and bottom right:
Two players using 19 pieces each

Bottom left:
Use this corner if three players and reduce to 13 pieces each.

HYENA CHASE

Players: any number can play
Age: all the family
Equipment: each player must have a piece or coloured counter which is different from the other players; another counter or piece totally different again; a dice and a board

1 Originally played in the marketplaces and villages of North African countries, the 'board' would have been drawn on the ground, but a board can be drawn on paper or light cardboard as shown below:

2 All the players' counters, plus the different one to represent the hyena, are placed in the village circle at the beginning of the game. Each player is aiming to get their mother from the village to the well and home again first – so entitling them to let loose the hyena on the other mothers trying to get home.

3 Moves are made in turn by each player, usually in a clockwise direction. Players must throw a 6 before their mothers leave the village

181

for the first circle, and from then on her progress to the well is deemed by the number on the dice. If a player throws a 6 after their mother is on her way, that player has another throw. If two 6s are thrown in succession, the player has one more throw. Two mothers can occupy the same 'day' or circle of the journey.

4 The well can only be reached by a direct throw, so if a mother is 4 circles away and the player throws a 5 or 6, she has to wait another turn to get there.

5 After reaching the well, the mothers wash their clothes and talk until the player throws a 6 to allow her to begin the return journey.

6 The first person to get mother back to the village (this does not need a direct throw) gains the hyena counter and must throw a 6 to get the hyena on the way back to the well. This is enhanced by the fact that the hyena travels at twice the speed of the mothers – if the player throws a 4, the hyena moves forward 8 circles or days.

7 Once at the well (again reached by a direct throw) the player must also throw a 6 to leave on the return journey to the village. However, this time, any mothers that the hyena passes on the way back to the village are 'eaten' and removed from the board.

8 The player who gains the hyena counter has won the game, but everyone always wants to see how many mothers they can eat too!

LEAPFROG

Players: two
Age: children love this game
Equipment: a board which is 10x10 squares; 50 different coloured counters each

1 There are some differences to Draughts, but this game follows similar principles. The main difference is that the board is plain (it does not have to bear a chequerboard pattern) and the players begin the game by placing their counters one by one in the positions they believe will be best. The aim of the game is to capture as many of their opponent's counters as possible by leapfrogging them.

2 Each player places 1 counter on the board into any square they like, taking alternate turns. Keep going until every square is filled. Now, each player, in turn, takes just 1 counter from the board, from anywhere they like.

3 Again in turns, players begin to leapfrog opponent's counters only into an empty space on the other side and removing the jumped counter. Players can jump once into an empty spot or, if it is possible, keep leapfrogging as many as possible as long as there is an empty spot on the other side of the opponent's counter.

4 When one player is unable to leapfrog at their turn, the game ends. Now add up the counters captured, and the winner is the one with the most pieces.

LUDO

Players: two, three or four players
Age: children and adults
Equipment: Ludo board; 4 different coloured counters for each player; one dice

1 Ludo is a modified, popular version of the 16th century Indian game called Pachisi. It uses a square-shaped cardboard board, marked with home bases, starting squares and homes for all, with the central columns leading to home. All the starting points are coloured for easy player identification, usually in red, blue, yellow and green.

2 Each player begins by choosing a colour and placing the appropriately-coloured counters on the matching starting square or corner. The objective is to beat the other players to race around the board, and to get all 4 counters safely to the home or finish.

3 The person who throws the highest number with the dice begins play. Each player must throw a 6 – which is the number needed to release a counter from its starting point to the starting square. Whenever a player throws a 6 another throw is taken. If this player has more than one counter on the circuit they can use the

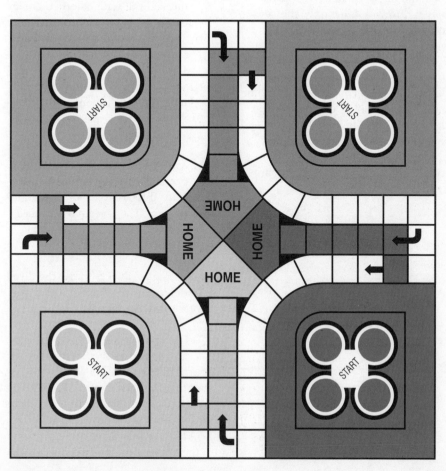

second throw to move the second counter. If two 6s are thrown in succession, another throw is allowed. Many people playing Ludo do not allow anyone who still has a counter at the Start to use the 6 for any other counter right throughout the game. It can be frustrating, but is a good rule!

4 If a counter lands on a square already occupied by an opponent's counter, the opponent's counter is returned to the start, and can only re-enter when a 6 has been thrown once again.

5 The Home base or finish can only be reached by a direct throw. If there are three squares left and the player throws a 4, the only choice is to await the next turn or move another piece if possible.

6 The winner is the first person to get all the 4 counters to the home base, and it is not as easy as may be thought, especially with 4 players and four counters from each moving around the circuit. It is very easy to get caught just when you think you are nearly home!

NYOUT

Players: two, three or four, although four is usual
Age: adults
Equipment: a specially marked board; pieces (called horses in the game) for each player – 4 each for two players, 3 each for three players and 2 each for four players; a dice

1 This game is from Korea where it is now mostly played for money, although it is an entertaining family game without the gambling element.

2 The game needs a board which is marked out with coloured circles. Twenty circles of two different sizes form a ring and enclose a cross made up of nine other circles as shown below. Note that the central circle and the four circles at the cardinal points are larger than the others. (On traditional boards these would be marked with symbols.)

3 Any counters or pieces may be used – 4 each for two players, 3 each for three players and 2 each for four players. The objective is to race each other to be the first to get the horses around the board.

4 To begin, players throw the dice to determine the starting order, the player throwing highest winning.

5 Each player then throws the dice and advances the horse the appropriate number of circles, counting the start circle as 1. (Note that 6 does not count in Nyout – if a player throws a 6 it is re-thrown to achieve a 1-5.) Players may have more than one of their horses on the circuit at a time.

Horses are moved in an anti-clockwise direction, leaving the ring at the exit circle.

6 However, there are three alternative routes which may be taken, rather than achieving the full circle. These are marked A, B and C on the above diagram. If a horse lands on one of the large circles, the player has a choice to take the alternative route, but is not compelled to do so, if for strategic purposes the usual way seems more prudent.

7 If a horse lands on a circle already occupied by an opponent's horse, the opponent's horse is 'taken' and returned to the start. The taker is allowed another throw.

8 If a horse lands on a circle already occupied by one of their own horses, the horses may be moved together as a double piece in subsequent moves. Of course, this raises the risk of being taken, when both pieces would be sent back to the start!

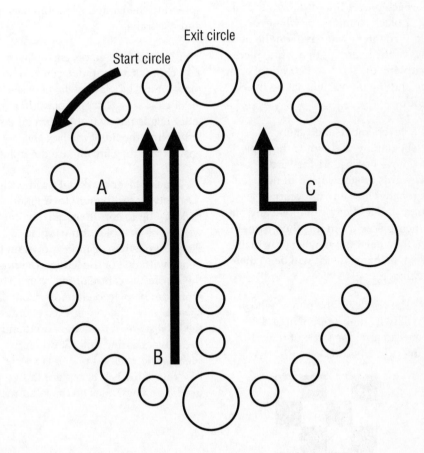

QUARTETTE

Players: two
Age: all the family
Equipment: a 4x4 square board; 8 counters, 4 in each of two colours – white or black is usual

1 An easy-looking game which has links to both Noughts and Crosses as well as Draughts, but which can take quite a bit of strategy to actually win. The aim is to create a straight, unbroken line of 4 in any direction – up, down or diagonally.

2 Each player lines up 2 white and 2 black counters (or whatever colour counters you have) on the outer rows of the board, with a white piece occupying the left hand corner of each side and the pieces alternating in colour.

3 Players move alternately, beginning with white. Each piece may move one square forwards, backwards or sideways (but not diagonally) into any unoccupied square and a player can move any one of their pieces when it is their turn. In fact, they must move when it is their turn, whether or not it will be to their advantage.

4 The winner is the player who outwits their opponent and creates an unbroken line of their 4 counters in any direction.

SCRABBLE®

Players: two to four
Age: adults and older children with good vocabulary skills
Equipment: Scrabble® board; four letter racks; letter bag; 100 letter tiles; a dictionary (optional)

1 All the above equipment comes with the proprietary board game bought in a box in a variety of editions, including the standard form. Scrabble® was invented in Depression-era America, but it became extremely popular in the early 1950s when it spread to the United Kingdom, Europe and Australia.

2 To begin the game, each player chooses a tile to determine who plays first. The player who chooses the letter closest to A begins play. (If a letter bag is not available, turn all the letters into the lid of the box and ensure that they are all face down.)

3 Each player picks out 7 letter tiles and places them in their letter rack, trying to sort them quickly into a word. The first player must place a word, two letters or more, down on the board with one of the letters covering the star in the centre of the board. The word can be placed either horizontally or vertically. The player then counts up the total score of the letters used and the player scoring notes it down. Meanwhile, the first player is taking tiles out of the bag to replace those used (keeping 7 tiles on the letter rack).

4 The next player (usually the player on the first player's left) has to use at least one of the letters already on the board now to create a word from their own letters. However, only one of their own letters need be used so long as it creates a new word, although that cannot be just an 's' to create a plural. If using an 's' a player must create a new word too. See example below – the first player put down PEAR, so the second player could add SING and be credited for creating both PEARS and SING.

]	P	E	A	R	S
					I
					N
					G

5 Play continues in this way, with players creating and adding words across the board, especially trying to achieve good scores with the premium squares, which give double and triple letter as well as double and triple word scores. A dictionary is usually kept close by in the event that a player challenges a word.

6 Socially, Scrabble® is a great after dinner game, however, there are many people who treat this game as far more than social entertainment. There are strategies to learn to become better and better. A wide vocabulary is necessary to enjoy the game in the first place, but if several of the tricky allowable two-letter words are learnt in addition, a distinct advantage will be gained.

SNAKES AND LADDERS

Players: two or more
Age: ideal for children
Equipment: marked board; one different coloured counter for each player; a dice

1 Even young children love this easy game, because it relies totally on luck and enabling them to compete with older children and adults on the same level. Its history is as a centuries-old Hindu game of religious instruction. The game represented the journey through life with the ladders representing virtuous acts and the snakes representing vices.

2 The board is marked with squares from 1-100 and the snakes and ladders are superimposed on the design, each linking two numbered squares.

3 Each player has a counter of a different colour which is advanced around the board by the throw of a dice. Each player must throw a 6 on the dice to begin the game.

4 If the counter lands on a square with the foot of a ladder in it, the ladder can be climbed (say from 9 to 31), but if the counter lands on a snake's head, it is necessary to slide down the snake, which could take the player from 49 to 11. If an opponent's counter is landed on, that counter returns to the start.

5 The object of the game is to safely reach the 100 square with an exact

throw. This is not as easy as it sounds, as, if a player was on 97 and threw a 5, they would advance to 100 and return to 98. This could be the head of a snake so the player would end up back at 78!

6 (A hint: if you are drawing up your own Snakes and Ladders board – designers always place a head of a snake around the 96, 97 or 98 square just for this purpose!)

SOLITAIRE

Players: one
Age: good for children and adults
Equipment: a Solitaire board complete with pegs or marbles

1 Solitaire is thought to have originated in France during the time of the French Revolution, so today there is a French board and also an English board on which to play Solitaire. The traditional French board has 37 shallow dips or holes to take pegs, while the English board has only 33 holes, as shown below:

3 There is only one move to make, and that is a peg has to jump an adjacent peg to an empty space beyond. The other rule is that the jump must be to the left or right, or up or down, never diagonal. The peg jumped over is removed.

4 Play is continuous, until either the goal is accomplished or two or more pegs remain which are isolated, which means the Solitaire has failed.

5 It has been proven by mathematicians that twenty-one different games can be played on the English board with between 15 and 19 moves to gain the Solitaire.

English

French

2 The basic Solitaire game is played the same, whichever board you choose to use. Every hole is filled except the centre hole, and the object is to remove all the pegs from the board except one, which should be in the centre hole.

TWIDDLEUMS

Players: two to six
Age: children and adults
Equipment: marked board; different coloured counters for each player

1 Each player takes a coloured counter and places it in the appropriate circle to begin. If only two are playing they may take up to 3 counters each; if three are playing they may have 2 counters each.

2 One person begins and then each player in turn places their counters on 1 in a circle in front of them. From now on players may move their counters in any direction into an adjoining circle which bears a number consecutive to the occupied circle. For instance, if a counter was in 2 it could be moved to a 1 or a 3 only. If a player cannot move, a turn is missed.

3 If the only appropriate circle is already occupied, a player may move the counter into this circle and 'take' the opponent's piece. (Players should decide whether it is returned to the Starting Circle again or removed completely from the board before commencing play.)

4 The winner is the player who successfully navigates across the board to the correct Finishing Circle for their particular colour.

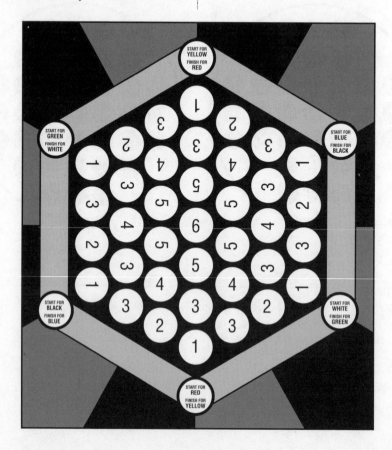

VORTEX

Players: two to four
Age: children and adults
Equipment: marked board; a different coloured counter for each player; a dice

1 Vortex is the game for those people who always seem to throw a 1 or a 2 when everyone else has thrown 6 and begun the game! This game rewards consistent low scoring.

2 Throw the dice to determine who plays first. It is usual for the player throwing the highest score to commence but, to continue the theme of the game, why not reward the lowest scorer by allowing them to begin?

3 Throwing the dice in turn, players take off towards the Vortex. If a player lands on a space already occupied by another player, they change places and the previous holder moves back to where the newcomer was.

4 When nearing the central area, there are marked coloured circles. If a player whose counter is red lands on (R) they are carried immediately into the Vortex and out of the game. (That happens to yellow, green and blue too.)

5 However, if the player gets past those and enters the Refuge area, they may rest and shelter in the Refuge until dislodged and sucked into the Vortex by throwing a 6. If the player lands on the Refuge of another, they stay and miss one turn provided the proper owner does not turn up, in which case they are immediately drawn into the Vortex. However, if another player, also of the incorrect colour arrives at that Refuge, the two players change places.

6 The winner is the survivor – the last one left outside the Vortex.

WOLF AND GOATS

Players: two
Age: adults and older children
Equipment: Draughts board and 13 counters, 12 of one colour and 1 of another colour

1 This game is another version of the old Fox and Geese, but has quite a strategy to enable a strong winning streak.

2 Set up the 12 counters as for Draughts – these are the goats. The wolf may be placed on any of the black squares on its back rank (row).

3 The goats can move one square forwards along a diagonal on any turn and, although the wolf can only move one square forwards or backwards diagonally, it can capture goats by jumping over them and landing on the empty square beyond.

4 To win, the goats need to crowd in the wolf so there are no legal moves left. The wolf wins if it manages to break through the goats to reach their back rank (row).

5 A simple-sounding game, but harder than it seems. Have a go!

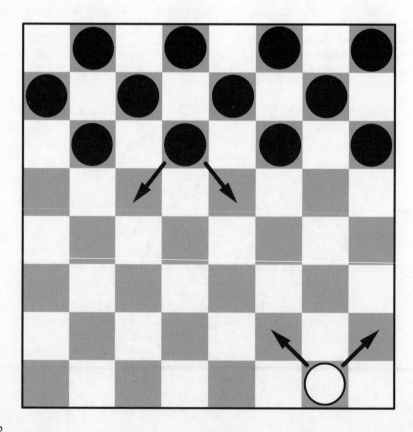

STRATEGIC GAMES

Although many games in the Racing Board Games section had strategic elements, the following are well known as war or territorial games whose players thrive on not only knowing how to play the game, but they also know how to think about the game.

Chess is often thought of as the ultimate in War Games and it is true that from its Hindu beginnings centuries ago (probably around 600 A.D), it spread with warring parties through Persia and into the Islamic world and thence into Europe and England, probably with the Norman conquests. It is believed that Chess (or Shatranj) was developed as a test of courage and mental flexibility and astuteness, but the warring element is certainly there. In Chess you do not surround the enemy, you capture and take him off the board!

ALQUERQUE

Players: two
Age: adults or children who love strategic games
Equipment: board; 24 counters, 12 each of two colours

1 Alquerque is thought to have originated in Ancient Egypt and was taken to Europe (Spain) by the Moors. Originally boards would have been carved from wood, or made from stone or marble, and the lines would have been carved into them.

2 The board consists of 25 points connected by horizontal, vertical and diagonal lines. Each player uses 12 counters arranged at the beginning of a game, leaving the centre point empty, as the illustration below shows:

3 Play is by alternate turns, and players may move one counter to any adjacent empty point, along any line. This means that the person to begin has a choice of four moves.

4 If any adjacent point is occupied by an enemy counter, and there is space immediately beyond it, the man can be captured by leaping. Further captures can be made in the same move so long as there are empty spaces to jump into – directional changes are acceptable.

5 'Prisoners' are removed from play and the winner is the player who takes all their opponent's team. Captures are compulsory, but if two captures are possible, the player can choose between them.

6 An advantage of only one man can seal the fate of the opponent. If men are reduced to two against one, it is extremely likely that the team with two will win.

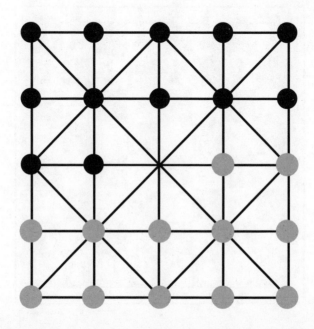

CHESS

Players: two
Age: children and adults
Equipment: 8x8 square board, coloured alternately light and dark (usually black and white; 16 pieces for each player in contrasting colours, usually black and white and consisting of two rooks (castles), two knights, two bishops, a queen, a king and eight pawns in each set

1 Chess is the world's most popular game of any type, either board or otherwise. There are Chess Olympiads held every two years and around one hundred nations take part However, family games are important too, and that is where champions are made! The game originated in India and is believed to be 1400 years old. It was brought to Europe by the Moors and has been a favourite game in the form known today since the 15th century.

2 The board is set between two players with white squares at each right-hand side and the pieces are set out as shown in the illustration below. The pieces next to the King are called King's Bishop, King's Knight and King's Rook and the pieces next to the Queen are likewise Queen's Bishop, Queen's Knight and Queen's Rook.

3 White always moves first, and then players take it in turn to move, moving only one piece in each turn. Once you have touched a piece, you must move it, and then it must stay where you placed it. Rows of squares across the board are called 'ranks' and the rows up and down are called 'files', while lines of squares running diagonally are called 'diagonals'.

Queen's side   Kings's side

e6

4 The first thing to learn in Chess is how the pieces are allowed to move on the board, as follows:

Pawns: can only move directly forwards. They have an option to go two squares on their first move, but only one square from then on. However, Pawns do not capture with the same move, but have to move diagonally one square to capture another piece – they cannot move directly forwards to capture.

PAWN – first move only

PAWN – capture move

Bishops: can only move diagonally, but in any direction and for any number of spaces. They cannot jump over other pieces.

BISHOP

Knights: can move in any direction (forward, backward, or to either side) and always have to move three squares at a time in a sequence of two squares in one direction and then one square to the side.

KNIGHT

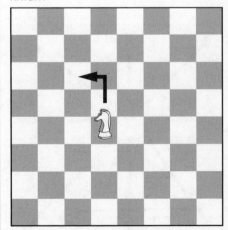

Rooks: can move in any direction (forward, backward, or to either side), and can move over any number of squares. They can only move in one direction in a turn, and cannot jump over other pieces.

ROOK

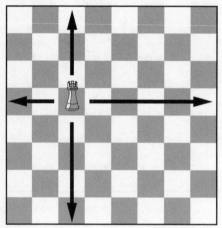

The Queen: can move in any direction (forward, backward, or to either side), and can move over any number of squares. It can move only one way in each turn, however, and cannot jump over other pieces.

QUEEN

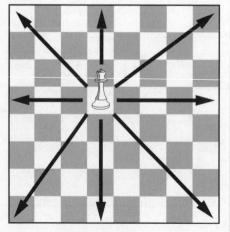

The King: can move and capture pieces in any direction, but can only move one square at a time. The King is the most important piece in the game, so must be guarded by each player as, if you lose your King, you lose the game.

KING

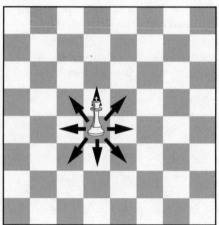

5 The object of the game is to trap your opponent's King, so it cannot escape being captured. This would mean that there are no squares for the King to escape to, no pieces which can be moved to protect it and no piece available to capture the piece doing the capturing. In Chess this situation is called a 'checkmate' and the piece doing the capturing is called the 'checking piece'. However, if either King is in a position where it can be captured it is said to be in 'check' and may be able to be saved. If this is the case, the player implements any of the three things above to stop the 'checkmate'. Either move the King, move another piece in front of the King or capture the checking piece yourself.

6 Castling is a special move for the King and the Rook which helps to keep the King safe in the early part of the game. Castling is the only time a King can move two squares (not just one) and the only time a Rook can jump over a piece. However, there are several rules for the move. The first is that this move must be the first for the King and the Rook. Second, there can be no other pieces between these two. Third, if the King is in check you cannot castle and finally if the King will be in check in the new position, or if the King passes over a square where it would be in check, you cannot castle. Whichever side you are on, Queen's side or King's side, you move the King two squares towards the Queen's or King's Rook and jump the Rook over the King – see illustration below:

7 There is also a special move for Pawns. It is given a French term en passant (pronounced 'on passon') which means 'in passing'. It can only be used when a player moves a Pawn two squares forward on its first move, and an enemy Pawn is in the right place to capture it as if it only moved one square. It has to be done by the enemy Pawn on its next move.

8 Another special thing happens to a Pawn if it arrives unscathed and uncaptured to the other end of the board – it can be Queened. If you still have your Queen, you can use another piece, such as a Rook inverted or another token altogether. It is possible therefore to have four or five queens on the board at the same time, say three black and two white.

9 Drawn games in Chess are common. Sometimes it just is not possible to checkmate the other side. It

CASTLING

CASTLING

can happen also that one side cannot make any more legal moves, but is actually not in check – this is a 'stalemate'. Other drawn games occur when one player continually puts the other in check. If this is repeated three times, the game is declared drawn. A game may also end in a draw with one player resigning or both players agreeing to end the game.

10 To play and improve your game you need to learn how experts write down moves in games of Chess, and then you can follow and practise

games yourself from books or magazines. There are two systems of notation (the code in which Chess moves are written down) – algebraic and descriptive. Algebraic is the most common and will be explained now.

Look back to the layout illustration on page 196. See how on the right hand side the ranks are numbered 1-8 and the files are lettered from right to left. Each square is therefore called by the letter and number of the rank and file it is in – see e6 is arrowed.

Each piece is given a letter, except for the Pawn – Queen (Q), King (K), Bishop (B), Rook (R) and Knight (N). To write a move, the letter of the piece is written first followed by the letter and the number of the square it moves to, and White's moves are always given first. For example, Ke6. For a Pawn you just write the square it moves to, such as, b4. When a piece captures another you write 'x' between the name of the piece and the move it makes, and check is written '+' – for example, Rxd6. Castling on the King's side is written 0-0 and on the Queen's side is written 0-0-0.

11 Now it is time to begin playing a game! There are many books devoted entirely to the opening moves in a game of Chess so, if you are determined to become an expert player, look for some of these. However, for the beginners, here are some tips and tactics regarding opening moves in Chess. White always begins the game.

The most important thing to remember is that your pieces are far more powerful in the centre of the board, not at the edges. They all have more

squares which they are able to move to and control, so a good first move is to move one of the centre Pawns two squares. (Remember, too, that your opponent will know this and will be planning on doing the same.) This move opens the way for the Bishops to emerge and, in your next few turns, plan on moving out the Knights and Bishops to good central positions. Once this is achieved, you are able to castle (see point 6). This keeps your King safely protected by Pawns at the side of the board. This is a strategy well worth remembering and practising to see its usefulness.

12 Try not to waste moves by moving the same piece too often or putting pieces on the wrong squares. Equally, you may be tempted to capture an undefended Pawn early in the game. This is fine if you are continuing to develop your own pieces, but it is not worth chasing that Pawn and neglecting the placement of your own pieces. Always have a reason to move a Pawn. They should be used to strengthen your central position, to defend your own pieces, as well as to attack enemy pieces. Keep practising and reading about Chess games in magazines or books and these and many more strategies can be learnt.

13 At the beginning of the game, remember to do these three things and you will be in a good position to continue and even win the game:

a) move the centre Pawns first to control the centre squares, defend your pieces and attack your opponent. Only move a Pawn if you have a reason to do so;

b) bring the Knights and Bishops out early in the game. Time should not be wasted in moving the Queen, and the Rooks are better left until the board is clearer later on;

c) look after your King (remember castling) from the beginning.

14 Now you need to ask yourself some questions. Try to understand what your opponent is trying to do. He will certainly be after your King as you are after his, but can you see his plan? Are your pieces defended or are any being attacked? Is your King well defended? Are your pieces working as a team? Are any of your pieces blocking your advance?

15 If neither player manages to checkmate in the middle game, both sides gradually lose pieces. In this case, you can remain powerful if you have any Pawns left in the game, as any one can make it to the other side of the board and become a Queen (see point 8). Also continue to keep all your pieces on open lines near the centre of the board because they continue to be most powerful here. This is also the time to bring out the King as an attacker, but guard it always.

16 There are many, many ways to force a checkmate whether you have many pieces remaining or not. Keep in mind that it is easier to create the situation for checkmate if the King is forced to the edge. However, it is recommended a beginner's Chess book be bought to continue the learning!

CONQUEST

Players: two
Age: older children and adults
Equipment: 9x9 square board; 9 different coloured counters each, 8 plain and 1 marked in some way to designate a king

1 The aim of Conquest (there is a hint in the title!) is to capture the central fortress according to one of four possible plans of occupation (see illustration below). Players must agree which plan they intend using before the game begins.

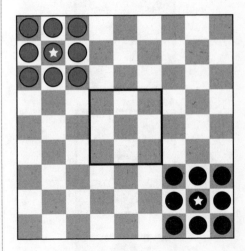

2 Players position their pieces as shown in the illustration to begin with eight ordinary counters surrounding one specially marked king.

3 Turns are alternate and only one move is allowed at a turn. The only permitted move for any piece is one square diagonally forward or backward (so that pieces stay on squares of the same colour throughout the game.)

4 If a player traps an opponent's piece between two of their own pieces in a diagonal line, so all pieces are on the same colour square, the player may exile the trapped piece to any other square of the same colour.

DRAUGHTS

Players: two
Age: children and adults
Equipment: 8x8 square chessboard (usually black and white); 12 counters or pieces for each player in different colours (usually black and white or red and white)

1 Draughts is known as Checkers in America but, whatever you know it as, a similar game was played in southern Europe in medieval times. It appears that the game was derived from an even older game played in the Middle East.

2 The aim of Draughts is to capture all your opponent's men, or ensure that they cannot move anywhere by blocking them. This means that draws can be a common result, as pieces can circle each other endlessly. The game is played on a standard 8x8 square chessboard, using only the dark (usually black) squares. Both players begin with 12 pieces or men each, set up as indicated in the illustration on page 203.

3 The player with Black begins by moving one piece one square forward in a diagonal direction only. This means that the pieces on the two back rows of each side cannot move at all until some of the pieces in the first row have been moved.

4 Draughts pieces can capture by jumping over an opponent's piece to the empty square beyond and then that piece is removed from the board. Captures are obligatory in Draughts. If the opportunity presents itself, the player must capture the opposing piece, even if it will result in that piece

itself being captured by the opponent in the next move. Multiple captures are possible too, so long as there are empty spaces for the capturing piece to land in on its spree.

5 When an opposing piece makes it to the back rank (or row) of the enemy it is rewarded by being crowned a king. Physically it means that a single piece receives another piece on top so it looks different. A king can move backwards as well as forwards, but still only diagonally on black squares.

6 The end of the game in Draughts can be subtle. Often, a player moves in for the kill to win the game and suddenly finds that the game can never be anything but a draw. On the strategic side, pieces are often sacrificed in order to create more opportunities to win outright, by making multiple captures.

7 The more you play Draughts, the more you will realise that the opening moves can mean all to a good game, and often whether or not you win or lose. Most social players do not think about opening moves, and move anything anywhere, however, tournament and club players often make things interesting by removing one piece for each player (the same one) and playing the game with 11 pieces not 12. Still others, usually tournament players, have cards written down with opening three move sequences. One is drawn at the beginning of the game, so everyone follows this opening for two games, playing once as White and once as Black.

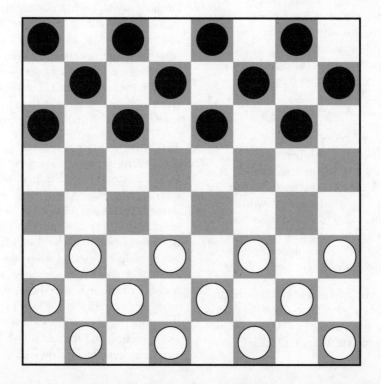

Variations: As versions of this game have been around since 1600 B.C. in Egypt, there are bound to be nationally-accepted differing rules and layouts. Following are some of the most common:

Italian: almost identical to the British and American versions, except that in Italian, Draughts kings cannot be captured by uncrowned pieces. Also, a player who has a choice between two or more captures must play the move that captures the most pieces, despite the outcome. If the choice is an equal number, but one piece is a king, the move must capture the king. Winning is the same as for British and American Draughts.

Spanish: the only difference between Spanish and Italian Draughts is in the power of the king. In Spanish Draughts, the king can move any number of squares along a diagonal in any direction, as long as it is unobstructed by its own pieces. The king can also land any distance beyond a captured piece but, having made that capture, his next capture should be on another diagonal if possible. Winning is the same as for British and American Draughts.

German: Spanish and German Draughts differ only with the capturing powers of uncrowned pieces. Uncrowned pieces can capture in both a forward and backward direction, and crowned pieces are called queens or dames, not kings. Winning is the same as for British and American Draughts.

Polish: virtually the same as German Draughts, Polish Draughts is played on a board measuring 10×10 squares and uses 40 pieces, 20 for each player,

which are laid out five each on the first four rows. Moving and winning is the same as for German Draughts, and also crowned pieces are known as queens.

Canadian: this version is identical to German and Polish Draughts except it uses an even larger board and consequently more pieces. A 12×12 square board is used with 60 pieces, 30 for each player, which are set up on the black squares in the five rows from, and including, the back row. Moving the pieces is the same as in German Draughts which introduces the concept of the uncrowned pieces being able to move and capture in a forward and backward direction. If an uncrowned piece reaches the back row but has not finished his move, he cannot be crowned on that turn. Winning is the same as for British and American Draughts.

Russian: this game is played in a similar way to German Draughts but a player with a choice of captures has just that, a choice, and does not have to take the larger number of pieces. Also, a piece is crowned a king as soon as it reaches the far row and acts like a king from then on. Winning is the same as for British and American Draughts.

Turkish: a traditional Turkish chessboard has no chequers but is the same colour all over, although this game can be played on a black and white board. Each player has 16 pieces set out on each player's second and third rows next to each other. Moves are directly forward or sideways and not diagonally and kings can move any number of squares directly forward, sideways or backward. Kings can therefore make multiple captures in any direction and for any number of spaces as long as their own pieces are not in the way. Pieces are removed when they are jumped. A player must make a capture when possible and must always take the greater number of pieces. Winning can be the same as for British and American Draughts but also, in Turkish Draughts, if a player has a king and the other player only has a single man remaining on the board the player with the king wins.

Other variations of the British and American version could include both the following:

Diagonal Draughts: this is an interesting concept away from the traditional game and good for those getting a little bored with the original! It can be played with either 12 or 9 pieces as shown on the two following layouts A and B, and the rules are the same as for the original except that pieces are crowned only when they land on the corner squares (marked k on the following illustrations).

Losing Draughts: an obvious concept brought about by boredom we expect! In this version of the great game the idea is the winner is the first person to get rid of all their pieces! It appeals particularly to young players. The board is arranged the same way as Draughts and the rules of movement and crowning are the same. The only difference is that in strategy – do not try to make kings, it nearly always means the other player wins in this version! Players are obliged to capture if they can, and the winner, as mentioned before, is the player who gets rid of all their pieces or is placed in a position where they cannot move.

Diagonal Draughts

A

B

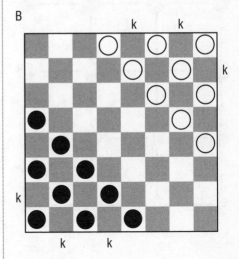

FOUR FIELD KONO

Players: two
Age: adults
Equipment: square board with sixteen points drawn 4x4; 16 counters, 8 each of two different colours

1 This game comes from Korea and is played on a square board containing sixteen points. Each player arranges their 8 counters as shown in the diagram.

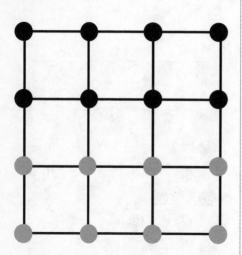

2 Players move in alternate turns. If a counter can jump a counter of the same colour and land on an opponent's counter, it can capture it. If no capturing moves are possible, the only move allowed is to move to an adjacent point along one of the lines.

3 The winner is the player who can capture all the opponent's counters, or who can block them so they are unable to move.

GO

Players: two
Age: mainly adults
Equipment: a Go board (called a go ban); Go stones which are made up of 181 black stones and 180 white stones (361 in all)

1 Go, or Wei-ch'i in Chinese, is considered one of the greatest strategic games. It originated in China at least 3000 years ago, and has been adopted by Japan and other Asian countries. It is gaining popularity in the West as well.

2 The board is made up of a 19×19 square grid, which yields 361 intersections or points. The nine darker points placed on the board are used as reference points, especially for placing of handicap stones (see point 4). As a game on a full size board can take hours, the game is often played on a smaller 13×3 board, while beginners can play on a 9×9 board. The rules and principles remain the same on the smaller boards, but the game is simplified.

3 The objective of the game is for each player to place their stones on the board to surround more unoccupied territory and enemy stones than their opponent.

4 Black plays first, so holds an advantage. The stronger player should then play White to equalise a little. If the stronger player continues to win, Go has a handicap system which can be implemented to enable the weaker player to place up to nine stones on the handicap points before play begins, as follows:

2-stone handicap	d4, q16
3-stone handicap	d4, q4, q16
4-stone handicap	d4, d16, q4, q16
5-stone handicap	As 4-stone plus k10
6-stone handicap	d4, d10, d16, q4, q10, q16
7-stone handicap	As 6-stone plus k10
8-stone handicap	as 6-stone plus k4, k16
9-stone handicap	d4, d10, d16, q4, q10, q16, k4, k10, k16

5 Players take alternate turns. A turn consists of placing a stone on an unoccupied point (not in a square), and it may be placed on any unoccupied point, except when a *ko* (almost eternity) situation arises (see point 6). Once in position, a stone is only moved if it is captured, when it is then removed from the board and retained by the capturing player.

6 Each player's aim is to form stones into connected groups or chains in such a way as to surround as many vacant points and opponent's stones as possible. When stones of one colour have nowhere to move to on adjacent points because stones of the other colour occupy the points, they are captured and removed. However, it is possible to win a game without capturing many, or even any, stones, as the objective is territorial gain.

Handicap Points

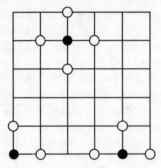

Capture of a single stone

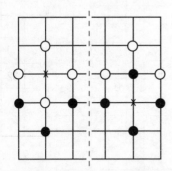

Two examples of capture of a group of stones

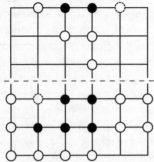

Two examples of a *ko* situation

A *seki* situation

7 A *ko* (almost eternity) situation is one which can be repeated indefinitely and means that the game would never be won or lost. So, the rules state that in such a situation the second player may not recapture until they have made at least one move somewhere else on the board. See illustration.

8 Another tactical situation occurs in which neither side can move without loss. This is known as *seki*. See illustration below. If either side moves on one of the two enclosed points, the other will occupy the remaining point to capture the opponent's group. These positions are neutralised at the end of the game, and neither side scores the territory.

9 Usually players utilising the whole board will mark out territories to the sides of the board with their first few moves. Once this phase of play begins to be crowded, the second or battle phase can begin. Both sides begin to build territory 'walls' to ensure opponents cannot enter.

10 When this phase of play draws to a close there only remains the tidying up of loose points here and there. Once both players 'pass' which means there are no more legal moves, the counting up begins. Neutral points are filled with stones of either colour and captured stones are returned to the board to fill points in the opponent's territory. Lastly, territories are adjusted into more or less regular shapes to facilitate counting. The unoccupied points are counted and the lower score is taken from the higher score. In the illustration on page 209, Black won by 3 points.

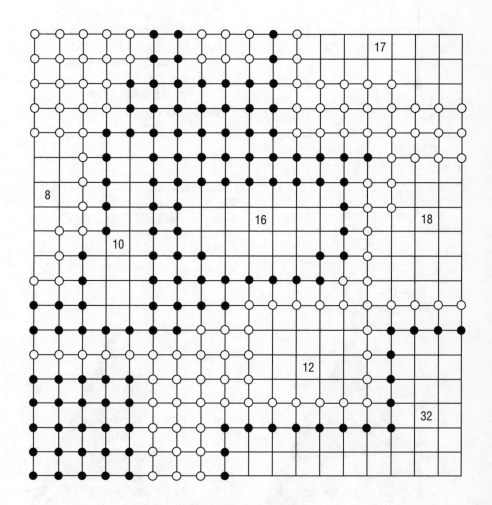

● black counters
○ white counters

white	black
8	16
17	10
18	32
12	58
55	

HEX

Players: two
Age: adults
Equipment: specialised board; 122 counters, 61 counters in black and 61 in white

1 A relatively little known game these days, Hex was invented by a Dane named Piet Hein in the 1940s. Traditionally, it has a board made up of hexagonal shapes, but triangles have also been used, and a board can easily be drawn on a piece of card. Samples of both shaped boards are shown below.

2 Firstly, a pair of opposite sides of the board are designated as black and white. The aim of the game is to form a continuous line of counters from one side of the board to the opposite side; thus, white moves towards white and black towards black.

3 Each player takes a set of pieces (counters) and the first player chooses where to place a piece on the board. Turns then alternate with each player placing a counter on any unoccupied hexagon. Once they have been placed, counters cannot be moved.

4 The game is won by the first player to construct an unbroken line of counters. This does not have to be a straight line, but must join the player's two sides of the board. Theoretically, the first player will always win, but if the other player can throw up a line of defence early on, they will win. There are no draws in Hex.

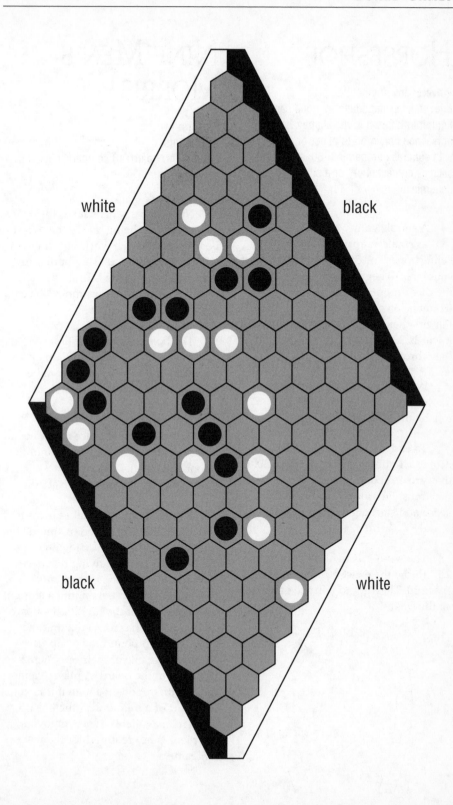

white

black

black

white

HORSESHOE

Players: any number can play
Age: children and adults – a good party game
Equipment: board in the shape of a horseshoe drawn on to paper or cardboard with squares numbered 1–30; a dice; treats such as confectionery or a small denomination coin

1 A simple game, where treats such as small wrapped items of confectionery or coins take the place of counters. To begin, each player throws the dice and places their stake (counter) on the corresponding space. Players then take it in turns to advance towards 30 in accordance with what they throw on the dice.

2 When a player lands on an occupied space, the original inhabitant is returned to space 1.

3 To end, a player must throw an exact number to reach space 30. If they are on space 27 and throw a five, they must go around the horseshoe space and start again from space 2, and so on.

4 The winner is the first person to throw the exact number to reach space 30. They get to win the game and all the stakes!

NINE MEN'S MORRIS

Players: two
Age: adults
Equipment: board; 18 counters, nine black and nine white

1 Nine Men's Morris takes the award for being one of the oldest board games in the world. It is known to have been particularly popular in the same form in the Middle Ages in Europe but could be around 3000 years old.

2 The board (see illustration page 213) can be drawn up on paper or card although they can be bought, usually made of wood.

3 The aim is to be the first to manoeuvre and place men to be in a position to capture all but two of the opponent's men, or to make it impossible for them to move at all.

4 Firstly, each player takes turns to place their nine men (counters) on the points of the intersecting lines. Then play turns to moving the pieces around the board to create a 'mill' – that is, getting three men into a straight line along one of the lines of the board. Once a player has formed a mill they are entitled to pound their opponent by removing one of their opponent's pieces from the board. A player cannot remove an opponent's man if it is in turn part of a mill, unless there is no other man available. Once removed, the piece is not required for the rest of the game.

5 It is allowable to form new mills by opening an existing mill (by moving one piece) and then re-creating the mill by returning the man at the next turn. Mills can be broken and reformed at any time, and each time it allows the creator to pound their opponent.

6 Play continues until one of the players is reduced to only two men on the board, or a player's pieces have been so blocked they are unable to move. Should a player's only remaining pieces form a mill, they still must move a piece even if it means losing a piece and therefore the game.

7 Optional rules include 'hopping'. For those players who only have three remaining pieces, some people play that they are no longer restricted to moving along a line to an adjacent point, but may hop to any vacant spot on the board.

8 The winner succeeds in blocking their opponent's men so they cannot be moved or has pounded the opponent so well, they only have two men left.

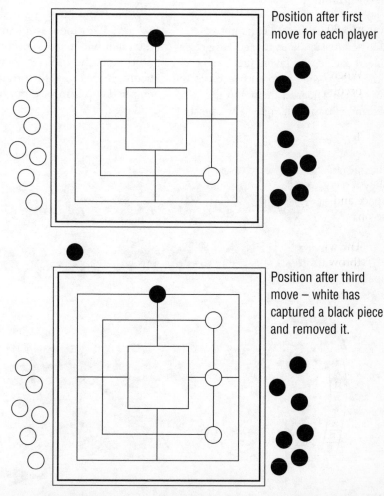

Position after first move for each player

Position after third move – white has captured a black piece and removed it.

OWARI

Players: two
Age: older children and adults
Equipment: board; 48 counters
(traditionally seeds, beans or stones)

1 This game comes from West Africa and is one of the family of games known as Mancala games. They have been played for thousands of years, traditionally played with a carved wooden board and seeds, stones or beans as counters. Sometimes, the games are played in hollows scooped in the ground.

2 The board has 12 cups in two rows of six, and two scoring cups, one at each end. Players face each other across the board and each has the row of cups nearest them and the scoring cup to their right. The object of the game is to capture as many seeds as possible.

3 Four seeds are placed in each of the 12 cups to begin (leaving the scoring cups empty). Players decide who moves first and then turns alternate.

4 The first player takes all the seeds from a cup on their side of the board and 'sows' or places them one by one in the cups around the board in a clockwise direction. Therefore, for the first turn, there will be 4 seeds in every cup and these are placed one by one in four more cups.

5 Play continues in this way. If there are 12 or more seeds in one cup then that will mean the sowing will need more than one circuit of the board. In this case, the original emptied cup is missed out when sowing.

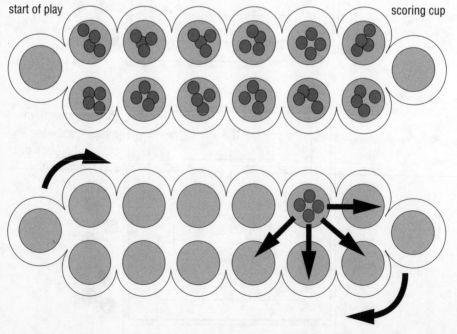

start of play   scoring cup

6 A player can capture seeds if they sow a seed into an opponent's cup so this cup then contains two or three seeds. The sower can remove all the seeds and place them in their scoring cup. After making a capture, the same player can capture seeds in adjacent cups if they also contain two or three seeds. However, a player cannot capture all the seeds in their opponent's cups (as they would then be unable to move when it was their turn), so one cup is left intact.

7 Play ends when a player is unable to make a move or when none of the remaining seeds can be captured. Seeds are then totalled in the scoring cups and the player who has the most seeds wins the game.

QUEEN'S GUARD

Players: two
Age: children and adults
Equipment: hexagonally-shaped board; two sets of pieces in different colours, each consisting of one queen and six guards

1 A board can be drawn (or computer-generated these days) on card or paper, with eleven hexagons as the central line and five lines each side which diminish one by one until a line of six hexagons is drawn. There should be 91 hexagons in all. The counters need to have a special marking drawn on one counter to differentiate the queen from the guards. See below.

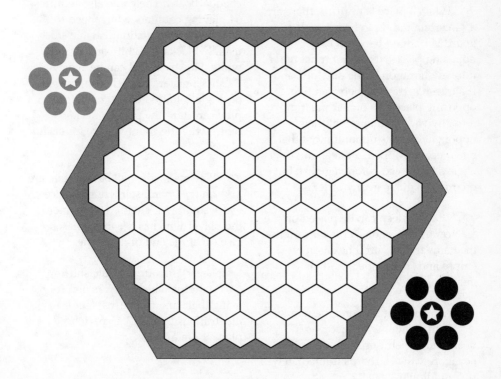

2 The game is won when one player succeeds in positioning their queen on the central hexagon and the six guards immediately surrounding it.

3 To start the play, there are two methods used. The first is that the pieces are positioned as shown in the illustration or players agree to position their pieces in turn, one at a time, anywhere they want to on the board.

4 Once the start of play has been decided, players then move one piece at a time, in turn. A piece can only be moved into a vacant hexagon and, except when a piece is trapped between opposing pieces, it may only be moved one hexagon sideways or toward the centre of the board. When a player touches a piece, that is the piece that must be moved.

5 When a piece is trapped, there are certain moves to be made. If a guard is trapped between two opposing pieces, its owner must move it to any hexagon in the outside band. If a queen is trapped between two opposing pieces, its owner must move it to any vacant square that their opponent decides upon. If more than one piece is trapped, a queen must always be moved before a guard, but guards can move in any order.

6 Only a queen can be placed on the central hexagon. A player forfeits the game if the central hexagon is empty and surrounded by their guards.

7 As mentioned before, the winner is the player who succeeds in positioning their queen on the central hexagon with six guards immediately surrounding it.

REVERSI OR OTHELLO®

(Othello is a registered trademark of Tsukuda in Japan)

Players: two
Age: older children and adults
Equipment: 8x8 board; 64 double-sided coloured counters

1 Reversi is a game of strategy that was invented in the late 19th century, but which has been revived as a proprietary game called Othello®.

2 The new boards of Othello® have 64 playing circles with interconnecting lines, however, Reversi can be played on a 64-square standard chequerboard. The game also requires 64 playing counters which need to have two easily distinguishable sides, usually black and white or red and white. However, this can be achieved by sticking stars or circles on one side of single coloured counters. Before play can start, the players decide which way the counters face for each player.

3 Play ends when all 64 counters are on the board, so there is a piece on every square (or circle). The winner is the player who has the most pieces face up at the end of the game.

4 There are four possible starting patterns which players aim for using their first two turns – see illustrations page 217. Experienced players prefer A.

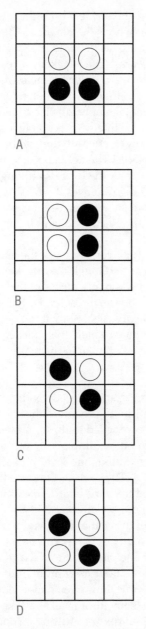

A

B

C

D

5 Once the first four pieces are placed, each player tries to make one move per turn. Only 'taking moves' are permitted, so if a player is unable to make such a move, they lose their turn. Both players are limited to 32 turns.

6 A 'taking move' is created by positioning a piece so that it is in a square next to a square containing an opposition piece; and it traps at least one opposition piece in a line in any direction between itself and another of the taker's pieces. Once a piece is taken, it is turned over to show that it now belongs to the other player. A piece may be turned over again and again throughout a game as it passes from one player to another – pieces are not removed from the board. Examples of taking moves are shown below:

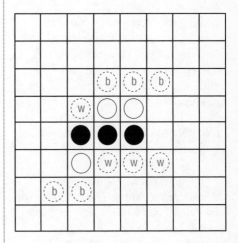

7 Multiple captures are possible, but strategic studies have shown that it is actually better to capture counters singly in the early and middle parts of the game.

8 It has been accepted by Reversi strategists that the corner squares are most valuable to control, with the band around the centre next best and so on outwards. Nevertheless, strategy changes and it is best to play just for fun and develop your own strategy along the way.

RINGO

Players: two
Age: older children and adults
Equipment: a circular board; one player (defender) has 4 counters, the other (attacker) has 7 counters – they must be of different colours

1 Ringo was invented in Germany and has certain similarities to Fox and Geese (page 180).

2 The board can be drawn on paper or card. It comprises a large circle which is divided equally into eight segments, one of which is shaded and called the neutral zone. The central circle or fortress is also a distinctive colour and six concentric rings of equal size spread out beyond it. The resulting sections of segment and rings are alternately coloured light and dark – see illustration.

3 Each player has counters in different colours. The defender (of the fortress) has 4 counters and the attacker has 7. See the illustration for the start of play layout. Nobody has a counter in the neutral zone – the defender's pieces are arranged around the fortress, and the attacker's are on the outermost ring.

4 The aim of playing Ringo is that each player tries to capture or immobilise as many of their opponent's pieces as possible to achieve their particular objective. The attacker's objective is to capture the fortress by getting two of their pieces safely into it; the defender's objective is to prevent this from happening.

5 Players decide who is the attacker and who is the defender. The attacker moves first and players then play in turns. The attacker moves their pieces forward (towards the centre) or sideways. However, the defender has the advantage of being able to move their pieces in any direction (except diagonally) – after all, they do have fewer pieces! The defender may not actually enter the fortress although is allowed to jump over it when capturing an attacker, as long as there is an empty section to land in.

6 Both players may use the neutral zone – although the attacker may only have as many pieces in the neutral zone as the defender has still on the board. Therefore, if the defender is down to two men, the attacker can only have two men in the neutral zone at any one time.

7 Both attacker and defender can capture the enemy, although they are not compelled to do so. A piece can be captured by jumping over it from an adjacent section onto a vacant section beyond it. The captured piece is then removed from the board. In capturing moves both the attacker and the defender move the same way as they do ordinarily. A player can only capture one piece in a move, and all pieces are safe from capture in the neutral zone. However, either player can use the neutral zone as a take off or landing point for capturing an enemy.

8 Play ends when the attacker successfully places two of their pieces into the fortress.

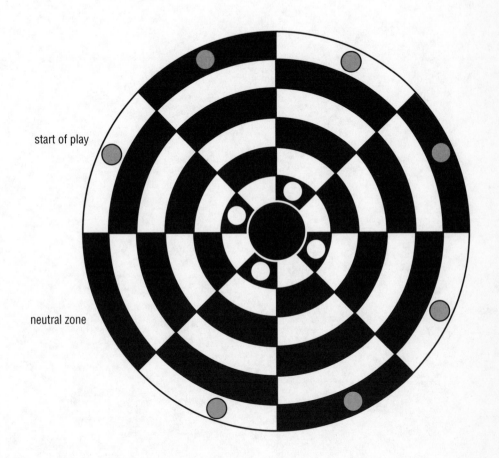

start of play

neutral zone

DOMINO, TILE AND DICE GAMES

In Western society we really only play one tile game, and that is Mah Jong – one of China's most popular games. Dominoes are the 'tiles' we play with most. They are of Chinese origin but have evolved over the years, so that many different sets are used around the world today.

Dice games usually give bad impressions of gambling dens and lost money, but dice games are actually really good fun for children. Because of the huge element of luck involved in any dice game, children begin on even terms against adults in any game. Enjoy them!

DOMINO GAMES

Dominoes are of Chinese origin but today many different sets are used around the world. The standard Western pack is called the Double-6 – this is because the highest domino in the set is the 6:6 (a double-six). The Double-6 originated in Europe probably from the early 18th century and the illustration below shows the 28 tiles which make up the pack. Individual dominoes are known as tiles, stones or even bones. However, we have included a number of games which use a Double-9 set (where the highest domino is the 9:9 – a double-nine).

These sets have 55 tiles in all, enabling more people to play. Each domino is divided into halves, each half-tile having a number of pips or none at all (blanks). If a tile has identical halves (such as 5:5) it is known as a double or doublet; all other half-tiles are called singles. Tiles are further designated by being in suits, named after the numbers 1-6 and the blank. Each suit consists of 7 tiles and all single tiles belong to two suits. Doubles, of course, only belong to one suit.

ALL FIVES

Players: two to four
Age: children and adults, but not suitable for younger children because of the complicated scoring
Equipment: a set of double-6 dominoes; scoring pad

1 Based on the game of Draw Dominoes, this game has a popular following in America. It is different due to its scoring system based on fives. It is also known as Muggins or Fives Up.

2 Players draw five dominoes each to begin. The first player leads with any domino (it does not have to be a doublet), and scores if its pips add up to 5 or 10 – see illustration (a).

3 The next player scores if a domino can be added, and the ends of the layout still add up to 5 or a multiple of 5 (b). (In this illustration the ends do not add up to 5 or a multiple, in which case the player does not score. However, the player could have chosen to take a tile from the 'boneyard' (spare pool of dominoes) to see if they could obtain a tile with which to score.)

4 A player now plays the first double of the game and opens a third end (c), although again there would be no score as the ends add up to 8 – 6+1+1.

5 The next domino placed opens up the fourth and final end of the game (and in this case would score as 6+1+1+2=10). See illustration (d).

6 Play continues on these four ends of the layout until one player finishes all their dominoes or the game is blocked.

7 A game of All Fives is usually 150 or 200 points (depending upon how many hands it is wished to play), and the scores accumulate as follows. A player scores 1 point when they place a domino and the layout's ends total 5 or a multiple of 5. The winner of a hand also scores points for the spots on their opponent's remaining dominoes.

However, some people play a variant in which players score one point if the layout totals 5, two points for 10 and three points for 15, and so on. In this game, the winning score is exactly 61 points, and a winner of a hand scores only a fifth of the value of their opponent's remaining dominoes.

a)

b)

c)

d)

225

8 If a player fails to claim their points after placing a domino in the layout, the first opponent to call 'Muggins' or 'Fives' claims those points.

Variations: A game called All Threes or Threes Up is played exactly the same way, but the scoring is based on multiples of 3. If you really want to tax your arithmetical brain, play Fives and Threes. As the name implies, it is a version where scoring is based on multiples of both 5s and 3s. One point is scored if the ends of the layout total five or three or a multiple thereof, or 2 points if the total of the ends is a multiple of both 5 and 3.

BERGEN

Players: two to four
Age: children and adults
Equipment: set of double-6 dominoes

1 The aim of this basic Draw Dominoes game is that players also score points when there are matching dominoes at the ends of the layout. For two or three players they begin with six dominoes each, and four players start with five dominoes each.

2 As usual the player with the highest double starts play. Subsequent play occurs on only two ends and a player who cannot or will not add a domino to the layout, draws from the 'boneyard' or spare pool of dominoes.

3 Players score 2 points whenever they add a tile that makes the two ends of the layout match (known as a double heading). See illustration below where the 5:2 and the 3:2 were added:

a)

The next player was lucky enough to be able to add a double-2, and so scored 3 points for a triple heading, seen below:

b)

4 Finally, a player scores 2 points for winning a hand. If no player actually finishes playing their dominoes and the game is blocked, the hand is won by the player not holding any doubles. If more than one player holds doubles, the player with the fewest doubles wins or the player with the fewest spots (pips) on their dominoes at the end wins.

5 A game of Bergen usually goes to 10 or 15 points.

BLIND HUGHIE

Players: two to five
Age: children and adults
Equipment: set of double-6 dominoes

1 If four or five are playing, each draws five dominoes without looking at them; if two or three are playing, each draws seven dominoes, again without looking at them.

2 Each player lays out their dominoes, face down, in a line in front of them. The first player begins by taking the first domino on their left and lays it face up in the centre of the table. Turns pass around the table and, at their turn, each player takes the domino on the left of their line and does one of two things:

a) if it matches at either end of the layout, it is played; or

b) if it does not match, the player lays it face down at the right of their line.

3 Play continues in this way until one player either finishes their dominoes, or the play is obviously blocked and can proceed no further.

BLOCK DOMINOES

Players: two to four
Age: children and adults
Equipment: a set of double-6 dominoes

1 This is the basic game of Dominoes, which is suitable for younger children. Draw Dominoes, sometimes known as Block and Draw Dominoes, is the basic game for a group of older players.

2 Two players usually draw seven tiles each, and three or four players draw five tiles each. The first player is the player with the highest double. They begin by laying this double domino in the centre of the table. Turns then pass around the table, with each player adding matching dominoes to either end of the line.

3 If a player is unable to add a tile because none of their dominoes matches, they miss a turn.

4 After one player has played all their dominoes (and called 'Domino!') the game ends. Spots are counted on the other players' dominoes, with the winner being credited for the total. Games are usually played to a set number of points, agreed beforehand – 100 to 200 points is usual.

5 The next game can start with the player who won, or by the player who draws the highest double.

CROSS DOMINOES

Players: two to four
Age: children and adults
Equipment: a set of double-6 dominoes

1 Read through the play for Block and Draw dominoes and then you will have enough knowledge to play this slightly trickier dominoes game, which is also known as Doubles.

2 Again, the player who draws the highest double starts. Then, however many players there are, the next four turns have to match dominoes to form a cross.

3 It is easiest to follow the illustration below. A double-5 was set to start, then the next players in turn laid out a 5:1, 5:6, 5:2 and 5:0 (blank) to create the four open ends needed for this game, giving a 1, 6, 2 and 0 available for play.

4 Until the cross has been laid, no other dominoes can be played and, if a player does not have the required numbered tile, they must draw a tile from the 'boneyard' (spare pool of dominoes) on their turn.

5 Play now continues as for basic Draw Dominoes, see page 231.

CYPRUS

Players: two to ten
Age: children and adults
Equipment: a set of double-9 dominoes
(55 dominoes in all)

1 This game is sometimes referred to as Sebastopol, and requires a set of dominoes known as double-9s, which has 55 dominoes instead of the normal set of 28. It is an interesting game for a large party of players.

2 The dominoes are shuffled on the playing surface and players draw according to how many are playing: for four players, 13 each; five players draw eleven each; six players draw nine each; seven players draw seven; eight or nine players draw six; and ten players draw five each. The player with the double-9 begins. If no one has drawn the double-9 the dominoes are shuffled and drawn again.

3 After the double-9 is played, the domino must be matched on both sides and ends to make a cross (as with Cross Dominoes), but then must also be matched diagonally to make an eight-pointed star (see illustration).

4 Play continues clockwise and, when the star has been created, play moves to the ends of the nines already played, which need to be matched.

5 The rules and form of play continue then as for Block and Draw Dominoes.

DOUBLE CROSS DOMINOES

Players: two to four
Age: children and adults
Equipment: a set of double-6 dominoes

1   This is a variation of Cross Dominoes, and firstly is set up as for Cross Dominoes. However, to make things just a little more difficult, a doublet must be played on one of the four cross arms before play can continue. See illustration.

2   A double-4 began the play, then 6:4, 2:4, 1:4 and 0:4 were played. Now the four ends of the cross are covered, a doublet must be played on one of them. In this case, a double-blank was added. If a player does not have a matching tile they take a tile from the 'boneyard' pile.

3   Play continues as for Block and Draw Dominoes.

DOUBLE NINE CROSS DOMINOES

Players: two to four or more
Age: children and adults
Equipment: a set of double-9 dominoes (55 in all)

1   If two or three players are taking part, they draw seven dominoes; four or more players draw five each.

2   The player holding the highest doublet begins the game, and then dominoes are matched to the two ends and two sides, as seen in Cross Dominoes.

3   In this game, whenever a doublet is played, two more ends are opened for play. Following the diagram below, the play opened with a double-7, then four dominoes (all with a 7 at one end) were laid at the four sides of the doublet. The next player laid a double-9, and two following players added 9:2 and a 9:6 as illustrated.

DRAW DOMINOES

Players: two to four
Age: children and adults
Equipment: a set of double-6 dominoes

1 Two players usually draw seven dominoes each, while three or four players draw five each.

2 Play is as basic Block Dominoes described previously, but there are some differences in Draw Dominoes, as follows.

3 For instance, a player who is unable or unwilling to add a domino to the layout, must draw dominoes from the 'boneyard' (spare pool of dominoes) until one is drawn that they are able or willing to play to the layout, or until only two dominoes remain in the 'boneyard'. If this situation occurs, when there are only two dominoes remaining in the 'boneyard', a player who cannot play a domino must end or miss a turn. Finally, if a player draws or looks at an extra domino by mistake, or turns up a domino so that other players see it, that player must keep the domino.

4 Many players, especially family players, consider this combination of Block and Draw dominoes to be the best basic form of Dominoes.

MALTESE CROSS DOMINOES

Players: two to four
Age: children and adults
Equipment: a set of double-6 dominoes

1 This is an even trickier version of Cross Dominoes (also known as Doubles). The doublet must be set to start and the four dominoes matched to both its ends and sides, just as in Cross Dominoes.

2 Then four more doublets have to be placed at each arm of the original cross before play can proceed. Only at that stage can play proceed as for Draw and Block Dominoes on all four arms of the Maltese Cross.

3 Players often have to raid the 'boneyard' (spare pool of dominoes) to get this game going.

MATADOR

Players: two to four, or more for larger sets
Age: children and adults
Equipment: a set of double-6 dominoes (for larger groups of players a set of double-9 dominoes would be better)

1 This is a slightly unusual game of dominoes, using the Draw Dominoes principle. Dominoes are played when they make a specific total with another domino at the ends of the layout. There are also wild dominoes known as matadors.

2 When playing with a double-6 set, the total of dominoes must be 7 and the matadors are the 6:1, 5:2, 4:3 and the 0:0. Two players begin with seven dominoes; three or four players take five each. When playing with the larger set, the required total is 10 and the matadors are the 9:1, 8:2, 7:3, 6:4, 5:5 and 0:0. Players begin with five dominoes.

3 To begin play the player with the highest (or heaviest) double starts. In this game doubles are not placed crossways on the layout, and the layout only has two ends at all times.

4 If a player is unable or unwilling to add a domino, they must draw a domino from the 'boneyard' (spare pool of dominoes). When only two dominoes remain in the 'boneyard', they must play a domino if they can.

5 Matador dominoes are played like wild cards, that is a matador can be played at any time and is the only tile that can unblock an end which, for example, has been closed with a blank.

6 As usual in dominoes, the first player to get rid of all their bones and shout 'domino' wins the game. Scoring is the same as in Block and Draw Dominoes. The player who calls 'domino' wins the total of the spots left in opponents' hands. If the game is blocked, the player with the lightest hand wins and scores the difference between their spot total and each opponent's total. The first to reach the agreed 50 or 100 points is the winner.

TILE GAMES

The only tile game we are including in this book which isn't a variation of Dominoes and which doesn't use a set of dominoes is Mah Jong. It's not a particularly old game in its present form, but has been derived from older Chinese games. The fascination for western players is in the quaint pieces and terms used in the game. When playing though, it is a simple game where players aim to collect sets of tiles in a prescribed way.

The three suits – circles, bamboos and characters – are unlike any we see in western games. When you add three dragons (white, red and green), east, south, west and north wind tiles and flower and season tiles, the mystery is complete.

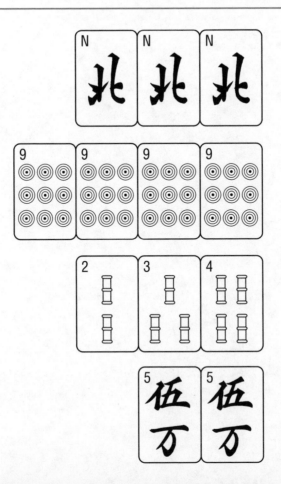

MAH JONG

Players: four
Age: older children and adults
Equipment: standard Mah Jong set of 144 tiles (tiles sold in the Western part of the world usually have numerals in one corner and letters denoting the four winds); two dice; racks to hold the tiles; scoring counters or a scoring pad and pencil; optional wind indicators

1 Mah Jong certainly has an aura of the mystic about it. The game is only about 100 years old, but its rules come from much older Chinese games. The mystical aspects, particularly to a Westerner, are found in the formalities of the game, the colourful pieces and the terms used. However, it is basically a simple game where players aim to collect sets of tiles to complete their hand in a prescribed way.

2 Firstly, it is a good idea to familiarise yourself with the playing tiles. They consist of three suits called circles, bamboos and characters. Each suit comprises tiles numbered 1 to 9 and there are four of each type of tile. See illustration below. Additionally, there are three dragons (white, red and green) – four of each of these tiles. East, south, west and north wind tiles also are represented with four of each type of tile. To complete the set there are four flower and four season tiles – just one of each. See illustration overleaf.

3 To begin play, each player is designated the name of a wind. Winds for the first hand are decided after the players are seated, when each player takes a turn to throw two dice. The player with the highest total becomes East wind, while the other players' winds are determined by where they sit in relation to East. West sits opposite East, South sits to East's right and North to East's left (the opposite to a compass).

THREE DRAGONS

FOUR WINDS

FOUR FLOWERS & FOUR SEASONS

4 The tiles are now shuffled face down on the table and players then build the tiles into four walls, each eighteen tiles long (with the tiles placed lengthways against one another) and two tiles high. The players then push the four walls together to form a square.

5 East throws the dice to determine who will breach the wall. The sum of the two dice is counted anticlockwise around the table by East, who counts as 1, South as 2 and so on. For example, if East throws an 8, North will break the wall. (See illustration right.)

6 North now throws the dice (usually within the walls) and the total thrown is added to the previous total. For instance, if North threw a total of 5, it is added to the previously thrown 8 and becomes 13. North counts thirteen tiles along their wall, starting at the right end. (If the count had exceeded 18, the player would turn the corner onto the left-hand neighbour's wall.)

7 North removes the thirteenth stack along and places both tiles on top of the wall to the right of the breach. Seven stacks of tiles are then counted from the right-hand wall, with the two tiles removed from the wall on top. These sixteen tiles are now known as the 'kong box' or 'dead wall', and are used to provide replacement tiles during play. (See illustration page 237.)

Live wall　　　　　　　　　　　Kong box (dead wall)

| 18 | 17 | 16 | 15 | 14 | 13 | 12 | 11 | 10 | 9 | 8 | 7 | 6 | 5 | 4 | 3 | 2 | 1 |

North

8 Now East takes four tiles from the wall (the live wall), starting at the left of the breach, and each player in turn takes four tiles until all players have twelve tiles in front of them. All players then take one more tile each, and finally East takes one more tile, so East ends up with fourteen tiles and the other players with thirteen tiles. Tiles are placed on the racks, out of sight of other players, and sorted into suits and/or runs.

9 The object of the game is to collect four sets, each of three or four tiles, and a pair. There are three types of sets to collect – the pung (three tiles of the same kind), the kong (four tiles of the same kind) and the chow (a run of three.) It should be noted that chows do not count when scores are tallied, so chows are only good when you go mah jong! Pungs and kongs can be of suit or honour tiles (dragons, winds) but a chow can only be made up of suit tiles (see illustration.) The first player to achieve this, calls 'mah jong', the game ends and the hands are scored.

10 Players in turn, beginning with East, now declare any bonus tiles they hold in their hands (seasons and flowers) by placing them face up on the table in front of them. They then draw replacement tiles from the kong box. If another bonus tile is drawn it is declared and another drawn. This occurs throughout the game from then on.

11 East now declares any kong held and places the tiles on the table, with the two end tiles face downwards to show the hand was 'concealed' (it came from East's hand). Replacement tiles are drawn as necessary. The other players do the same. East completes the turn by discarding any tile and declaring it ('red dragon', 'four circles') as it is discarded.

PUNG

KONG

CHOW

PAIR

237

12 In theory, play passes now to South, however, any player who wants the discard tile to complete a pung or a kong, or to declare mah jong, can announce the fact and pick up the tile. The set is immediately placed in front on the table, including the discarded tile. All tiles are face up to indicate the set is 'exposed' (it included a discard). The player who picked up the discarded tile then discards, and the play passes to the player on the right. This can mean some players will miss a turn. Only the player to East's right (that is, South) can claim the discarded tile to complete a chow. It is done in the same way, laying down the tiles face up or exposed in front of the player and then discarding a tile.

13 When scoring, a concealed pung or kong is worth double, so a player should keep any on their rack as long as possible.

14 If a player does not want to pick up the discard of the previous player, they take the first tile from the live wall. If this is a bonus tile, it is declared and another tile is taken from the kong box. If it is not a bonus tile, the player decides if their hand could benefit from it and chooses a discard tile.

15 When a player has collected four sets and a pair, either by drawing the final necessary tile or collecting it as a discard tile, they declare 'mah jong' and lay the concealed hand face-up on the table. If no one declares mah jong, the game is said to be a draw when the wall is reduced to the last fourteen tiles. In this case, the game is abandoned, the tiles are reshuffled and the same player remains East wind for the next round.

16 There are other prescribed special hands which are accepted by some as alternatives to going mah jong. These usually score 300 points. Other scoring systems differ so the scores for these special or limited hands should be agreed before playing. Some players only accept a few, which are listed below:

a) Heaven's blessing – East holds a mah jong after any loose tiles for kongs or bonus tiles have been drawn, but before discarding.

b) Earth's blessing – any player who similarly goes mah jong with East's first discard.

c) Thirteen Grades of Imperial Treasure – comprises a 1 and a 9 of each suit (six tiles), one of each dragon (three tiles), one of each wind (four tiles) and a pair to any of these tiles (one tile). (These all must be kept concealed in the hand, of course, as there are not any pung, kong or chow to lay down.)

d) Imperial Jade – pungs or kongs of green tiles (the green dragons, 2s, 3s, 4s, 6s and 8s of bamboo only), plus a pair.

e) Wriggly Snake – 1 to 9 of any suit, plus one of each of the winds, with any suit tile paired.

f) Gates of Heaven – a pung of 1s, a pung of 9s, plus one each of tiles 2-8, any one of these being paired, and all tiles being of the same suit.

g) Four Joys – a set of each of the winds, plus any pair.

h) Seven Twins – any seven pairs (fourteen tiles in all). This scores half the mah jong limit (150).

17 After a player has declared mah jong, players calculate the value of their hands according to a scoring table. The players also settle with each other in the following way:

a) If East wind goes mah jong, that player receives double the total value of their score from each of the other players, (either in counters or cash, or in points on a scoring pad);

b) If another player goes mah jong, double the value of their score is received from East wind, and the value of the player's score from each of the other players;

c) Each loser also settles with every other loser. The player with the lower score pays the difference between their score and the other player's score. If East wind is the loser, that player pays or receives double when settling with another loser.

TILE VALUES

All players	Exposed	Concealed
Any chow	0	0
Pung of tiles 2-8 in any suit	2	4
Pung of 1 or 9 in any suit	4	8
Pung of winds or dragons	4	8
Kong of tiles 2-8 in any suit	8	16
Kong of 1 or 9 in any suit	16	32
Kong of winds or dragons	16	32
Any season or flower	4	
Player going mah jong		
Pair of any dragon	2	
Pair of player's own wind	2	
Pair of wind of the round	2	

BONUS SCORES

Player going mah jong	
For going mah jong	20
Winning tile drawn from the wall	2
Winning with only possible tile	2
Winning with the last piece from the wall	10
Winning with a loose tile	10
For having no chows	10
For having no scoring value (except flowers or seasons)	10

DOUBLING

All players	Number of times doubled
Pung or kong of any dragon	1
Pung or kong of player's own wind	1
Pung or kong of the wind of the round	1
Player's own season or flower	1
Four seasons or four flowers	3
Player going mah jong	
Hand with no chows	1
Hand with no scoring tiles except flowers/seasons	1
Hand all one suit except for winds and/or dragons	1
Hand all 1s and 9s except for winds and/or dragons	1
Snatching a kong to go mah jong	1
Hand all one suit	3
Hand all winds and dragons	3
Original hand (only East wind's 14 tiles when play begins)	3

DICE GAMES

If gambling card games have had bad press, then the same must be said for for dice games. They have a reputation for being the most venal and heart-wrenching of games, that is, of course, if you use them to bet your house and lose!

If, however, you play at home for matchsticks, the luck of the winning streak creates competitiveness, even addictiveness, but fortunately, the house will stay intact. For those deep thinkers picking up dice, they may well wonder if life and luck is just random – or is there divine will at work? The turn of the dice may simply be luck, but throughout centuries men have looked to them for divination of the god's will or making decisions.

Dice are actually great fun for children. Because of the huge element of luck, they begin on even terms against adults in any game. The only skill found in dice games is in understanding the likelihood, or mathematical probability, of throwing a specific combination of numbers – for instance, with two dice there are 36 possible combinations of numbers which will fall with every roll. So, there are six ways to throw a seven (4-3, 3-4, 5-2, 2-5, 1-6, 6-1) with the odds against throwing a seven being calculated as 5 to 1 by the simple formula of 36 (total possible combinations of the dice) minus 6 (the number of ways to throw a 6), which leaves 30 to 6 or 5 to 1.

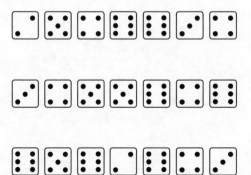

ACES IN THE POT

Players: two or more
Age: all the family
Equipment: two dice, dice cup and counters

1 Each player takes 2 counters and then takes it in turn to throw one dice. The highest number goes first, and then play moves clockwise around the table.

2 If a player throws an Ace (a 1) they put one counter in the 'kitty' or pot in the centre of the table and, if two Aces are thrown, both counters go into the pot and they are out of that round.

3 Similarly, if a player throws a 6, they give a counter to the player on their left. If a player throws two 6s, both counters are given to the player on the left. All other throws do not count.

4 Only players who have counters can continue to throw the dice. When the dice come to the last player to hold a counter, the dice are thrown three times. If there is no 6 in those three throws, the player wins the pot. However, if a 6 is thrown, the last counter and the dice are passed to the player on the left. The first player to throw the dice three times without throwing a 6 wins the pot.

5 In the next round, everyone is given two more counters, and the person to the left of the first player in the last round begins.

CENTENNIAL

Players: two to eight
Age: older children and adults
Equipment: three dice; board or paper marked with a row of boxes numbered 1–12; one differently coloured counter for each player

1 The objective of the game is to be the first to move their counter from box 1 to box 12 and back again, according to the throw of the dice. Play begins after a preliminary roll of the dice for all players has determined who is the first shooter, which is usually the player with the highest score.

2 Each player in turn throws the three dice once. Their throw must contain a 1 before they can begin to play, by placing their counter on the box numbered 1. The dice are passed in turn after each throw.

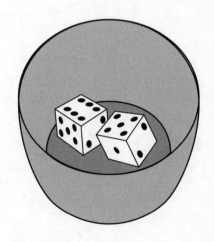

3 When a player has their counter in box 1, they are now trying to throw a 2, and so on. These numbers can be made by throwing a 2 or by throwing a 1, 1, and 6 for instance (the 6 does not count). However, if a player is lucky enough to throw a 1, 2, 3 on their first throw, they can move through boxes 1, 2, and 3 obviously, but also through box 4 (1+3), and box 5 (3+2) and box 6 (1+2+3).

4 Keeping an eye on your opponents is useful in Centennial too. If another player throws a required number, but overlooks it, that number can be claimed by any other player who needs and can use it immediately.

5 The first player to finish the journey up from box 1 to 12 and back again to box 1 is the winner.

CRAPS

Players: two to ten or more
Age: all the family (no one has to bet!)
Equipment: two dice, counters, an optional backstop

1 When playing Craps at home any large flat surface will be useful, for example, the floor or large table with an optional solid backstop (so the dice have something to rest against). In casinos there is a large playing table with a stencilled layout to show where bets can be placed and there are two main layouts used in the world – the British and the American (Las Vegas). It is certainly the biggest gambling game in America.

2 Players decide what the maximum bet will be (say, 5 or 10 counters) and the first player (known as the shooter) announces the amount they will bet and places the counters into the centre, by saying, 'I'll shoot five', which means they are betting 5 counters to win. Now the other players can 'fade' or bet against the shooter by covering that player's bet and putting their money with the shooter's in the centre pot. One player can cover the whole bet or several players can cover parts of it, say by five players all putting in 1 counter. Any part of the shooter's stake that is not covered must be withdrawn before the dice are rolled. Players do not have to bet every time.

3 When the shooter's bet has been covered or faded, that player takes up the dice and throws them. Both dice have to be able to be seen by all those betting and if one dice has

landed in such a way that it is doubtful which side is showing, the throw is declared void.

4 So how does the shooter win? If the first roll of the dice is a 7 or 11 (a natural) the shooter wins; if it is a 2, 3 or 12 (known as craps) the shooter loses. However, if the shooter rolls a 4, 5, 6, 8 ,9 or 10 they have what is known as a point to make. This means they have to roll the dice again and again until the same number is rolled. If the shooter throws a 7 before they make a point, the bet is lost and the dice is passed to the player on the left. Between rolls the shooter can voluntarily pass on the dice at any time.

5 When the shooter wins they take all the counters in the pot. If the shooter loses, those players who faded each take double the amount they put in – so they get back their original bet plus their share of the shooter's stake. In our example above, where the shooter bet 5 counters and five separate players faded one counter each, when the shooter loses, each of the betting players receive 2 counters back and the shooter loses all 5.

6 Additionally, players can bet among themselves as to whether the shooter will win (come right) or lose (come wrong). Players can also bet separately with the shooter.

7 Remember, craps is a game of chance. The only way of knowing the sort of odds you have of winning is if you concentrate on learning the mathematical probabilities of each throw – and for family fun you don't really need to do this!

Total possible combinations

	Number of ways	Odds Against
2	1	35-1
3	2	17-1
4	3	11-1
5	4	8-1
6	5	31-5
7	6	5-1
8	5	31-5
9	4	8-1
10	3	11-1
11	2	17-1
12	1	35-1

DIX MILLE

Players: as many as possible
Age: older children and adults
Equipment: six dice; pencil and paper

1 The name of this game gives away both its origin and the object. Dix Mille is French for ten thousand, so we know it is French in origin and the purpose is to build a score of 10,000.

2 A single dice is thrown by all the players to determine the order of play, with the lowest score playing first. Then play moves clockwise.

3 On a player's turn all six dice are thrown. For the next turn, the player first removes the scoring dice or the combination of scoring dice, then picks up and re-throws the remainder. The player continues in this way, removing the scoring dice each time, until a throw is made in which there is no score. (The player also does not have to take every scoring dice after each turn, see point 6.) The turn now ends and if a turn ends like this the player loses any accumulated score from the previous throws. However, a player may stop at any time after a scoring throw (with one exception, see below), so it is vital to know when to be satisfied with a score and to stop.

4 The exception to being allowed to stop a turn at any time, is when a player rolls three pairs or a straight – when all six dice must be rolled again. However, if six of a kind is thrown, it need not be counted as three pairs. It could be counted as three of a kind twice, in which case the player can end the turn.

5 When a player is down to one dice, two throws are allowed to score with it. If the player succeeds, there is a 500-point bonus score. If the player continues the score and again is reduced to one dice and, with the two scoring chances, scores again, a 1000-point bonus is scored. This way of playing can continue throughout that turn, and the player scores a bonus which increases by 500 points every time.

6 As mentioned before, most players will take each dice that scores every turn, however, a player does not have to take every one. Perhaps with four dice remaining, a player throws 4, 4, 4, 5. Four hundred could be scored for the three of a kind and 50 for the 5, but the player may want to gamble and keep the one dice and score 400 for the three 4s, and throw again twice to try for a 1 or a 5 and score a bonus of 500 points.

SCORING TABLE

Single dice: 1 or 5	100 points or 50 points
Three of a kind: three 1s	1000 points
three of any other number	100 points x number
Three pairs (six of a kind or four of a kind plus a pair can count as three pairs, but see Disaster below)	1500 points
Straight: 1, 2, 3, 4, 5, 6	3000 points
Disaster: four or more 2s	wipe out complete score, not just the score for that turn

7 All players must have the same number of turns so if one player reaches 10,000 they may opt to continue scoring, especially if other players are close in total. The winner is still the first to reach or exceed 10,000 points once all players have had an equal amount of turns.

A good build up, followed by a crash

Throw		Score	Accumulated Score
1		300	3000
2		100	3100
3		50	3150
4		700	3850
5		1500	5350
6		50	5400
7		0	0

Nice and steady gains a good score

Throw		Score	Accumulated Score
1		100	100
2		100	200
3		150	350
4			350
5		600	950
6		400	1350
7		100	1450
8		50	1500
9			1500
10		1050	2550
11		250	2800
12		100	2900

DROP DEAD

Players: any number can play
Age: older children and adults
Equipment: five dice; paper and pencil

1 Each player throws a single dice to decide the order of play – lowest goes first. The aim of the game is to make the highest total score.

2 The first player throws the five dice, and if no 5s or 2s appear, scores the total thrown. (The chances of not scoring a 5 or a 2 is only one in seven, so a player would be probably on their way to a good score.)

3 However, if a 5 or a 2 appears, nothing is scored. The player takes out the dice showing the 5s or 2s, and re-throws the remainder. Play continues for this player until all the dice have been eliminated, when the player is said to have 'dropped dead'.

4 Of course, it is possible for a player to drop dead in the first throw, if they throw 2, 2, 2, 5, 5; or equally they can keep throwing for many throws with just the one dice.

5 The game is won by the player with the highest score after every player has had a turn.

Variation: The game can also be played with each player having just the one throw per turn with one dice only and passing it on to the player on the left after each throw. Scores are tallied on a score card, to include the actual running total as well as how many dice the player has left.

EVEREST

Players: two to eight
Age: older children and adults
Equipment: three dice; paper and pencil for each player; a differently coloured counter for each player

1 A similar game to Centennial, but with a slightly different scoring system and layout.

2 Again each player throws to determine the order of play, with the highest scorer leading play. Each player is given a piece of paper on which they draw twelve boxes twice, side by side, and number them 1-12 and 12-1.

3 The objective is still to be the first to score all 24 numbers, but this time the numbers do not have to be scored consecutively as with Centennial rules, but when they come up on the dice. However, in Everest you can only use each dice in a throw once. For example, if a 5, 3, 1 is thrown you could cross off 5, 3, 1 or 8 and 1, or 4 and 5, or 6 and 3.

GENERAL

Players: any number can play
Age: older children and adults
Equipment: five dice; paper and pencil to score

1 This is known as one of the 'category' dice games, others include Yacht on page 257.

2 Players throw one dice to determine the order of play – lowest goes first. The turns then go clockwise with players having up to three throws each in a turn.

3 The first player throws the five dice, and may set aside any dice they may want to keep, and then re-throws the remainder. This may be done again but, after the third throw, the five dice represent that player's score for the turn. The score is then entered for the appropriate category, as illustrated below:

Scores for the categories are as follows:
Big General – this is five of a kind made on the first throw of any turn. It is not put on the score sheet because it wins the game immediately and the likelihood of it happening is rare!

Small General – this is five of a kind made on the second or third throw. It scores 60.

Four of a Kind – scores 45 on the first throw, 40 on subsequent throws.

Full House – scores 35 on the first throw, 30 on subsequent throws (need three of one score, and two of another, such as 4, 4, 4, 6, 6).

Straight – scores 25 on the first throw, 20 on subsequent throws (either 1, 2, 3, 4, 5 or 2, 3, 4, 5, 6 are counted).

Sixes, 5s, 4s, 3s, 2s and aces (1s) – all score their spot value.

4 Note that if a player throws Four of a Kind on the first throw, but keeps one dice to throw for Small General and fails, only 40 is scored for the Four of a Kind, not 45.

Categories	John	Kate	Lisa	Tom
Small General				60
Four of a kind			40	
Full House	35			
Straight		20		
Sixes	18			
Fives		15		
Fours				12
Threes	6			
Two				
Aces (ones)				
Total				

HEARTS OR HEARTS DUE

Players: two or more
Age: children and adults
Equipment: six dice; paper and pencil for scoring

1 Special dice marked with the letters H, E, A, R, T, S instead of numbers can be found to play this game, however it is easy to play with numbered dice too. Just substitute the numbers for the letters, so that H=1, E=2, A=3, R=4, T=5 and S=6.

2 Players can either agree that the winner is the person to score more than the others over a decided number of rounds, or in a single round, or up to an agreed total, say 150.

3 A preliminary throw of one dice per player decides who is to throw first – the highest or lowest scorer usually has the honour. Each player in turn rolls the six dice once and calculates their score according to the following:

1 (H)	5 pts
1, 2 (HE)	10 pts
1, 2, 3 (HEA)	15 pts
1, 2, 3, 4 (HEAR)	20 pts
1, 2, 3, 4, 5 (HEART)	25 pts
1, 2, 3, 4, 5, 6 (HEARTS)	35 pts

4 If a double (such as two 4s) or a treble (such as three 5s) is scored when the six dice are thrown, only one of them counts. However, if three 1s (or Hs) appear, the player's whole score is wiped out and they have to begin again.

HELP YOUR NEIGHBOUR

Players: two to six
Age: children and adults
Equipment: three dice; 10 counters for each player

1 This is a fast, fun and furious old game fit for all the family – in fact, you can win or lose a fortune (of counters) in an hour or so!

2 Each player is given 10 counters to begin. If there are six players, each person chooses a number from 1 to 6; if there are five playing, players take numbers from 1 to 5 and 6 is not in play and is ignored when it comes up in a throw; with four players both the 5 and 6 are ignored, but with three players, each takes two numbers and if only two are playing, each takes three numbers.

3 Play moves clockwise around the table, beginning with the player who is number 1. Each player throws the three dice and when a player's number comes up they must put a counter in the pot, one for each number. So, if there are six players and one throw sees 6, 4, 2 come up those players put in one counter each. However, if there is a throw which has 3, 3, 5, the player who is number 3 has to put in two counters.

4 This is good, as the first player to run out of counters wins the round! The next round will begin with player number two.

INDIAN DICE

Players: any number can play
Age: adults
Equipment: five dice

1 This is a popular bar game in America (as is Poker Dice, from where it originated).

2 The objective is to make the highest possible poker hand using the dice. The hands rank as follows: five of a kind (highest); four of a kind; full house; three of a kind; two pairs; pair; no pair. Note that a straight does not rank in Indian Dice.

3 After the order of play has been decided by the roll of the dice – the highest scorer becomes the first shooter, who then has up to three throws to establish a hand. They can 'stand' on their first throw, or pick up any or all of the dice for a second throw. Again, they may stand on that throw or pick up any or all of the dice for a third and final throw. No subsequent player can make any more throws than the first player.

4 A game usually involves two rounds or legs, with the winners of each playing off for the stakes if they are involved. If no stakes are involved, often the lowest scorers play off for the win. If there are only two players, the winner is the one who wins two out of three legs.

Five of a kind

Four of a kind

Full house

Three of a kind

Two pairs

Pair

No pair

LIAR DICE

Players: three or more
Age: adults
Equipment: five dice; or a set of Poker Dice; each player needs 3 betting chips or counters

1 It can be assumed from the title of this game that lying or at least bluffing and deception are part of this game – and they are! It can be played with ordinary dice, but is more enjoyable when Poker dice are used.

2 As with the card game Poker, and Poker Dice and Indian Dice games, learning the ranking of the hands is useful. In Liar Dice the hands rank the same as in Poker Dice, and are as follows: five of a kind (highest); four of a kind; straight (can be either a, k, q, j, 10 or k, q, j, 10, 9); full house (three of a kind and one pair); three of a kind; two pairs; pair; no pair.

3 The order of play is established by each player throwing one dice – the highest scorer becomes the first shooter. The second highest scorer sits to the left, and so on.

4 Each player has three betting chips in front of them. The first shooter throws all five dice and keeps them covered so no one else can see what they are. The player declares the throw in detail, such as, 'full house, nines on fours' (9, 9, 9, 4, 4), however, this call may be true or completely false, and it is for the player at the left either to accept or challenge the call. The declaring player may call below the actual value of the hand if so wished.

5 There are two things the player to the left can now do. If they think the caller is lying they can challenge, and the dice are exposed. If the caller has lied, one chip must be paid into the pot by that person but if, in fact, the value of the throw is equal to or higher than the call, it is the challenger who has to pay into the pot. In either case, it is now the challenger's turn to throw.

6 However, if the challenger accepts the call, this player takes over the dice (still covered) and may now throw any or all of them, but must truthfully say how many are thrown. Keeping the dice covered, the player makes a call, which must be higher than the accepted call. It does not have to be a higher rank, but just a higher hand. The call may be accepted or challenged by the player to the left, and so on.

7 When a player has lost all three of their chips, that player is out of the game, but play continues until there is a sole survivor, who is declared the winner and collects the pot.

PIG

Players: any number can play
Age: children and adults
Equipment: one dice; pencil and paper for scoring

1 In this simple dice game, the winner is the first player to reach an agreed score – usually 100.

2 To decide who throws first (and there is a slight advantage in doing so), each player throws the dice once and the player with the lowest score becomes the first shooter. The highest throw is last, but again this has a slight natural advantage.

3 The first shooter (and subsequent players) may roll the dice as many times as they wish, adding their score throw by throw until they elect to stand their turn. However, if a player throws a 1 at any time, they lose the entire score they have made on that turn and play passes to the next player.

4 Play continues in this way until someone reaches the agreed total. Given a little luck, that could well be the first or last player. The first player's advantage, however, can be counteracted by allowing all players to have the same number of turns. The last shooter still has a slight advantage because they know the scores made by all their opponents. Provided they steers clear of 1s, they can continue throwing until they have beaten all those scores.

5 A fair way of organising the game is to ensure each player gets to be the first shooter of a round.

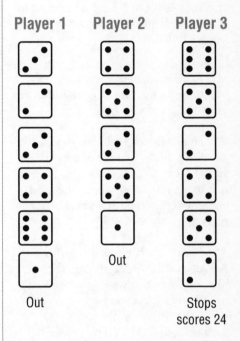

Player 1   Player 2   Player 3

Out   Out   Stops
scores 24

POKER DICE

Players: two or more
Age: adults
Equipment: five dice, usually special Poker dice marked with a, k, q, j, 10 and 9 instead of the numbers 1 to 6, but the game can be played with ordinary dice when 1 ranks highest, then 6, 5, 4, 3, 2

1 As the name suggests, the aim is to make the best poker hand in not more than two rolls of the dice.

2 Hands rank as follows: five of a kind (highest); four of a kind; straight (can be either a, k, q, j, 10 or k, q, j, 10, 9); full house (three of a kind and one pair); three of a kind; two pairs; pair; no pair.

3 Each player rolls a single dice to decide the order of play. The highest scorer throws first in the first round and the second highest scorer sits to that player's left, and so on. Play goes clockwise and a new player commences each round.

4 The first player rolls the dice. They can accept the hand produced by this first throw or may elect to pick up one or more of the dice and throw again in an attempt to improve their hand. The second throw completes their hand. The player notes it down or memorises it, and passes the dice to the next player.

5 The highest hand in the round wins. If there are only two players, the best two out of three rounds wins.

6 Poker dice can be played with aces 'wild', meaning that they can rank normally or count as any other value the player wishes. For example, a throw of j, j, j, j, a, could rank as five jacks.

SHUT THE BOX

Players: two or more
Age: children and adults
Equipment: two dice; pencil and paper; or specially made Shut the Box equipment consisting of a rectangular box complete with sliding covers to open or shut the boxes, which have numbers 1 to 9 either in view or covered

1 Players aim to cover as many of the numbers as possible in accordance with the throws of the dice. The aim should be to cover high number boxes first, as it is the player with the lowest score who wins.

2 After a preliminary round decides the first shooter (the highest score usually wins this honour), that player throws the two dice and adds the total value of them. Say the total thrown is 9, this would allow the player to cover 9, or 8 and 1, or 7 and 2, or 6 and 3, or 5 and 4. They then throw again and once more close appropriately numbered boxes that are still open.

When a player has shut boxes 7, 8 and 9, they can, if they wish, continue to throw with only one dice. This player continues to throw until the total rolled cannot be matched against any combination remaining open. The turn then ends and the boxes open are totalled to become the player's score. Thus, if 1 and 3 were still open, the score would be 4.

3 The numbered boxes are once more opened and then it is the turn of the next player, and so on. When every player has had a turn it is the player with the lowest score who wins.

4 It may be difficult to find a Shut the Box tray, but it is easy to score this game by ruling up columns of the numbers 1 to 9 for each player and crossing them out as they are thrown. Or, alternatively, rule up nine boxes on a piece of paper using numbers of a size which can be covered by counters or coins when they need to be covered.

THIRTY-SIX

Players: any number can play
Age: children (who can add to 36) and adults
Equipment: one dice; pencil and paper; counters for a pot

1 In this simple family dice game, the lowest scorer in a preliminary round plays first.

2 The object is for players to score a total of 36 points. Any player scoring more than 36, however, is eliminated from the game. The winner is often the player whose score is nearest to 36 and that player takes the pot.

3 Each player puts in an agreed amount of counters into the pot, say five each for four players, and the first player rolls the dice once. That player keeps note of the score and passes the dice to the next player, who does the same thing.

4 Play continues around the table round by round. As a player nears 36 they may choose to stand on their score, especially if it is 33 or more.

5 In the event of a tie, the pot is divided.

Player 1

30 points

Player 2

33 points

Player 3

31 points

YACHT

Players: any number can play, but best for five or six
Age: older children and adults
Equipment: five dice; paper and pencil

1 Yacht is known as a category game among dice games. Many people will know it as Yahtzee® which is its commercial form. It is similar to the game General, a favourite game in Puerto Rico.

2 Players throw one dice to determine who goes first, with the lowest score beginning the game. The first player then rolls the five dice, sets aside any dice they wish to keep, and throws for a second and third time to try to improve their hand. The following table shows the hands to aim for and the scores they achieve.

3 When the first player has thrown three times, they must then decide the category into which to place the total score. Play proceeds clockwise.

4 Play in one game continues for twelve rounds, when each player must have entered a score for each category, even if that score is zero (this will often be the case). When a score is entered in a category it stays, and cannot be superseded by a superior score in that same category later on.

5 One strategic hint is to try for larger scores early on.

6 Players add up their scores at the end of the twelve rounds and the highest total wins the game.

Hand	Points
Yacht (five of a kind)	50
Big Straight (2, 3, 4, 5, 6)	30
Little Straight (1, 2, 3, 4, 5)	30
Four of a Kind	Pip value
Full House (any three of one kind, and two of another)	Pip value
Choice (any five dice of no specific pattern)	Pip value
Sixes, fives, fours, three twos and aces (ones)	Pip value for every dice thrown in each category

ACTIVE GAMES

In the following pages we have presented active games for everyone, both children and adults. We've included some of the most popular sporting games in the world, giving a brief overview of how they are played and a very basic introduction to scoring and rules. Enough to get you started in the wonderful world of competitive sporting games.

Some of these games require skills that cannot be learnt from a book. If you or your children want to get involved in them it is best to find a club near you. Clubs provide coaching, teams to join and instruction in the finer points of the rules of each game.

Active games are terrific for letting children run and play off some energy in a supervised way. Kids will also develop motor skills and social skills while they're enjoying themselves. Parents and other adult supervisors are sure to find they are having lots of fun too!

GAMES OF SKILL

Some of the following games require quite large and even expensive equipment and perhaps, because of this, games like billiards and table tennis may seem to be out of reach. How about going along to a pool hall as a family during the school holidays or, alternatively, buying a table with friends or neighbours to share the cost?(Or hiring first to see if you like it!) Alternatively, you could buy a second-hand table if you decide as a family it would be a good investment.

These games are all good opportunities to have fun together as a family.

Also, Table Tennis sets can be bought in plastic for younger players and perhaps be kept on a flat area just outside the family room doors. Or a table top can be created fairly cheaply from craft board (available at hardware stores) and painted. Once your children have discovered how much fun these games can be, the investment of time and money will be well worth it.

BILLIARDS OR ENGLISH BILLIARDS

Players: two players, or four playing in pairs
Age: older children and adults
Equipment: specially marked billiard table; a cue for each player; three balls (one white, one white spot and one red)

1 Play lasts an agreed length of time, or until one side reaches an agreed number of points. Each game is known as a frame.

2 To determine the order of play and which of the cue balls (white or white spot) is used for the duration of play, players 'string' for choice. That is, each player strikes their cue ball up the table from the 'D' with the player winning the choice if the ball stops nearest to the end cushion.

3 The red ball is placed on the spot (marked on the table) and the striker places the cue ball at any point in the 'D' and plays their first shot. The striker scores points for winning hazards, losing hazards and cannons (noted further on). Each time a player scores from a shot they are entitled to another shot. Only when they fail to score does play pass to the other player. If a striker makes a foul shot (noted further on) they lose their turn, plus any score they have made in that turn (or break). In addition, they concede points to their opponent (noted further on).

4 Strikers score points for the following:

Winning hazards

a) if the cue ball hits the other white (or cue) ball into a pocket – 2 points;

b) if the cue ball hits the red ball into a pocket (allowed a maximum of five times in succession) – 3 points.

Losing hazards

a) if the cue ball is pocketed 'in off' the white ball – 2 points;

b) if the cue ball is pocketed 'in off' the red ball – 3 points. Only fifteen consecutive hazards may be scored.

Cannons

a) if the cue ball strikes both other balls – 2 points;

b) if the cue ball goes into a pocket after the above – 2 additional points if the white ball was struck first, or 3 additional points if the red ball was struck first.

Only 75 consecutive cannons may be scored.

5 Fouls in play include the following and mean the striker's opponent scores the points:

a) touching the ball more than once in a stroke – 1 point;

b) forcing a ball off the table – 3 points;

c) not playing from the 'D' correctly – 1 point;

d) making a push shot (not striking the ball) – 1 point.

The following fouls mean the striker loses a turn, but they do not incur any penalty points:

Starting position

KEY

Red ball

Cue ball

White ball

a) playing with both feet off the floor:

b) playing the balls before they are still;

c) striking the ball with anything but the cue;

d) playing the wrong ball;

e) playing out of turn;

f) playing from outside the 'D' when should be playing inside it.

6 There are some other rules to remember:

a) When a striker brings a cue ball into play, no shot may be made directly at any ball within the balk area (see diagram);

b) if both balls are in this area, the cue ball must strike a cushion outside the balk area before it can touch either ball;

c) in a break, if the non-striker's cue ball is pocketed, it remains off the table until the next break;

d) when the red ball is pocketed, it is immediately replaced on the 'spot';

e) when the cue ball is pocketed the striker brings it back into play by playing from the 'D';

f) if the striker's ball comes to rest against another ball, the red ball is replaced on the 'spot'. The non-striker's ball, if on the table, is placed on the centre spot.

g) Players may use a rest to support the cue.

CAROM BILLIARDS

Players: two or more in pairs or teams
Age: older children and adults
Equipment: specially marked carom billiard table; a cue for each player; three balls (one white, one white with two spots and one red)

1 This type of billiards is played on a slightly smaller table, with no pockets. The table also has a different set of spots and markings to a regular billiards table (see page 266).

2 Order of play is decided by a system known as 'lagging'. The red ball is placed on the foot spot, with each player in the lag taking a cue ball and playing it against the foot cushion from behind the head string. Players lag separately to the right and left, with choice of cue ball, and playing order going to the player whose cue ball comes to rest nearest the head of the table without interfering with the red ball in any way. The lag is repeated until there is a clear result.

3 The break or opening shot is made with the red ball on the foot spot and the white object ball on the head spot. The cue ball is played from the head string within 15 cm (6 in) of the white object ball. The cue ball must contact the red ball first for this first break shot only (see point 5). If the first player manages this shot, a point is scored and the turn continued.

4 A player's turn continues until they fail to make a score or foul in some way, when not only do they lose their turn, but also a point. Fouls include: making a shot while any ball is still moving; touching the cue ball more than once in a shot; pushing the cue ball; touching an object ball with the cue; using the wrong cue ball; or having both feet off the ground when making a shot.

5 The object of Carom Billiards is to make a 'carom shot', that is, to make the cue ball hit the red ball and then hit the other white ball. Apart from the break shot, it does not matter if the cue ball bounces off a cushion before doing the above. A point is awarded for any carom shot, however, a point is deducted if such a contact is not made and the player's turn ends.

6 There is one exception to the above rule! If a player makes a successful 'safety shot' – for example, the cue ball is struck in such a way it comes to rest in contact with a cushion after hitting a white object ball, or the object ball rests against a cushion – no points are deducted, but the player loses a turn. However, only one safety shot is allowed in any session at the table.

7 If a player's cue ball jumps off the table they lose one point and a turn. The cue ball is replaced on the head spot, or, if it is already occupied, on the foot spot. If the red ball jumps off the table it is replaced on the foot spot. If the white object ball jumps off the table it is replaced on the head spot. However, any score made before this ball jumps off the table is kept and the player continues the turn. If all three balls jump off the table, the

player loses one point and a turn and the incoming player makes a break shot.

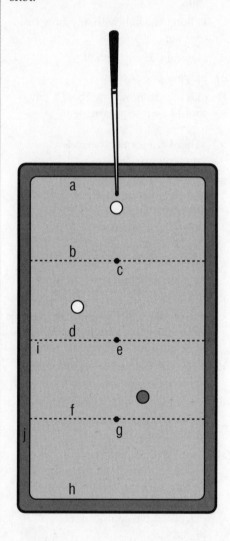

KEY

Red ball

White with two spots

White ball

DARTS

Players: two or more, in pairs and teams
Age: older children (but be careful, darts have very sharp steel points) and adults
Equipment: standard dartboard; three darts per person; chalkboard or paper for scoring

1 Darts now has enthusiasts, indeed professional competition players, in many countries throughout the world, but it was traditionally played in English public houses ('pubs'). Often, one pub would play against another pub, or the local cricket team would play against the cricket team of the next village or suburb. It was not unusual for teams to travel in buses through dreadful weather to compete in weekly events, usually on Friday nights.

2 Safety is one issue that must be mentioned, whether families are playing at home or in a club situation. Darts can be dangerous. Be careful where the dartboard is positioned (so no one will walk unexpectedly nearby), and remember that darts can bounce off the wire on the board, so a wide, clear space needs to be given to the game. Also, no one should ever attempt to catch a dart! Young children should be kept away from the darts and a game in progress. Never play in sandals as a dart through the toe or instep means a trip to hospital! Hopefully, no one has been scared off, because darts is a great team and family game that will be enjoyed over and over again. In addition, players can play alone to create personal best scores!

3 Set up the dartboard so that the top – the 20 wedge – is 173cm (around 6ft) above the ground and decide on a throwing line for the ability of the players which should be marked with tape – either 237cm or 293cm (around 8ft or 10ft) from the base of the board. Set up a board and paper or a chalkboard for scoring.

4 General rules and scoring are fairly easy to learn, whether played by two people or teams. If playing in teams, players from each side take alternate turns, one after the other. Each turn consists of three throws, then the darts are retrieved by the player who threw them and the next player stands on the line. A dart only counts if it sticks in the board. Leaning over the line is acceptable, although no player's foot can extend across the line.

5 Each player or team throws one dart at the board aiming for the bull's eye to decide who plays first. The player throwing a dart closest to the bull's eye starts.

6 There are many variations of darts, but the standard tournament game is called 301. (There are 501 and 1001 too, but beginners will do best to stick to 301.) This means that each player's score is deducted from 301 with the aim of reducing the score to exactly zero.

7 The first dart thrown must be a double in 301, and sometimes this means an individual player can give a head start to an opponent who has no luck in achieving that elusive double. (Teams are good for beginners for this reason. Some people are good at doubles and can be relied on to start and finish!)

8 The last dart thrown to achieve the zero score must also be a double. (Players' mental arithmetic will sharpen the more they play darts as they will always be tallying up mentally the best double to try to achieve, or the best combination of numbers to reach that magical zero score!) If any dart in a turn (even the first thrown) reduces the score to less than zero or busts, the turn ends without scoring. For example, if there was 31 left, a player could go for 11 and then double 10, or 1 and double 15. However, if while going for 11, 14 was hit instead, a player would need to do some quick mental arithmetic to ascertain that 17 was left and a 7 and double 5 would be needed. This all means that players are really kept on their toes mentally!

Variations: There are many variations of darts, but a simple one if you are bored with 301 or 501 is called Around the Clock. Each player throws three darts in a turn and, after beginning with the almost compulsory double (of any value), the idea is to throw a dart into each of the wedges, in order, from 1 to 20. Most games allow darts in the double or treble sections of the correct number to count. The winner is the first person to finish.

Irish black

Narrow Five

Target

JACKS

Players: two or more (or alone for practice and personal bests)
Age: children probably enjoy it more than adults (and have more time to practise)
Equipment: set of five stones, or commercially sold sets which are now usually plastic

1 Some people will know this game as Fivestones, while others will say that Jacks is a game which is played with five small, six-legged metal objects and a rubber ball. This game is known to them as Knucklebones. Anyone who originated in parts of the north of England actually may call this game Tally, derived from the name Tali as it was known in ancient Asian times. Knucklebones was also a very popular game in ancient Rome.

2 Whatever you call it, it is a fun game for one, but even better for two or more, to gain dexterity in throwing small objects in the air and catching them in various ways which gain in difficulty as you proceed.

3 The objective is to complete a series of set down throws in an agreed sequence. Each throw must be completed successfully before proceeding to the next. For two or more players, it is usual to play turn and turn about, and a player's turn ends when they fail to complete a particular throw. That player's next turn begins with another attempt at the failed throw.

4 There are hundreds of throws, but those following are the most commonly known.

5 The basic throw is where a player holds all five stones in the open palm of the hand, then tosses them in the air (not too high!). While the stones are in the air, the player turns their hand over and catches the stones on the back of the hand. Any that fall must be left on the ground or table. Then the player tosses the stones in the air again and quickly turns their hand over and catches the stones in the palm of the hand.

a

b

c

throwing hand before the single thrown stone is caught with the same hand. When this is complete, the two caught stones are transferred to the other hand and the stone is thrown and the catching hand sweeps up the final two stones.

8 Threes and fours follow the same pattern, except of course, firstly one and three stones need to be swept up and then all four before the thrown stone is caught.

9 There are three throws, which are commonly achieved following ones, twos, threes and fours. They are called Pecks, Bushels and Claws, and the great thing is that they never have to be actually achieved if the basic throw is mastered first. If this basic throw is achieved, every time a player has a turn for the above-named throws, they move on to the next one.

10 Beginning with Pecks – if the basic throw and catching of all five stones is achieved, move on to Bushels. If not, this is what to do. Keep all the caught stones in the palm of the throwing hand, moving one to hold between the forefinger and thumb (see illustration). Then toss that stone into the air, pick up one stone from the ground with the same hand and catch the thrown stone with the throwing hand (the same hand again). Repeat this procedure until all stones are picked up.

6 If this basic throw is completed by catching all the stones the player continues with 'twos'. If even one stone falls in the basic manoeuvre, the player moves to 'ones' before 'twos'. This means that the dropped stones are left on the ground and the player transfers the other stones except one to the other hand. This single stone is then thrown in the air and the player picks up one stone from the ground with that throwing hand and then turns the hand over and catches the thrown stone. The player repeats this procedure until all the stones have been retrieved.

7 'Twos' entails the player scattering the five stones on the ground, taking care not to let them land too far apart. One stone is then selected (experience will help to choose which stone) and thrown up in the air while two other stones are picked up from the ground with the

11 Bushels is achieved if the basic throw is successful. If not, continue with Bushels by throwing all the caught stones into the air, pick up one stone from the ground with the throwing hand, and catch the thrown stones. Repeat until all stones are picked up.

12 Claws is the next test. Again, if the basic throw is successful, move on to some trickier throws, such as Ones under the Arch (see below). However, if it is not successful, continue with Claws by tossing all the stones from the palm of the hand to the back of the hand (same movement as in the basic throw). If all five are caught, the player attempts to complete the basic throw again, and if successful moves on. However, if no stone is caught on the back of the hand, the player's turn ends.

13 If one or more are caught on the back of the hand the player leaves them there. The stones on the ground are then picked up between the outstretched fingers of the throwing hand, holding one stone between any two fingers, or a finger and thumb, and tossing the stones from the back of the hand, catching them in the palm. This is achieved without dislodging the stones between the fingers, or finger and thumb, and in fact they are then manoeuvred into the palm to complete the move.

14 After successfully completing Claws, there are several harder throws to try. Ones under the Arch is a good one. The player scatters the stones on the ground and makes an arch near them with the thumb and forefinger of the non-throwing hand. One stone is selected and thrown into the air. While it is in the air, the other stones are knocked through the arch and the thrown stone then caught. When all four stones have been knocked through the arch, the player throws the final stone and, before catching it, must pick up the other four stones. Twos under the Arch follows, as does Threes under the Arch and

Fours under the Arch, except that in all cases the stones must be knocked through the arch as twos, threes and fours.

15 A similar game is Horse in the Stable where the stones are once again scattered on the ground and the non-throwing hand is placed near them with the fingers and thumb spread out, fingertips on the ground and palm raised. The gaps become stables. One stone is thrown in the air and before catching it, the player knocks a stone into or toward one of the stables. Only one stone may be knocked into any one stable. The player continues throwing, knocking and catching in this way until all four stables are filled, then moves the hand away and tosses the throwing stone. Before catching it, all four stones must be picked up from the ground with the throwing hand.

16 Toad in the Hole. Scatter the stones on the ground and make a 'hole' by joining a forefinger and thumb of the non-throwing hand together on the ground. One stone is then thrown in the air, and before catching it, the player must pick up one of the other stones (a 'toad') and drop it into the hole. This is repeated until the four stones are in the hole when the player moves the non-throwing hand, tosses up the single stone and before catching it must sweep up all four toads.

17 Threading the Needle is similar to the above game, but this time the forefinger and thumb make a circle about 20cm (8 in) above the ground. This is where the stones are to be 'threaded' through.

18 Over the Line. Place the non-throwing hand with the palm on the ground, and scatter four stones to its outer side. The player then throws the fifth stone in the air, and before catching it must transfer one of the other stones to the other side of the non-throwing hand. This is repeated until all four stones on the ground have been transferred 'over the line'. (Try to keep the stones together as you go.) Now the player throws up the fifth stone and, before catching it again, must pick up the other four stones in the throwing hand. A turn ends if the stone does not make it to the other side, or a player does not pick up the four stones at the end.

19 Over the Jump is a similar game, where this time the non-throwing hand is placed on edge so it makes a 'jump' for the stones to be placed over – a little more difficult.

20 Building a Tower. This can only be played if the Jacks used are cubes. The player scatters four stones and throws the fifth into the air. Before catching it, one of the stones on the ground is moved away from the others. At the second throw one stone is picked up and placed on top of the first, and so on. A turn ends if the tower is knocked over or a stone fails to stay on the preceding stone.

21 Demolishing a Tower is, of course, self-explanatory. At each throw the player removes a stone from the tower.

22 Backward ones, twos, threes and fours are similar to the original ones, twos, threes and fours, with the difference being that four stones are scattered on the ground and the player throws the fifth stone in the air and catches it on the back of the throwing hand. The fifth stone is then tossed into the air from the back of the hand and, before catching it in the normal way, the player must pick up one stone from the ground. These two stones are then thrown in the same way and a third picked up, then the fourth. In backward twos, threes and fours the player must pick up the required number of stones in each throw.

PICK-UP-STICKS

Players: any number can play; equally amusing for one
Age: children (with good motor skills) and adults
Equipment: a set of sticks can be bought at any toy store; they are sometimes known as Jackstraws or they can be made

1 Long ago, Pick-up-Sticks were made of ivory or bone, and it seems the game originated in ancient China. Today, a set of Pick-up-Sticks consists of 50 coloured or designed sticks about 15cm (6 in) long. Each colour or design designates the value of each stick, usually one to five. Often there is a single stick which, when collected, can be used to help get sticks out – sometimes it is black and its value is usually 10.

2 One player drops all the sticks on the floor or table by holding them in a bundle at one end and letting go. That player is then not able to touch any stick unless trying to collect it. Obviously, the first player has some advantage as there are always sticks which roll or move away from the bundle as it drops and these are easy pick-ups. Hence, each player needs to have a turn being the first player. Once a player's fingers touch a stick, it must continue to be collected. If another stick moves, the turn is over. If nothing moves, the player can continue until a stick does move, and then it is the next person's turn.

3 Play continues until the last stick has been picked up and then everyone calculates their score from the sticks they have collected. The winner is the person with the highest score.

POOL

Players: two individuals, pairs or teams
Age: older children and adults
Equipment: specially marked pool table; a cue for each player; fifteen numbered balls and one white cue ball

1 The object of the game is to be the first to score an agreed number of points, usually 125 or 150 in title play. One point is scored for pocketing a called ball in a called pocket, and an additional point is scored for every other object ball pocketed in the same stroke.

2 Order of play is decided by a system known as 'lagging'. The choice goes to the player whose cue ball comes to rest nearest the head of the table after being stroked against the foot cushion from behind the head string (see page 276). The cue ball may touch the side rails. The winner usually chooses to play after their opponent.

3 The break shot is important in setting up a game, but the opening player has three choices. They must either:

a) drop a called ball into a called pocket, then the turn continues;

b) drive the cue ball and two other balls to a cushion, then the turn ends and the opponent accepts the balls and plays on; or

c) play (scratch) the cue ball into a pocket and two other balls into a cushion, then the turn is ended and a point lost.

Failure to achieve any of the above incurs a foul and the player loses two points. Upon agreement, the turn could be ended or the balls reframed and the break tried for again. Two points are lost for each consecutive failure to meet the break requirements.

4 As the object of the game is to score points for pocketing called balls, a player must always designate the ball they are aiming to pocket and in which pocket they are aiming to score. If a ball bounces from a pocket back onto the table, it is not considered pocketed, the player ends the turn, and the ball remains in play where it landed.

5 If a player misses the shot called, the turn ends, although a miss carries no other penalty provided that the cue ball hits a cushion after hitting an object ball; or drives at least one object ball to a cushion; or at least one object ball into a pocket. If this does not happen, the player is deemed to have fouled, ends the turn and loses a point.

6 If a player pockets fourteen balls consecutively, known as continuous play, the fifteenth ball is left in position on the table and becomes the break ball. The cue ball is also left in position, and the fourteen pocketed balls are racked with space for one ball left at the foot spot apex of the triangle. The player then continues the turn by either calling and pocketing a ball, or trying to pocket the break ball in a designated pocket and carom the cue ball from the break ball into the triangle of racked balls. (The rules of the break shot apply.) If successful the turn continues; if not, rules for misses above apply.

Set up for break shot in Pool (see point 3)

7 Scratches are incurred when a player plays the cue ball into a pocket at the break shot or during continuous play. Scratches are also incurred during safety play when a ball is frozen to a cushion or when a player's cue ball jumps off the table. The first time, a player's turn ends, a point is lost and one scratch marked against them. If a ball is pocketed at the next turn or a legal safety shot played, the first scratch is removed. If the player scratches a second time (without the penalty being removed as above), the turn is ended, a point lost and two scratches marked against them. At the third scratch, the player loses one point for the scratch and then 15 points for the three successive scratches. The player must then break the balls as at the start of a game.

8 In attempting a safety shot, the player must either:

a) drive an object ball to a cushion; or

b) cause the cue ball to strike a cushion after contacting an object ball; or

c) pocket an object ball. Failure to achieve any of the above is a foul shot and incurs a 1 point penalty.

9 Other penalties include:

a) jump shots, caused when the cue ball rises from the bed of the table by the player digging under the cue ball with the tip end of the cue;

b) jumped balls; if the called object ball jumps off the table it is counted as a miss and only ends the player's turn and the ball is returned. If a player scores the called ball and causes another ball to jump off the table, a legally pocketed ball is scored and the player continues the turn;

c) balls in motion; any stroke made before all balls on the table are completely stopped is a foul and the player loses a point and ends the turn. The incoming player has a choice of whether to accept the balls where they are or insist upon a return to the state before the foul occurred;

d) cue ball within the string; if, after a warning, a player fails to shoot from within the head string it is a foul and the player ends the turn and loses a point. The incoming player can accept the balls in that position or return them to the positions they were in before the foul;

e) frozen cue ball; when the cue ball is in contact with an object ball, a player can play directly at the object ball so long as the object ball is moved and the cue ball strikes a cushion, or the object ball in contact with the cue ball is driven to the cushion. If neither condition is met a foul results with a 1 point penalty;

f) ball frozen to a cushion; if a player stops the cue ball in front of an object ball frozen against a cushion a 1 point penalty is incurred. When playing such a shot the player must either pocket the object ball, ensure the cue ball contacts a cushion or drive the object ball to another cushion;

g) if both feet are off the floor when playing a shot or there is interference by a player of a ball, both instances incur a 1 point penalty and loss of a turn;

h) if a player touches a ball with any part of the cue but the tip, 15 points are lost and the player must break as at the start of the game at the next turn.

SNOOKER

Players: two players, pairs, or teams
Age: older children and adults
Equipment: can be played on a pocketed billiard table; triangular rack; cues for each player; 22 balls (one white cue ball, fifteen red balls, one yellow, one green, one brown, one blue, one pink and one black ball); scoreboard

1 Another popular table game in the same vein as Billiards and Pool, Snooker is a good family game as there is often lots happening.

2 The balls are positioned as shown on the illustration opposite to begin. The toss of a coin can determine order of play. The game's objective is to score points by pocketing balls and also to force an opponent to give away balls through 'snookers'.

3 Each ball therefore has a scoring value. They are as follows: red, 1 point; yellow, 2 points; green, 3 points; brown, 4 points; blue, 5 points; pink, 6 points and black, 7 points.

4 The initial stroke of any turn (including the first player's) must strike the cue ball against a red (as long as there are red balls remaining on the table). If the player succeeds in pocketing a red, they score that ball and continue the break by attempting to pocket any non-red ball. The player nominates which ball is being aimed for and must hit the cue ball against that ball. If it is pocketed, the player receives the value of that ball on to their score.

5 Once a red ball is pocketed it stays there, but while there is still a red ball on the table, each coloured ball is immediately re-spotted on its appropriate spot (see setting up illustration) after it is pocketed. The player who pockets the last red ball may attempt to pocket any coloured ball and if it succeeds, that coloured ball is re-spotted.

6 After the last red ball has been pocketed, the coloured balls must be struck by the cue ball and pocketed in strict ascending order of value, and they are not re-spotted once they are pocketed now. A player's break ends once they fail to pocket the ball of lowest value left on the table.

7 The ball that is next to be struck is referred to as 'on'.

8 The player with the highest score when all the balls are cleared from the table is the winner. When only the last ball (black) is left, the first score or penalty ends the game – unless a draw is the result. Then the black is re-spotted and the players draw lots to play at the black from the 'D' – the next score or penalty wins.

9 A snooker occurs when a ball a player must not play obstructs a straight line between the cue ball and the ball that is 'on'. The player must attempt the shot and will be penalised for missing the 'on' ball or for hitting another ball. If, however, the player is snookered by an opponent's foul stroke any ball nominated may be played. If it is pocketed, it is treated as a red, unless all the reds are already off the table, when it is treated as the 'on' ball.

10 Fouls and penalties abound, some of which have been

Snooker Layout

KEY

1 White cue ball
2 Yellow
3 Green
4 Brown
5 Blue
6 Pink
7 15 Red
8 Black

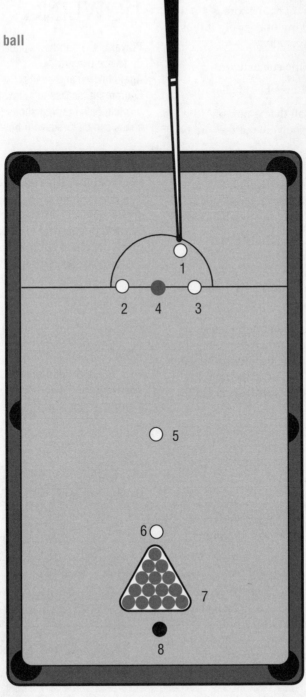

mentioned already. After any foul shot the striker loses the turn and any score made on that particular turn, or break. The minimum penalty score is 4 points and the following only apply if they give a higher penalty:

a) pocketing the cue ball;

b) missing all the object balls;

c) hitting a ball that is not 'on' (the penalty is the value of the 'on' ball);

d) for striking two balls together or pocketing with one shot (other than two reds or the 'on' ball and a nominated ball). The penalty is the higher value of the two balls struck;

e) for a push stroke, jump shot or playing out of turn, the penalty is the value of the 'on' ball or of the ball struck or pocketed, whichever is the higher;

f) for forcing a ball off the table, or moving a ball when the cue ball is touching it, the penalty is the value of the 'on' ball or of the ball off the table or moved, whichever is the greater;

g) for pocketing the wrong ball, the penalty is the value of the 'on' ball or the ball pocketed, whichever is the greater;

h) for playing with other than the cue ball, or playing at two reds with successive shots, the penalty is 7 points;

i) for playing with both feet off the floor, or playing balls before they have come to rest or for playing the ball without anything but the cue, the penalty is the value of the 'on' ball or the ball interfered with, whichever is greater.

TENPIN BOWLING

Players: any number – usually two teams of up to five players
Age: children and adults
Equipment: access to a bowling rink; bowling ball; bowling shoes (balls and shoes can be hired from bowling rinks)

1 Tenpin bowling, often called 'tenpins', is a fun indoor game that can be played by people of all ages and skill levels. Friends can form bowling teams and take part in tournaments or leagues if they wish. Or they can just as happily go along for a bowl at their local rink any time and play as individuals.

2 Tenpins is a variation of the ancient game of skittles, which dates back several thousand years. The ancient Egyptians played a form of skittles and it was very popular in Europe in the Middle Ages. Skittle

games are still played today, of course. Skittles are often thought of as a children's game but in England, skittles is often played as a pub game and the rules vary in different parts of the country. The modern game of tenpin bowling was developed in the United States and is extremely popular in that country.

3 Tenpins is played on a long, flat indoor alley just over 1 metre (1.09 yds) wide and 18.2 metres (60 ft) long. At one end of the alley is a runway for bowlers and a foul line, which bowlers cannot cross. At the other end of the alley stand the ten pins, set up in a triangle formation, with a pit behind them for balls and pins to fall into after a player has had a throw. Heavy bowling balls have two or three holes in them so bowlers can grip the ball as they prepare to throw it. Bowling balls come in different sizes and players choose one that suits them.

4 The aim of the game in tenpins is, of course, to knock the pins over. A game usually consists of ten 'frames'. That is, ten sets of pins are set up for each player. Ten boxes on a scorecard or scoreboard correspond to the number of frames bowled. Bowling centres have automatic scoreboards so if you're not familiar with the scoring system, don't worry. You will easily be able to keep track of the scores via the scoreboard.

5 Players have two balls per frame in which to knock down all the pins. To begin a game, a player steps up to the alley and bowls a ball down it, being careful not to step over the foul line and onto the alley. If he knocks all the pins over with his first ball, it is a 'strike'. A strike is worth 10 points plus a bonus of all the pins that the bowler knocks down with the next 2 balls.

If a player knocks down some of the pins with one ball and the rest with the second ball, it is a 'spare'. A spare is worth 10 points plus a bonus of all the pins that the bowler knocks down with the next single ball.

A player can also score a 'double' by bowling two strikes in succession. The score for a double is usually twenty plus the number of balls knocked down for the first ball of the next frame.

It is also possible to score a 'turkey' by knocking down three frames with three balls! The maximum total score that a bowler can score in ten frames is 300. A bowler would have to bowl twelve strikes in a row to earn such a score.

An 'error' occurs when the bowler does not knock down all of the pins in a frame with his two balls. When this happens he gets no bonuses and just adds the total of the number of pins knocked down to his previous score.

6 Tenpins is a game that is fun for all the family. It makes for a great night out and we highly recommend it. If you have not tried tenpin bowling before, why not look up your nearest alley and book a lane? Enjoy!

TIDDLYWINKS

Players: two to four
Age: children and adults
Equipment: four 'winks' per player and one 'shooter' each (in a different colour for each player); a target cup

1 Essentially a standard children's game, Tiddlywinks has now been taken over by adults and there are associations throughout the world, plus many Internet sites devoted to its play.

2 Tiddlywinks sets have everything you need provided, including the winks and a slightly larger circular plastic disk known as a shooter. The standard game sees two, three or four players given a set of four winks and a shooter in a different colour for each player. The objective is to be the first player to get all four tiddlywinks in the cup and win the game.

3 Order of play is often decided by one shot each. The nearest to, or in the cup, wins, and then turns travel clockwise.

4 Each player shoots a wink towards the cup and if successful in getting it in, another turn is taken. A wink is shot from where it lies after the player's previous turn.

5 In play, any wink that is partly covered by another is considered out of play. A player whose wink is covered must either wait until their opponent moves the wink or can attempt to shift it by hitting it with another of their own winks. A wink laying against the cup is considered out of play until it is knocked by another wink, however, a wink that is shot off the table during a turn is not considered out of play – it is replaced on the table at the point where it went off.

6 Tiddlywinks is won by players counting the number of games they win overall or by scoring one point for each wink in the cup when every game ends.

Variations: The simple game described above can become boring, so create a series of drawn circles on a large piece of paper and put the target cup in the centre. Now draw on scores for each circle – perhaps 5, 10, 15 and 20 for the cup. If a wink lands on the line between two it always scores the lower score. A wink is only shot once and thus when it lands that is its total score. The winner is always the player with the highest score.

SIMPLE OUTDOOR GAMES

Most of the games in this section need a large area in which to play. A garden, park or playground is ideal for them. Many of these games don't require a great deal of specialised equipment and have very simple rules. They are great for keeping groups of young children amused. As you read through the games, you will probably recognise some of them from your own childhood. They've been played and enjoyed by children for many generations!

CALL THE BALL

Players: six to eight players
Age: any child who can manage a ball –
including catching it
Equipment: a soft, bouncy ball; optional
high brick wall

1 The high brick wall is optional, so long as there is a paved area to play on where the ball can be thrown up high with safety. This is a good game to play with groups of active children at a party or family get-together. There is no real winner, but the game will certainly burn off a lot of excess energy!

2 Each player is given a number or the name of a day of the week, or month of the year. If there are less players than days of weeks or months of the year, players can double up and be 'Monday and Thursday', or 'April and October', for instance.

3 The first player throws the ball, either high up in the air or high up against the wall, and calls out a number, day or month.

4 The player whose number, day or month has been called has to run and catch the ball before it bounces more than once.

5 If he successfully does this, he calls next. If, however, he misses, the first player throws and calls again.

CALLING THE COMPASS

Players: four or more is best
Age: anyone who knows east from west
Equipment: a large, flat, paved area; chalk

1 Mark a big cross on the paved area with the chalk. The cross must have the four points of the compass – one on each end of the cross. (Hint: for education as well as fun, take a compass outside and mark the cross according to the real compass points.)

2 The points need to be about 20 metres (65.6 ft) apart.

3 All the players stand in the centre of the cross to begin, and one player is chosen to call out a compass point. Everyone must then run to that point.

4 The last player to make it (an adult can be judge if required) calls out the next compass point to run to, and everyone runs there.

5 The last player again calls another compass point, and so on.

6 The player who is never last, and never gets to call a compass point themselves, is the winner.

285

HIDE AND SEEK

Players: as many as possible
Age: children love this game
Equipment: none

1 Players choose something as 'home' – a chair, or a doorway perhaps. They also choose the first seeker, who then shuts their eyes and counts to 40 while all the other players hide.

2 When the seeker reaches 40, they shout 'Ready' and go to look for the other players. When a player is found, that player tries to reach home before the seeker can touch them.

3 The first player to reach home untouched becomes the next seeker.

HOPSCOTCH

Players: two to ten
Age: all ages can play and enjoy this game, but seven- to 10-year olds love it
Equipment: chalk; one small stone

1 This game has been entertaining children of all ages for hundreds of years, both in schoolyards and quiet streets outside homes.

2 A level site which is preferably paved is needed, on which you use the chalk to draw a hopscotch grid. There are many ways to draw this grid, but one way is shown in the illustration below:

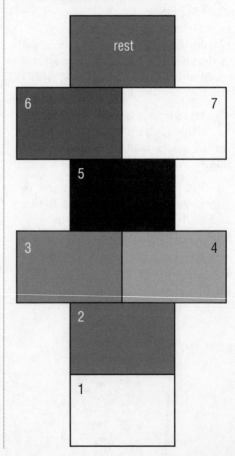

3 The first player throws the stone into box 1 and hops into it, staying on one foot. The player stays on one foot, picks up the pebble and hops back to beyond the starting line, not standing on any lines, and without letting the other foot touch the ground. If this is done successfully, the stone is thrown into box 2 and the player hops after it (using box 1 as a step if necessary).

4 The first player continues their turn until a foul is committed. This can be either by throwing to the wrong area, or missing the correct one; by hopping on to a line; by losing balance and allowing both feet to touch the ground at the same time. When this happens the player's turn is over.

5 To win, the first player to have played the stone into each box and returned to the start, hopping from box to box with only one foot, is the winner.

MARBLES

Players: two to six
Age: all ages, skill is developed with practice
Equipment: five marbles and a 'shooter' for each player; chalk

1 Marbles were once made from clear or coloured glass, but nowadays they are also made from plastic. Somehow, it does not matter what they are made from, players become attached to 'lucky' marbles. It is a tradition that marbles are played for 'keeps', that is they can be won or lost permanently, so it is as well to establish the rules for your particular game before it begins.

2 Players select a reasonably level area of ground and mark out a circle around 2.5 metres (8 ft) in diameter. Each player places a marble on the perimeter of the circle, ensuring they are spaced out fairly equally. Out from the ring approximately 1.8 to 2 metres (6 ft to 6 ft 7 ins) another line is drawn. This is the shooting line.

3 Each player now takes their shooter and rolls it to the centre of the circle to determine the order of play: the player whose shooter rests closest to the circle's centre starts the game.

4 The first player kneels behind the shooting line (knees must not touch the line) with the aim of hitting one of the marbles on the circle's edge with sufficient force that both the target marble and the shooter end up outside the circle. If this happens the player captures that marble and has another go. However, if the shot is

unsuccessful the turn ends and one of that player's marbles must be placed on the edge of the circle.

5 The game ends when there are no more marbles left on the circle's rim and the winner is the player who has captured the most marbles.

MOON AND STARS

Players: good for a crowd of up to ten
Age: younger children – this is an especially good party game
Equipment: none, but the sun has to be out and there is a need for a large wall, or building or tree, to throw a big shadow

1 Choose one person to be 'It'. In this game they are the Moon and must stay in the shadow of the large wall, building or tree.

2 The Stars, or the other children, stay mainly in the sun, but dance in and out of the shadow.

3 The aim is for the Moon to tag or catch a Star when it comes into the shade. This child then becomes a new Moon.

4 This game doesn't necessarily have to have a winner, but the winner could be the child who doesn't get tagged during the game.

QUEENIE

Players: up to six or eight
Age: any age
Equipment: a soft, bouncy ball

1 Along with skipping, ball games have been around for hundreds of years. However, the first 'balls' weren't balls as we know them. They may have been round stones, just for throwing and catching. Then there were balls made from leather strips and stuffed with horsehair and feathers. More often than not these were found in country towns and villages, although they would have made their way to cities, too. So it's not surprising to know that the first ball games were simple games of catch, like Queenie.

2 Queenie is a very early game of catch – it's also known as Queen Anne and her maids. One player is chosen to be Queenie. Queenie stands with her back to the other players and throws the ball backwards (without looking!) over her head.

3 The other players then scramble to catch the ball and when one has it, they all stand with their hands behind their backs, singing 'Queenie, Queenie, who's got the ball?'

4 Queenie then turns and tries to guess who has the ball. If she's right, she is Queenie again. If she's wrong, the person who has the ball becomes Queenie.

QUOITS

Players: two
Age: any age
Equipment: set of quoits; two stakes

1 Quoits is well known in England and probably began around 1000 years ago, associated mainly with rural people. Quoits were made from poor quality, left-over metal and this is why many areas of quoit playing are centred around mining communities.

2 The home game is known as Sward Quoits because the other games are played on a pitch with target pins embedded in soft clay at either end, and the home game is usually played on a lawn with the pins as far away as the participants think is good. A championship game in England has the pins 19 metres apart or (21yds), but this may be too far for beginners and younger family members, so try 10 metres (11yds) or so to begin and see how the family likes it.

3 To play is very simple. A single game is played by two people and each person throws two quoits alternately each turn. The players then walk to the other pin and, standing next to it, throw two quoits at the opposite pin. The player with the quoit nearest to the pin wins the end and scores two points if both quoits from that player are nearest to the pin.

4 A game is won by the first player to reach 21 points.

ROUND HOPSCOTCH

Players: good for two to four
Age: children of any age
Equipment: chalk and a large area of pavement

1 Draw a snail shape on to the pavement and divide into 20 or so squares (see illustration). For younger children make the squares smaller, so they are easily jumped into or over.

2 The aim of the game is to hop around the pattern, jumping clearly into each square without stepping on any lines and keeping balance on one foot.

3 When the player reaches the centre, they may rest on two feet before they hop right out again.

4 Each time a player successfully completes this hopping marathon without stepping on a line or putting their other foot down (except in the middle to rest) they can write their

initial in any square. This space becomes their Home Space and they can rest there on two feet from then on.

5 Nobody else can hop into a players' Home Space – they must hop over it.

6 Once each player has had three or four successful turns, it does get harder to hop into the centre without stepping on a line or invading someone else's Home Space.

7 As soon as any player hops on a line or rests their foot in the wrong spot, or can't jump the required Home Spaces, they are not able to score a Home Space. But they can have another turn to do so, in sequence.

SHADOW TAG

Players: good for a crowd of up to ten
Age: younger children, especially good party game
Equipment: none, but the sun has to be out and there is a need for some hiding places

1 Another version of Tag to keep young children happy. This version is similar to Moon and Stars but you need to have some hiding places, as well as lots of space.

2 Choose one person to be 'It'. The rest of the crowd moves around so that It doesn't step on their shadow. This is the one time that players themselves aren't tagged.

3 Perhaps an adult could adjudicate, if someone claims their shadow has not been stepped on.

4 When a players' shadow is stepped on, they become It, and the game continues.

SIMON SAYS

Players: as many as possible
Age: any age, including the very young
Equipment: none

1 This is a great children's party game. One player (or an adult) is the leader and the others spread around that person. The leader orders the others to do various actions – such as marching on the spot, or waving their arms above their heads. They only obey these orders if the leader precedes the order with the words 'Simon says'.

2 If the leader just says, 'Hands on heads' they must not carry out the action. If a player makes a mistake they are out of the game.

3 The leader will encourage mistakes by giving orders very fast in succession, or developing a pattern of movements and then breaking it, or doing the actions for others to follow.

4 The last person left in the game is the winner and becomes the next leader.

SKIPPING GAMES

Players: one can play, or join in with any number of friends
Age: any age, but children around seven to twevle really enjoy skipping
Equipment: a skipping rope – short for one person but much longer if there is a group of friends playing

1 When skipping ropes first became popular with children, it was mainly boys who played with them. They made up many tricks which skippers still do today, such as skipping with crossed hands. Girls soon started playing, often in groups. They then added rhymes which they taught their friends.

2 When playing alone with a skipping rope, children could try saying the very old rhyme:

Ipsey, Pipsey,
Tell me true,
Who shall I be married to?
A, B, C, D, . . .

Then the skipper continues to skip, going through the alphabet until they stumble or tire. The letter they stop on becomes the first letter of their future sweetheart's name!

Of course, groups of friends can play this game too, but they take turns at skipping one at a time.

3 It's good to begin skipping along when you first learn to skip, because it gives you a chance to practice a lot and become good enough to take part in group skipping games. However, when you skip with a large rope with friends, you usually run in

and out of the rope. This also takes practice, so friends must practice together. It's also acceptable for a skipper in a group to begin by standing in the middle of the rope and getting their friends to start turning the rope on the count of three.

4 Here is another old rhyme that can be used by skippers playing on their own. However, it can also be used by groups of skippers.

The idea of this skipping game is that at first, the rope is turned slowly on the word 'salt', then faster for 'mustard' and 'vinegar' and the fastest possible on 'pepper'. Try this rhyme now:

Bluebells and cockleshells,
Eevy, ivy, over.
My mother sent me to the store
And this is what she sent me for:
Salt, mustard, vinegar, pepper!

5 Two still-popular schoolyard skipping rhymes for lots of people are the following:

House to rent,
Enquire within.
When I jump out,
Let ——— jump in.

With this rhyme (one of the oldest known in skipping), the skipper calls in a friend on the last line, then they jump together about twice and then the first person jumps out, leaving the other to say the rhyme and call someone else in. The other well known old rhyme for many skippers is this:

Apples, peaches, pears and plums,
Tell me when your birthday comes.
January, February, March . . .
(continuing) First, second, third . . .
(continuing)

The person reciting the rhyme continues and the others jump in on their birthday month and jump out again when the date is called.

STATUES

Players: as many as possible
Age: under-sevens love it
Equipment: none

1 Another really good children's party game for the garden. It is probably best to have an adult as the 'grandmother' standing with her back to the rest of the children.

2 The children begin about 15 metres (16 yds) away from the grandmother and, while grandmother's back is turned, they creep up quietly. However, every so often grandmother turns around suddenly and immediately the children see her turn they stop and freeze into statues.

3 If she spots anyone moving they are out of the game.

4 The first child to touch grandmother, or the last child left in the game, wins and (especially at parties) they are awarded a prize. Then another round can start.

TAG

Players: as many as possible (up to 20 or so)
Age: six- to ten-year olds love it
Equipment: none

1 Usually about 20 minutes of this good children's party game is probably enough. Children like to be entertained, but should not become over-excited.

2 Form the children into a circle about 8 metres (9 yds) in diameter. One child, the chaser, stands in the middle of the circle and calls out the names of two of the children. These children have to get up and run across to exchange places with each other. They have to reach their new position and sit down without being touched (tagged) by the chaser.

3 If the chaser succeeds in tagging a child, that child becomes the chaser for the new round.

4 Just a hint. It is wise to have adult supervision so there are fewer disputes and every child gets their name called out at some point.

TOM TIDDLER'S GROUND

Players: best with several players
Age: younger children, good for a party game
Equipment: a length of rope; a selection of sweets

1 A section of ground is marked off with a rope, as Tom Tiddler's ground, which is supposed to have gemstones (or gold) scattered all over it. The sweets are scattered all over the area within the rope, and they are the gemstones (or gold).

2 One player is chosen to be Tom Tiddler.

3 The rest of the players venture on to Tom's ground, picking up the sweets and saying, 'Here I am on Tom Tiddler's ground, picking up gems (or gold)'.

4 Tom defends his kingdom by rushing at anyone he likes who is trespassing on his ground. However, he cannot leave his ground. If he succeeds in tagging a player, that player takes his place as Tom Tiddler.

5 The winner of the game is the person who collects the most gems (or gold) from Tom Tiddler's ground, once they have all been picked up.

TOUCH TAG

Players: good for a crowd of up to ten
Age: younger children, an especially good party game
Equipment: none

1 Again, an 'It' must be chosen.

2 This time, however, when a player is tagged by It, they can stay in the game without becoming It, but must run around holding on to the place on their body where they were tagged.

3 This is the part of the game where It can really have some fun! Tag one person on top of the head, then another on the knee, then another on the ear perhaps, and all players will end up dissolving into laughter when they see each other looking really silly.

4 Once everyone is tagged, another player gets to be It and the game starts over.

WALL BALL

Players: fun for one or more
Age: older children with good ball skills
Equipment: a hand-sized bouncy ball

1 This is a game where you throw the ball against the wall and then do something before you catch it again – the idea is to catch it on the full, but for younger children, it's okay to allow it one bounce. You can spend countless hours of fun and practice on your own, as you achieve PBs (personal bests). Alternatively, Wall Ball can be played with a few friends.

2 There is a sequence of moves in Wall Ball which you must complete. They get harder and more complicated the further you go, so let's begin:

3 Ordinary – throw the ball against the wall and catch it.

Moving – throw the ball and catch it without moving your feet.

Laughing – throw the ball and catch it while keeping a straight face, but thinking of something funny (easier to do when you're alone).

Talking – throw the ball, touch your mouth, then catch it.

One Hand – throw the ball with one hand, then catch it with the other.

One Foot – throw the ball while standing on one foot, then catch it while standing on the other.

Clap in Front – throw the ball, clap your hands, then catch it.

Clap at Back – throw the ball, clap your hands behind your back, then catch it.

Clap Front and Back – throw the ball, clap in front and behind your back, then catch the ball.

Clap Back and Front – throw the ball, clap behind your back, then in front, then catch it.

Twirl Front – throw the ball, twirl your right hand away from your body and around your left hand, then catch the ball.

Twirl Back – throw the ball, twirl your right hand around your left hand behind your back, then catch the ball.

Spin – throw the ball, spin yourself around, then catch it.

4 Once you've mastered this sequence of moves, you can begin to add variations. For instance, after clapping in front and behind your back, you can add a sequence where you clap twice, then three times, then four times and so on (throwing the ball ever higher to give yourself more time to complete the movement), until you reach your limit.

5 Another variation of this game is also to do with clapping. This time, you throw the ball, then raise your right leg and clap once underneath it, then catch the ball. Next you throw the ball, raise your left leg and repeat the clapping movement. You can continue adding claps until you reach your limit.

The moves for this game are limited only by your imagination.

Groups of friends playing Wall Ball can set rules and hold competitions, to see who is the most skilled player.

COIN TOSSING GAMES

Tossing a coin usually plays a part in a game only to decide whether a player serves or has first turn. However, there are a small group of games played around the world which revolve around the coins themselves. Here are just three to enjoy.

BROTHER JONATHAN

Players: two or more, as individuals or in teams
Age: any age
Equipment: coins for each player; a board upon which numbers have been written in sections

1 The board for Brother Jonathan can be drawn either on the ground, or on a large sheet of paper and laid on the ground. There are five rows in a rectangle and then sections need to be divided off across each row. Any numbers can be used, but the smaller numbers should be put in the larger sections and the large numbers in the smaller sections to make it harder to score high.

2 Each player takes it in turn to pitch a coin from a previously agreed point onto the board. Most games would consist of five throws each. If a coin touches any of the dividing lines it does not count towards the player's score.

3 To win, the first player or team to score an agreed total takes the coins, or the player or team with the highest score after an agreed number of games or throws. Of course, it doesn't have to be played for the coins as stakes, it can be played just for fun.

COVER IT

Players: two or more
Age: children and adults
Equipment: coins for each player; a wall

1 The first player throws a coin against a wall and leaves it where it rests on the ground.

2 Each player then takes it in turn to throw a coin against the wall. If the coin is touching another coin when it comes to rest, the player who threw it picks up both coins. If it is not touching another coin, the coin is left on the ground. (The game can also be played with cards.)

TWO-UP

Players: any number can play
Age: mainly adults
Equipment: historically two pennies; a kip (a flat piece of wood used for throwing)

1 In Australia, Two-Up was an illegal gambling game for many years. Groups of men (known as 'schools') were found almost anywhere and police raids on the better known schools were a common occurrence.

2 These days, souvenir sets of old pennies and a wooden kip can be found in games shops as well as souvenir shops in many cities.

3 In professional games, Two-Up was controlled by a 'boxer' who was in charge of the spinning of the pennies and the betting. The person spinning the coins (known as the spinner) bets on their ability to throw heads, and the others playing will cover that player. Of course, spectators wager side bets either for or against the spinner. The boxer collects a percentage, or rake-off, from all these bets, win or lose.

4 The spinner is provided with a small, flat piece of wood known as a kip. That player then places two pennies on this and, when all bets have been placed, the boxer calls 'Come in, spinner', and throws the coins. If the pennies come down heads the spinner has won, and loses if they come down tails. If the throw shows one head and one tail it is declared a no throw and the spinner repeats the toss.

5 The spinner keeps tossing while heads continue to show. Heads must be spun three times before the spinner can take the winnings. After that this player can bet if desired or retire and the next spinner takes a turn.

6 At home, scoring can be done on how many times each player wins a round – the best of three, or the best of five perhaps?

SWIMMING POOL GAMES

It is fair to say that most of the games played either in the pool or at the beach are watery versions of old, land-based favourites. No doubt you will recognise many of your childhood games in this selection, but it is surprising how much more difficult they can become when you need to swim everywhere to win!

Obviously, games in the pool are fun, but good adult participation and close supervision at all times is an absolute MUST. The adult should take an active part in the games (even joining in the fun in the pool) and definitely should not be reading or talking, away from the action.

DOLPHIN CHALLENGE

Players: two or more
Age: any age
Equipment: eight quoits

1 Everyone gets to be a Dolphin, but if more than two are playing, select two Dolphins first.

2 All eight quoits are thrown anywhere in the pool.

3 Someone says 'Go' and the Dolphins, who can start either together at one end of the pool, or at opposite ends, swim underwater and try to be the first to collect four quoits each.

4 The winning Dolphin is the one who places the four quoits on the side of the pool and yells out 'Finished'.

5 In games where there are more than two players, another Dolphin now challenges the winning Dolphin.

LOCH NESS MONSTER

Players: five to ten
Age: any age
Equipment: a whistle

1 This fun swimming pool game is great for parties, where there are a large number of players. An adult or older child can act as referee.

2 First, all players join hands and form a long line in the swimming pool. The first player in the line is the head of the fabled Loch Ness Monster. The player at the end of the line is the tail.

3 The aim of the game is for the player who is the head of the Loch Ness Monster to try to 'bite', or tag, the tail.

4 The referee blows the whistle and then all players between the head and tail of the monster twist and turn, to try to prevent the head tagging the tail.

5 After the tail is bitten, the head moves to the end of the line and the next player in line becomes the head of the Loch Ness Monster.

6 The winner of this game is the person who avoids being bitten the longest, as judged by the referee.

MARCO POLO

Players: three or more
Age: any age
Equipment: none

1 Choose a Marco Polo.

2 While the other players are spreading out around the pool, Marco Polo counts to ten with eyes shut.

3 Keeping eyes closed, Marco Polo moves slowly around the pool trying to tag the other players. Whenever Marco Polo calls out 'Marco' all the other players must say 'Polo'.

4 One player at a time may leave the pool and enter at a different spot, but if Marco Polo calls out 'Fish on the beach' the player who is out of the pool becomes the new Marco Polo.

5 Or, if Marco tags a player, they become the new Marco Polo.

NEPTUNE SAYS

Players: five or more
Age: any age
Equipment: none

1 A watery version of a land-locked favourite, especially for younger children – make sure they are wearing their safety jackets (or 'floaties').

2 If the person chosen as Neptune calls out 'Neptune says . . .' and tells the other players to touch the ladder, touch the bottom, do a duck dive, blast off or gather a quoit from the bottom, everyone does it.

3 If Neptune leaves out the magic words 'Neptune says . . .' and players still carry out the command, then they are out of the game.

4 The aim is to be the last player in, and that person is the new Neptune.

PIRATE'S TREASURE

Players: two or more
Age: confident swimmers
Equipment: lots of small coins; waterproof marker; a bag of sweets such as chocolate buttons or jelly beans

1 All children who are reasonably confident swimmers love to dive for coins. In this simple, variation of the game, they receive a reward for finding the 'Pirate's Treasure'.

2 Using a waterproof marker, first mark about a third of the coins with an X (or if you want to be really inventive, a skull and crossbones!). Then throw the coins evenly around the bottom of the swimming pool.

3 Now players jump in together and dive for the coins, each player collecting as many as they can. At this point it's a good idea to ensure that an

adult acts as a referee, so no underwater squabbles break out over the coins!

4 Once all the coins have been collected, check each person's collection and count how many marked coins they have. For each marked coin, the player receives a replacement sweet treat. (Hint: when the game is finished, ink on the coins can be removed with methylated spirits.)

SEAL IN THE MIDDLE

Players: three or more
Age: any age
Equipment: a large waterball

1 Select one player as the seal, who goes into the middle of the pool.

2 All the other players split between the opposite ends of the pool and throw the waterball over and past the seal who continues to try to catch the ball.

3 The seal can swim to touch a player who is holding the waterball, and then that tagged player becomes the seal.

4 If the seal catches the ball, the player to throw it becomes the new seal.

SEAWEED

Players: six or more
Age: any age
Equipment: none

1 Choose one player as the judge.

2 All the other players are spread out around the pool.

3 On 'Go' from the judge, all the players move around the pool swaying like seaweed caught in a current.

4 The judge then calls out a number and a part of the body, such as three elbows, or five feet. Players rush to find other players to place that exact number of the correct body parts together. Players who cannot make up the number are out and help the judge.

Select a new judge from one of the last two players left in.

SHARK

Players: up to twelve
Age: any age
Equipment: none

1 The aim is to not be caught by the shark. A player, selected as the shark, chooses one end of the pool.

2 All the other players scatter around the pool.

3 The shark, with back turned to the pool and with eyes closed, counts to 20 aloud and then calls out 'Still pond'. Everyone must be still, although they can slip underwater but not leave the spot they are in.

4 The shark moves around with eyes tightly closed. The first player the shark touches becomes the new shark.

SOAKING SOCK RELAY

Players: up to twelve – more if the pool is large
Age: confident swimmers
Equipment: two pairs of old socks, large enough to fit on everyone's feet

1 In this fast and furious relay game for confident swimmers, two teams of players battle it out to see who can get to the finish first.

2 Divide a group of players into two teams and give each team a pair of old socks.

On 'Go!' players jump into the water, pull on both socks while in the water and then swim to the other side of the pool.

3 Once players reach the other side of the pool, they are met by the next member of their team who must also jump into the water and pull on the wet socks. Pulling on the wet socks while in the water creates much hilarity and is rather hard to do!

4 The winner of the race is, of course, the team who finishes first, after each player has swum a lap of the pool wearing the socks. (Hint: for younger children, pulling on a single sock may be sufficient. Alternatively, an old t-shirt can be used instead of a pair of socks.)

SOGGY SPONGES

Players: six to eight – more if the pool is bigger
Age: any age
Equipment: two large sponges (the kind used for washing cars is best); rope or volleyball net

1 The aim of this fun pool party game is to keep two large sponges in play, going back and forth across a net or rope that has been strung across the pool, to divide it in half.

2 First, players are divided into two teams and each team is positioned on either side of the net, or rope. A referee (usually a supervising adult) gives one wet sponge to each team and on 'Go!' players must toss the sponges over the net at the opposing team.

3 Players on each team must catch the wet sponges every time. If one team member drops a sponge, then that player leaves the pool (leaving fewer team members to throw and catch the soggy sponges!).

4 Eventually, only one player will be left in the game, holding both soggy wet sponges. This player's team is the winning team.

TASTY ICE-CREAM

Players: three or more
Age: any age
Equipment: none

1 The aim is to reach the ice-cream seller who is standing at one end of the pool. Choose a player to be the ice-cream seller and all other players line up at the other end of the pool.

2 The ice-cream seller turns around with eyes closed and calls out one letter at a time with the name of an ice-cream flavour, such as 'C is for Chocolate', or 'L is for Liquorice'.

3 Players who have that letter in their name – both first and last names – can step up one step closer to the seller, so Cathy Cook can move up two steps when 'C' for chocolate is called.

4 After five letters (this will depend on home rules and the size of the pool!) the ice-cream seller can look at how close players are before saying another letter.

5 The first player to reach the seller, becomes the next seller. Ask Mum or Dad if there is an ice-cream in the fridge because this is tiring work!

THREE STRIKES AND YOU'RE OUT

Players: four or more
Age: any age
Equipment: one large waterball

1 All players take a number and stand in a circle.

2 Player number one throws the waterball in the air and calls out a number.

3 As the number is called, such as 'Number 4', all the other players swim away from the waterball. But as soon as player number 4 gets the waterball they call out 'Stop' and all the other players must stand still.

4 Player number 4 with the waterball now throws it gently at any player. If the player is hit, that player is given one strike. Three hits, and therefore three strikes – well, you're out!

5 All players go back to the centre and player number two takes the waterball and calls out a number and so the game continues until only one player is left.

WATER STATUES

Players: four or more
Age: any age
Equipment: none

1 A judge is selected from the players and stays outside the pool.

2 Everyone else enters the water and when the judge says 'Go' all the players in the water move around.

3 When the judge says 'Stop' everyone freezes.

4 The judge then chooses the player who froze last, and this player comes and stands with the judge to help.

5 The game continues until one player is left; this player is the new judge.

WHIRLPOOL WIPEOUT

Players: six to twelve – ideal for parties and large groups of children
Age: any age, but best for confident swimmers or older children
Equipment: garden hose

1 This is a fun, rough and tumble game, where children do their best to dodge cold water from a garden hose, while walking in a circle and forming a whirlpool in the water. The aim of the game is for players to avoid water from the hose, while changing direction in the pool.

2 First, one person is chosen to be Caller. This person will stand at the pool's edge with a garden hose, switched on. The rest of the players join hands in the pool and begin to walk around in a large circle, clockwise, as fast as they can.

3 After the players have walked around a few times, a good current of water will be flowing in one direction – especially if the pool is round. Now the Caller yells 'Wipeout!' Everyone must turn around as fast as they can and begin to walk in an anti-clockwise direction.

4 Here is the fun part for the Caller. She must aim the hose into the pool and try to squirt one of the players, as they turn around and commence walking in the opposite direction. The player can avoid being 'wiped out' by ducking under the water – but they must keep hold of other players' hands and keep on walking. Needless to say, this is very hard to do!

5 If the Caller's target is able to avoid a direct hit with the water from the hose by ducking under after the turn, she may continue on until the next call of 'Wipeout!' If the target is hit, however, she must take the place of the Caller and the game begins again.

FOOTBALL GAMES

Football games are some of the most popular sporting games played around the world today. They are fast, action-packed and great fun for children and adults alike. As a spectator sport, football is hard to beat. Millions of people attend professional football matches each week, cheering on their favourite teams. Children and families can also become involved with their local football clubs, learning the skills of the particular code they choose to play and making new friends amongst their team mates.

Although football games are generally played on a football ground or pitch, children love to kick the ball around and practise their skills just about anywhere – in backyards, quiet streets, local parks and at the beach. Football is a game for everyone. All that is needed is a ball.

AUSTRALIAN RULES FOOTBALL

Players: two teams of up to twenty-two; eighteen on the field at any given time
Age: juniors to adults
Equipment: an oval shaped Australian Rules football; access to an oval or playing field; good quality football boots, shorts and jumper if playing with a club; a mouthguard to protect teeth

1 Australian Rules Football is one of the most popular team sports in Australia. It was first devised and played in Melbourne in 1858 during the winter months, when cricket was not played. It quickly became popular and today it is played in all parts of the country, and watched by millions each year.

The football season runs from autumn through to spring in Australia but the game is now so popular that training and play often begins in the summer months.

2 Australian Rules is played on a grassed oval 135 metres (147.6 yds) wide and 185 metres (202.3 yds) long, although junior players often play on a smaller oval (see diagram page 320). Umpires supervise the field of play, the goal posts and the boundaries of the oval.

3 There are two sets of four goal posts at each end of the football oval. Players score goals by kicking the ball through the centre sets of their opponents' posts and 'behinds' by kicking the ball through the outer sets of their opponents' posts. The aim of the game is for each team of 18 players to score more points than the other side, by kicking goals and behinds.

Goals are worth 6 points each.
Behinds are worth 1 point each.

To score a goal, the ball must pass cleanly over the goal line and through the centre goal posts – it doesn't matter if it bounces, as long as it doesn't touch the posts.

To score a behind, the ball must pass through one of the outer sets of posts. A behind is also scored when a player kicks the ball and it hits a goal post, even if it goes through the centre posts. And if the ball is touched by another player on its way through the posts, it also scores only a behind.

4 A game of Australian Rules is played over four quarters of 20 minutes. However, each quarter often lasts a little longer than this when extra time or 'time on' is added, for time lost while the ball is out of bounds (when the ball bounces out of the playing area), or for other interruptions to the game.

5 There are a number of different playing positions on the field in a game of Australian Rules. Players in various positions are generally responsible for contesting the ball in their area on the field, and depending on their position, they have a different job in the game.

There are also three players who can follow the ball anywhere on the field. They are the ruckman, the ruckrover and the rover.

6 A game of football is started when the field umpire bounces the ball in the centre circle. Players from each team then try to grab the ball. They can run with the ball in their hands, as long as they bounce it every 15 metres (16.4 yds). They can also pass the ball

to other team members by either kicking it, or handpassing it to other players. Handpasses are done in a special way – one hand is held underneath the ball, while the fist of the other hand is used to hit it on. This move is called handballing.

To obtain the ball, players may 'tackle' another player by grabbing them above the knees and below the chest. If a player is tackled, he or she must pass the ball to another player with a kick or a handpass. If the ball is kicked out of the playing area (out of bounds), then the opposing team takes the ball and the game continues.

7 When a ball is kicked in the air, players often catch it by 'marking' the ball. There are several different ways to mark a ball, but the easiest one is the chest mark. Players catch the ball and hold it close in to their chest, to stop opponents from snatching it from them. If a player marks the ball they can choose to kick it to another team member, or handpass it, or begin to run with it.

8 Kicking the football requires lots of practice. Experienced footballers can kick a football long distances with great accuracy and a coach can help you or your children learn this skill, along with the others we've mentioned, such as marking.

9 Australian Rules Football is a dynamic and exciting game for everyone. To learn more, check out some of the many websites about the game, on the Internet. Join a local Australian Rules football club and visit some local football matches. Or perhaps you might prefer to watch one of the many professional games screened on television, or visit a big football match.

10 You could also modify the rules so that you can have an enjoyable game with family members in a park, or a short match at a children's party. In its simplest form, all you need is a ball to enjoy a game of Aussie Rules. Have fun!

GAELIC FOOTBALL

Players: two teams of fifteen
Age: juniors to adults
Equipment: a Gaelic football (like a soccer ball, only slightly smaller); access to a playing field, marked for Gaelic football; good quality football boots; shorts and jumper if playing with a club; a mouthguard to protect teeth

1 Gaelic football is an Irish code of football and it is one of the most popular sports in Ireland today. The rules for Gaelic football are very similar to those of the other Irish national sport, hurling. Gaelic football is also played in many other countries and several clubs can be found in Australia.

2 Gaelic football is similar to Australian Rules in many ways and could also be described as a cross between the games of rugby and soccer. However, different forms of the game have been played for more than 500 years!

3 The rules of modern Gaelic football were first written down in the 1880's. The sport is played on a grassed pitch or field, approximately 137 metres (150 yds) long and 82 metres (90 yds) wide. Juniors often play on a smaller pitch. A referee, two linesmen and four umpires supervise the field of play.

4 There are two sets of goal posts at each end of a Gaelic football pitch, and they are similar to those found on a rugby pitch – that is, they consist of

two posts joined by a crossbar. Players score goals by getting the ball under the crossbar of their opponents' posts. They can do this by either kicking the ball or knocking it through with their hands. Points are scored by getting the ball over the crossbar of the opponents' posts.

The team who scores the most points at the end of the game is, of course, the winner.

Goals are worth 3 points each.

Each point is worth 1 point.

A green flag is raised by an umpire when a goal is scored and a white flag is raised when a point is scored.

5 A game of Gaelic football is played over two halves, or periods of 30 minutes at local level. Championship games are played over two periods of 35 minutes. Extra time may be added by the referee, if there is a draw at the end of the game. Extra time usually runs for two extra periods of 10 minutes each.

6 Each of the fifteen players in a Gaelic football team has a position on the pitch. There are forward positions, midfield positions, back positions and of course, a goalkeeper. Defending players are responsible for contesting the ball in their particular area on the pitch. Attacking players must be careful not to enter the defending player's area before the ball when they are playing, or a foul can result and the opponent gets the ball! This is called a 'square ball'.

7 When playing a game of Gaelic football, players must not pick the ball up straight off the ground. Instead, they must lift it up with the toe of their

321

boot and then they are permitted to handle the ball. However, players are not permitted to take more than four steps with the ball in their hands. They must drop the ball from hand to foot as they run across the pitch. This requires a great deal of practice and skill, as players must 'solo run' with the ball in this fashion while being pursued by their opponents. Many fast hand and foot passes between players are used in this game, to get the ball from one end of the pitch to the other.

8 Players tackle their opponents with their shoulders to try to unbalance them and take possession of the ball. They also try to hit the ball from an opponent's hands, but only with the open palm of their own hand. In other words, they cannot punch the ball out of an opponent's hands.

9 There are many ways to 'foul' and lose the ball to your opponent in Gaelic football, such as if the ball goes out of bounds, or if players tackle each other in any but the accepted way of using the shoulders. Special free kicks are also sometimes awarded, and these are called a '45', as it is taken from the defending teams 45 metre (50 yd) line.

10 All in all, the exciting game of Gaelic football is fun to both watch and play. Why not try to find a club in your area? Many Gaelic football clubs have websites on the Internet. Gaelic football is also occasionally shown on some television channels – both free-to-air TV and pay TV. Watching a match or two will give you a good idea of what an excellent spectator sport Gaelic football is, and why it has been popular in Ireland for hundreds of years.

GRIDIRON (AMERICAN FOOTBALL)

Players: two teams of eleven with several extra specialised substitute players
Age: juniors to adults
Equipment: an oval shaped American football; access to a playing field, specially marked for the game; appropriate safety gear – helmet, boots, mouthguard and protective padding; team outfit if playing for a club

1 Gridiron, or American football as it is known outside the United States, is arguably the most popular game in that country. Only baseball comes close. Gridiron may appear a very disorganised game to the first-time spectator, but it is actually the opposite – extremely complex and almost scientific in the way that it is played. Only a brief description of Gridiron will be given here, as to play this game informally is not really possible and to play with two teams in a formal manner requires the help of a good coach.

2 Gridiron originally developed from the English game of rugby and it was first played in schools and colleges in the United States. The first professional games were played in the late 1800s. The early game of Gridiron was quite violent, with lots of dangerous tackling. Some players even lost their lives on the field! New rules and protective clothing were introduced to make Gridiron the much safer game that it is today.

3 Gridiron is played on a field 110 metres (120 yds) long and 49 metres (53.3 yds) wide. The field is divided into lines every 4.5 metres (5 yds) and marked with numbers every 9 metres (10 yds) (see diagram page 325). Special hash marks also run the length of the field. The whole appearance of the marks on the field gives the sport of Gridiron its name, as the field resembles a large grid.

4 Gridiron is played over four quarters of 15 minutes each but the game goes for much, much longer than this, as the clock does not run continuously and there are many clock stops, depending on what is happening on the field. There are two sets of goal posts at each end of the Gridiron field – large U-shaped structures resting on a single pole.

5 The aim of the game is for each team to try to score as many points as they can. Teams may play an Offence or Defence position. The Offensive players are in possession of the ball and try to score, while the Defensive players, of course, try to stop them. The Offensive team often meets in the famous Gridiron 'huddle', to plan their strategy before they make their next play. Teams can score points in one of four ways: By scoring a 'touchdown', by crossing the other team's goal line while holding the ball. By a 'conversion', which can occur after a touchdown, when the scoring team has a second chance in which to kick the ball over the goal posts or run over the goal line again. By scoring a 'field goal', by kicking the ball from the field and through the goal posts. By scoring a 'safety', when the defensive team tackles the person from the other team who is carrying the ball in their own end zone.

Touchdowns are worth 6 points.
Conversions are worth 1 point.
Field goals are worth 3 points.
And a safety is worth 2 points.

6 Each Gridiron team is made up of almost two separate teams of specialist players and it depends on whether they are playing an Offence position or a Defence position as to which players take the field. Players are regularly substituted throughout the game, depending on how the team is faring and what part of the game they are playing. Playing positions are:

Offence –
1 Quarterback (he is in charge of the moves his players make)
2 Running backs (half-back and full-back)
2 Wide receivers
1 Tight end
1 Centre
2 Guards
2 Tackles

Defence –
2 Tackles
2 Ends
3 Linebackers
2 Safeties
2 Cornerbacks

7 So how does this complicated and exciting game begin? Most plays in the game begin with a 'scrimmage'. Players from opposing teams face each other across a 'Line of Scrimmage', which is as wide as the ball. The Offence have four plays to get the ball a minimum of 11 metres (10 yds) down the field, towards the opposing team's goal line. They do this by passing the ball between the players and running. If they are able to do this, they are able to have what is called a 'first down' and they start the series of plays again, all with the aim of getting to the Defence's goal line. Players may also kick the ball in an attempt to score a field goal, or to 'punt' the ball to another player when too far away from the goal.

If the Offence team cannot move the ball the required distance in four plays, the opposing side gets the ball.

8 Seven officials supervise the game of Gridiron – a referee, an umpire, line judge, linesman, field judge, back judge and side judge. They each have a yellow flag and a whistle, which they use if one of the many rules of the game are broken, such as players being out of their position before play commences or if an interference to a pass takes place.

9 The Gridiron season run by the National Football League in the United States runs from late summer, through autumn and into the middle of winter. It ends in a grand final between the two top teams called the Super Bowl, on the last Sunday in January each year.

10 The description of Gridiron we've given here has simply touched on the basics of an amazing game that if watched once, will never be forgotten. There are local Gridiron teams in most areas and they can often be found on the Internet. Why not look

one up and go along and watch a local game? Alternatively, Gridiron games can regularly be seen on television during the American season and the Super Bowl is viewed by millions around the world each January. Gridiron is an exciting game to both watch and play.

110 m
(120 yd)

Hash marks
(college)

Hash marks
(professional)

Goal post

Goal line ▶

9 m
(10 yd)

End zone

49 m (53.3 yds)

INTERNATIONAL RULES FOOTBALL

Players: two teams of up to twenty – no more than twelve on the field at any time
Age: children and adults
Equipment: access to a playing field; a regulation Australian Rules football; mouthguard, good quality football boots; shorts and shirt

1 International Rules football is a new game with rules which are basically a mix of Australian Rules football and Gaelic football.

It was devised in recent years so that players from Australia and Ireland who played the two different codes of football could compete against each other with a consistent set of rules. Australian and Irish teams had played matches for some years, using a number of different, informal sets of rules. Finally, in 1998, a formal set of International Rules was drawn up.

2 International Rules is currently played annually between the two countries. Two matches, or tests, are played each year, with players taking it in turns to travel either to Ireland or Australia. Any elite football player in each country may be put forward to take part in the international game. In the future, young players who hope to play at a professional level of their local code when they are older may also get the chance to join an International Rules team.

3 International Rules is played on a field 100 to 120 metres (110 to 130 yds) in length and 60 to 70 metres (65 to 76 yds) wide. There are two goal posts at each end of the field and each has a crossbar between them. A goal net is strung between each set of posts, also.

4 International Rules is played over four quarters of 20 minutes and just like Australian Rules, each quarter often lasts a little longer than the 20 minutes when extra time or 'time on' is added, for lost time when the ball is out of bounds, or for other interruptions to the game.

5 The aim of the game is for each team to try to score points. The team with the most points at the end of the game is the winner. Points are awarded as follows:

Goal (when the ball is kicked under the crossbar of opponent's goal) – 6 points

Over (when the ball is kicked over the crossbar of the opponent's goal) – 3 points

6 There are a number of different playing positions on the field, and they are very similar to Gaelic football. Players move the ball about the field in much the same way as Australian Rules, being able to 'mark' the ball, tackle other players for the ball and kick the ball using the same kicking methods as for Australian Rules. Players may also pick up the ball directly from the ground, which they cannot do in Gaelic football. Play on the field is fast, furious and athletic, as the attacking and defending teams vie for control of the ball.

7 Eight officials oversee a game of International Rules football – two referees, two linesmen, and four goal umpires (two at each end). The goal umpires use two red flags to signal a

goal, one red flag to signal an over and one white flag to signal a Touchdown (when a player with control of the ball places it on the ground in the 'End Zone' area of the opposing team's goal). A score may also be registered for a Touchdown – usually 1 point.

8 International Rules football is a new and growing code of football. It is hoped that in the future, an American team may join in a series with the Australian and Irish teams. This would increase the competition and bring about more matches, creating a greater public awareness of this new and exciting game.

9 International Rules football is a fantastic spectator sport. The game combines the best of its two parent codes. It is fast, exciting and there is never a dull moment on the ground. If you get a chance, it is definitely worth going along to an International Rules match or watching it on TV. And any child who enjoys playing Rugby or Australian Rules will enjoy watching or participating in a game of International Rules football.

RUGBY LEAGUE

Players: two teams of thirteen plus four extra substitute players – less for an informal family game or a modified version of the game for young children
Age: children and adults
Equipment: an oval shaped ball, usually leather; a mouthguard, helmet and optional shoulder pads – essential for young players in particular; good quality rugby boots and team jumper, if playing with a club

1 Rugby League is a fast and exciting game that is played all over the world. It is particularly popular in Australia, Great Britain, South Africa and New Zealand, where millions watch and play the game each year.

Rugby League is the youngest of the two types of Rugby game. Adapted from Rugby Union, it was first played in the late 1800s in Northern England. Rugby League is a complex game with many rules, moves and strategies, and our description here will simply be a basic introduction.

2 Rugby League is played on an oblong grassed pitch, 100 metres (109.3 yds) long and 68 metres (74.3 yds) wide (see diagram page 329). Junior teams taking part in a modified game often play on a smaller field. A referee controls the field of play and the referee is assisted by two judges.

3 There is a set of goal posts at either end of the rugby field, each with a bar between them. The field is also divided into lines – a halfway line, two 20 metre (21.8 yd) lines and two goal lines, behind which is a special 'in goal' area. The aim of the game is for each team of thirteen players to score as many points as they can, by scoring 'tries' and goals. Players move down the field with the ball by running forward with it. They must never kick or pass the ball forwards – they can only do this sideways as they move down the field.

4 Players score a try when they ground the ball (literally contacting the ball with the ground whilst holding it in their arms or hands) over the opposite team's goal line and inside the in-goal area. If a team scores a try, they can then attempt to kick the ball over the crossbar between the goal posts. This is called a 'conversion' and will give them further points.

Tries are worth 4 points each.

Conversion goals are worth 2 points each.

Field goals (goals kicked over the goal crossbar from the field) are worth 1 point each.

Penalty points are also awarded to the opposite team, if a player breaks one of the game's many rules.

5 A game of Rugby League is played over two halves of 40 minutes. However, each game lasts a little longer than this when extra time is added to compensate for interruptions to the game, such as injury to players. As in all football games, there are a number of different playing positions on the rugby field and they are divided into Back players and Forward players.

6 Tackling and the ability to avoid being tackled is probably the most important skill in Rugby League. Players must be strong, fast and agile!

When a player with the ball is trying to make their way down the field towards the opponent's goal line, they can be tackled by being grabbed around the waist, legs or ankles and pulled to the ground. A team who has control of the ball can be tackled six times whilst trying to score. Then they must give up the ball to the opposing team. Of course, they try to avoid this at all costs! On certain occasions after the opposing team has made an illegal move, a seventh tackle is allowed.

7 Another feature of Rugby League is the famous 'scrum'. A scrum must take place after some rules of the game are broken, such as knocking the ball forward – a 'knock-on', or the ball goes out of the playing area. In a scrum, certain players in each team, the Forward players, form a special huddle of three to six. The ball is placed between them and then each team tries to get possession of the ball, once play recommences.

8 Rugby League is a fantastic spectator sport – one that the whole family will enjoy and quickly become involved in, choosing their favourite teams from premier leagues and supporting them every week during the playing season. Youngsters can also learn to play and take part in games by joining a local club. Coaching is essential in this vigorous sport, to teach safe play and good skills.

Dead Ball Line

Goal Line

20m Line
(21.8 yd)

Halfway Line

100m (109.3 yds)

In-goal Area

68m (74.3 yds)

RUGBY UNION

Players: fifteen for most games. Games can also be played with less players on each team.
Age: children and adults
Equipment: as for Rugby League, an oval shaped ball, usually leather; a mouthguard, helmet and optional shoulder pads – essential for young players in particular; good quality rugby boots and team jumper, if playing with a club

1 As mentioned in our section on Rugby League, Rugby Union was the first rugby game to be played. It is said that the game began in 1823 at Rugby School in England, when a young schoolboy by the name of William Webb Ellis picked up a soccer ball during a match and ran with it towards the opposing team's goal. Today, Rugby Union is played all over the world and is popular in countries such as Australia, New Zealand, Great Britain and South Africa, to name just a few. Every four years, teams of the best players from different countries gather to compete for a Rugby Union World Cup, which is a spectacle not to be missed for rugby fans.

2 The game of Rugby Union is, of course, very similar to that of Rugby League. And like Rugby League, we will only touch on the basics here. However, there are some differences in Rugby Union that bear mentioning.

3 Rugby Union is played on a grassy pitch of similar dimensions to that of a Rugby League, being 100 metres (109.3 yds) long and 69 metres (75.5 yds) wide. The field

of play is slightly different to that of Rugby League in that lines are marked at 10 and 22 metres (10.9 and 24 yds), rather than 20 metres (see illustration page 331). Again, a referee officiates.

4 The aim of the game is for each team of players to score more points than their opponents by scoring tries and goals. Players move down the field with the ball by running forward with it, in the hope of scoring a try by grounding the ball inside the opposing team's in-goal area. In Rugby Union, tries are worth 5 points each. Goals scored after a try are worth 2 points each. A goal from a penalty kick is worth 3 points. Other goals are worth 2 points.

5 Rugby Union is also played over two halves of 40 minutes. However, each game lasts a little longer than this when extra time is added to compensate for interruptions to the game, such as injury to players. Again, there are a number of different playing positions on the field and they are divided into Back players and Forward players.

6 As well as players tackling each other and the scrum, there are also two other important moves in Rugby Union which are used at different times during the game. The first is called the 'ruck'. This occurs when a player or players from each team push together over the ball, which is on the ground. Both teams are attempting to gain possession of the ball in the ruck, and it is quite a sight! The second move unique to Rugby Union is called the 'maul'. The maul takes place when a player has possession of the ball but the opposing team has him blocked and he is unable to pass the ball on.

Then other team members come together to surround him and protect the ball. Of course, the opposing team also surrounds him and you have a maul, which is also exciting to see. Rucks and mauls can happen at any time.

7 To learn how to play Rugby Union, it is essential to join a club and receive coaching. A coach can effectively teach young players how to play the game both safely and skilfully. There are local Rugby Union clubs in many areas and the game is also taught in some schools. As a spectator sport, Rugby Union is equally as exciting as other football sports and more so, according to fans of the game. Why not go along to a game and see for yourself!

SOCCER

Players: two teams of eleven
Age: juniors to adults
Equipment: a round soccer ball; a playing field or pitch; good quality soccer boots; mouthguard; shin guards, at least for junior players; uniform, if playing with a club

1 Soccer, or football as it is known in many European, African and South American countries, truly deserves to be called 'the world game'. It is played in almost every country and is arguably the most popular game in the world today. It is also an Olympic sport.

Soccer has its origins in England. A form of soccer was played in the streets of English towns and villages during the Middle Ages. In the mid 1800s, the first formal set of rules were written down for the game and it was fully recognised as a code of football separate from games such as Rugby and Gaelic football. At first, soccer was called Association Football. Eventually it was simplified to just football. The word 'soccer' itself is a shortening and twisting of the word 'assoc', used instead of 'association'. Every four years, teams from over 100 countries gather to compete in the soccer World Cup. The finals of this competition are always a spectacular affair, with much pageantry and many thrilling soccer matches. The World Cup is an event every soccer fan looks forward to.

2 Soccer is played on an oblong grassed pitch or field, approximately 90 to 120 metres (100 to 130 yds) long and approximately 90 metres (100 yds) wide. Different pitches can be different sizes, as long as the pitch is always longer than it is wide. Junior teams often play the game on a smaller pitch (see diagram page 334).

3 There is a large goal frame at either end of the soccer pitch. The goal is usually covered with netting. A goal area is drawn on the pitch around each goal and a second larger square, called the penalty area, is marked further out from the goal. A large circle is drawn in the middle of the pitch and this is called the centre circle. The game always begins in the centre circle.

The aim of the game is for each team of eleven players to score as many goals as they can. One player from each team is the goalkeeper, or 'goalie' and he stays within his team's penalty area, defending the goal.

4 Once the game begins, players from each team try to take possession of the ball and move it down the pitch to score goals, by kicking the ball into the opposing team's goal. The ball can be moved down the pitch with any part of the body except the arms and hands. Soccer players must be very skilful at moving the ball with their feet, knees, chest and even their head!

Only the goalkeeper is allowed to actually pick the ball up with his hands, when he is defending his goal area. The goalkeeper can also play on other areas of the pitch but when he does, he cannot use his arms and hands.

5 There are a number of different playing positions within a soccer team and each player is responsible for their area of the pitch. There are Fullbacks, also known as Defenders, Forwards, Midfielders and the Goalkeeper.

6 A game of Soccer is played over two halves of 45 minutes, with a 15 minute interval in the middle of the game. If a match is drawn at the end of the second half, then two 15 minute halves of extra time may be played. And if the match is still drawn at the end of extra time, an exciting 'penalty shoot-out' may take place. Each side chooses five players to take a turn at kicking the ball from the penalty line into the opposing team's goal, defended only by the goalkeeper. The team with the most goals at the end of the shoot-out is the winner. On some occasions, teams may still be deadlocked at the end of the penalty shoot-out. If this happens a 'sudden-death play off' may take place. Then teams choose one player each to take a turn at trying to score. Some of the most exciting games in soccer's history have been won in this way.

7 A referee and two linesmen officiate at a game of soccer. It is their job to award free kicks and penalties, should the rules of the game be infringed. Rules include no inappropriate tackling of other players, as this is a serious offence in soccer. If the ball goes out of play or is deemed 'off-side', a kick is awarded to the other team. If a player commits a foul against another player by interfering with him or doing something else against the rules, he may receive a 'yellow card'. This is a warning. However, if the player does something more serious to another player he may receive a 'red card' and be sent from the pitch altogether. A player who is sent off the field cannot be replaced by another team member, thus leaving the team short of players.

8 One of soccer's greatest appeals is that it can be played anywhere in an informal setting, by anyone. All that is needed is a field, two teams of players (and the teams don't have to be eleven in an informal game) and a round soccer ball. In many parts of the world, soccer is the main pastime for children when they are not at school or helping around the family home, or farm.

Soccer is also an incredibly exciting spectator sport. There are many soccer clubs around and you are bound to find one in your local area. Take a look in the phone book or do a search on the Internet if you or your children wish to participate in the sport more formally.

Soccer matches are regularly played in most places and they are also regularly screened on TV. Why not take a look at the world game? Your family is sure to enjoy it.

45–90m (49–100 yds)

Corner Flagpost

Penalty Area

Penalty Mark

Centre Circle

Halfway Line

Centre Mark

Touch Line

Penalty Arc

Goal Area

90–120m
(100–130 yds)

Optional Mark

Goal Line

BAT, RACQUET AND STICK GAMES

Games where a bat, racquet or stick is used to hit a ball are popular and fun. There are a large number of these games to choose from and they can be played in a club setting or just informally, with the family or a group of friends. There are games such as tennis and badminton, for those who enjoy playing as individuals. And there are also team games such as hockey and cricket.

Many bat, racquet and stick games are extremely popular spectator sports and are equally as popular as football games. We'll take a look at some of them here. Then you and your family can have fun trying a few of them out, or going to watch them played.

BADMINTON

Players: two or four
Age: older children and adults
Equipment: racquets; some shuttlecocks; a net and a clear area to play on

6.09m (20ft)
76cm (2ft 6ins)
3.96m (13ft)
1.98m (6ft 6ins)
13.4m (44ft)
top of net 1.52m (5ft)
5.18m (17ft)

1 Badminton originated about 2000 years ago in the Far East, and the rules we know today were laid down by British officers in India in the 1800s.

2 The court is laid out as shown in the illustration, but for a home game measurements can be a little lax and the game will not suffer!

3 To play a singles game a coin is tossed and the winner chooses to either play at a particular end or to serve first. The server stands in the right-hand service court. To start serving, the server holds the racquet so that it is pointing down and holds the shuttlecock above waist height in the other hand. The shuttlecock is then dropped and must be hit below the waist with the racquet still pointing downwards. (It sounds hard but a little practice will see the action improve.)

4 The serve is good if it crosses the net and falls between the long and short service line for singles in the receiver's service court. The shuttlecock can touch the net (no let is called) but the racquet may not. If a server touches a boundary line or fails to serve into the required area, the serve passes to the receiver. However, the receiver loses the point automatically if a foul is committed while receiving the serve.

5 If the serve is good, the receiver must return the serve. It must be hit only once and must fall within or on the boundary lines for singles. The server then must return the shuttlecock correctly – clearly over the net in one hit and into or onto the boundary lines of the opposite court.

6 When each rally is finished, the player moves to the other service court, as does the receiver. If three games are being played to decide the match, the players change ends at the end of the first two games. Fifteen points are required to win a set between two men, but women's rules hold that 11 points will win the game for them. However, if the score is 14-14 (or 10-10) the player who reached 14 (or 10) first has the choice of whether the game ends at 15 or 17 points for men, and 11 or 12 points for the women.

BASEBALL

Players: two teams of nine
Age: children and adults
Equipment: baseball bat; baseball; selection of specialised baseball gloves for catcher and other players; chest and leg protectors for the catcher; helmet and mask for the catcher; helmets for the players; a protective box for male batters; team uniform and shoes

1 Baseball is the most popular sport in the United States, apart from Gridiron. As well as being an exciting spectator sport, it is played in every part of the country at a local level. And a major league baseball competition is played nationally each year.

Baseball is also one of the world's most popular games. It is now played in more than 60 countries around the globe.

2 Although the history of baseball is relatively short compared to some sports, its exact origins are uncertain. It is very likely that the game was developed from the English bat and ball game of rounders in the early 1800s. However, it is also claimed that an army cadet in New York invented the game in the 1830s. What is certain is that the game originated in the United States and the first official national rules were drawn up in 1845.

3 Baseball is not really a game that can be played informally. To pitch a baseball and also to bat involves skill and practice, and requires coaching. However, those who enjoy playing the game love to spend their spare time out in the back yard or at the local park, practicing their pitching and

catching. This applies to children and adults alike!

4 As with many of the more complex ball games featured in this book, we will give you a brief outline of how baseball is played. Then you will be able to enjoy it as a spectator or look for a local club in your area, if you think you or your children will enjoy playing it.

5 Baseball is played on a large field. Inside the field is a specially marked 'diamond'. The area inside the diamond is known as the infield. Areas beyond the diamond are known as the outfield and the foul territory (see diagram). There are bases on three of the diamond's points and a home plate and batter's area on the fourth point. In the centre of the diamond, 18 metres (60 ft) away from the batting area, there is a special pitcher's mound. Here the pitcher throws the ball to the batter.

6 The aim of baseball is for each of the two teams playing to achieve as many runs as they can during a game. Runs are made by players hitting the ball with the bat and travelling around all bases, before returning to the batter's plate. Each full trip around the diamond equals one run.

7 A baseball game consists of nine innings. During each innings, both teams bat and field once. An innings ends when three players on the batting team have been dismissed.

8 During an innings, the batting team works hard to get as many players around the diamond as possible and score as many runs as they can. A batter takes his position on the home plate and the pitcher throws

a ball to him. If the batter does not hit the ball and the ball is good, then it is a 'strike'. If the batter hits the ball into the foul area of the field, it is counted as a strike. And if the batter gets three strikes before he hits the ball and runs from the home plate, then he is out until the next innings. This is the 'three strikes and you're out' rule.

9 If a batter hits the ball, then he must drop the bat and run to first base. Players on the other bases all run to the next base after the batter has hit the ball. So the batter goes to first base, the player on first goes to second, the player on second goes to third and the player on third goes to home base, thus scoring a run. Bases are not always full, however. Sometimes players on the bases may have run between more than one base, leaving a base empty.

10 If the batter hits a particularly good ball, there may be time for all players to run around each of the bases and make it home. If the batter does this, it is called a 'home run'. This is not as easy as it sounds. The fielding team works hard to prevent batters from scoring. If a batter is tagged by a member of the opposing team while running between bases, he is out. Each base has a man from the opposing team guarding it, ready to tag the batter out the moment he receives the baseball. The batters are only safe from being tagged while they are actually standing on the base plates at each point of the diamond.

11 Each player on a fielding team has their own particular position on the field (see diagram page 340). They may play infield, outfield or on one of the bases. The pitcher is

arguably the fielding team's most important weapon. Pitching must be accurate. The ball is thrown overarm in baseball and it is done so with great speed. It must pass through the 'strike zone' when it is thrown. The strike zone is directly above the home plate, higher than the batter's knees and lower than the batter's armpit. If the pitcher throws a ball that travels outside the strike zone, the umpire will call out 'ball'. If the pitcher throws four 'balls' then the batter is permitted to walk to first base.

12 The catcher is positioned behind the batter and it is his job to pick up the ball after it has been pitched, if it is not hit by the batter. He must get the ball back to the pitcher or to another member of the team if it is needed elsewhere on the field.

13 Four umpires supervise the game of baseball and every one of them is needed! Although the game sounds very straightforward and simple, it is actually very complex. Players from each team use many strategies to try to win. Pitchers have a number of different ways of throwing the ball at the batter, and they tailor their throws to each type of batter. Batters try to sneak between bases when the fielding team is otherwise occupied, to get closer to scoring a run. This is known as 'stealing' a base. Players also practice sliding onto bases so that if a ball is thrown to the base they are running to and they are tagged, sometimes they are able to get their foot on the base before the opposing player tags them. Then they are not out of the game.

14 At the end of nine innings, one team is usually declared a winner. Sometimes, though, the game

is tied. If a game of baseball is tied, an extra innings is played. Some of the greatest baseball games of all time have ended with an extra innings. An extra innings is riveting for the spectators and nerve-wracking for the two opposing teams.

15 If you think you or someone in your family might enjoy playing baseball, we strongly recommend that you look up a local club in your area and check it out. Baseball fans all around the world would agree that this is one of the greatest ball games of all time!

CRICKET

Players: two teams of eleven – less for an informal family game
Age: children and adults
Equipment: cricket ball; bat; leg pads for batsmen; cricket shoes; batting gloves; protective box for male players; helmet or mouthguard for batsmen; white cricket clothing if playing with a club

1 Cricket is an extremely popular game that is played in most countries of the British Commonwealth. It is also one of the most popular spectator sports in these countries during the summer months, when it is played. The exact origins of the game of cricket are lost in time but we know cricket-like games were played several hundred years ago in England, in the Middle Ages. The modern game of cricket was first recorded in the late 17th and early 18th centuries in England. There, matches were played with great gusto between neighbouring towns and counties, and in front of very rowdy crowds. Today, cricket at the highest level is played in two forms – the 'test match' and the 'one-day match'. Test matches are usually played over three or five days and often involve great battles of strategy with the bat and ball between the two opposing teams. One day matches are more popular as a spectator sport and matches are won and lost within a few hours.

2 The game of cricket can be played on a field of any size or shape, but is generally played on a large oval. The edge of the field or oval must be marked out, so the field of play is clearly defined. At the centre of the field is a pitch – an oblong hard patch of ground 20.12 metres (22 yds) long.

This can be shorter for younger players.

3 At each end of the pitch is a 'wicket'. Wickets consist of three stakes placed side by side in the ground, with small wooden pegs called 'bails' balanced on top of them. Several lines are drawn on the pitch, in front of each wicket. These are called the 'creases'. The creases show where the bowler must bowl the ball from and where the batsman must stand while being bowled to.

4 At the edge of the field, some distance behind each wicket, is a 'sight screen'. The sight screen helps the batsman to see the cricket ball coming towards him after it has been bowled (see diagram page 343).

5 The aim of a game of cricket is for each team to score as many 'runs' as they can, by hitting balls bowled to them by the opposing team. Teams consist of specialist batsmen and bowlers, as well as some good all-round players. A coin is tossed to decide which team bats or bowls first in a game. Batting and fielding turns by each team are called 'innings'.

6 Two batsmen from a team take the field at one time. The batsmen must defend their wickets and prevent the bowler's ball from hitting them. One batsman is 'on strike', being bowled to by a bowler from the opposing team.

After hitting a ball bowled to him, the batsman must try to run between the two wickets and score runs by doing so. He swaps places with his partner, who also runs at the same time.

One run is scored for each length of the pitch the batsmen run.

Four runs are scored if a batsman hits the ball and it travels outside the edge of the field without being stopped by a player from the opposing team. Six runs are scored if a batsman hits the ball and it travels outside the edge of the field without touching the ground within the field of play.

7 Each team takes a turn to bat and a turn to field. The fielding team concentrates on trying to get the batting players out. One team member at a time bowls to the batsmen and the rest of the players return the ball from the field. There are more than 30 different fielding positions and the team captain shifts his players around the field on a regular basis, depending on how the game is progressing and how the batsman is playing.

8 Batsmen may be got 'out' in several ways. They can be:

Bowled – this happens when the bowler bowls to the batsman and the ball goes through to the wicket, hitting it and dislodging the bails.

Hit Wicket – if the bails are accidentally dislodged by the batsman himself, before he runs.

Stumped – if the wicketkeeper (a specialist fielder from the opposing team who stands directly behind the wicket) knocks the bails off when a batsman has left his crease.

Caught – if a fielder catches the ball after it has been hit and before it bounces on the ground.

Run Out – if the batsman doesn't make it back to his crease before someone from the opposing team knocks the bails off the wicket (similar to stumped).

Leg Before Wicket – if the player accidentally stops a bowled ball with any part of his body other than the bat, when that ball would have gone through to the stumps behind him.

9 Two umpires officiate at a game of cricket and there is often a video replay 'third umpire' in matches at the highest level, to help settle close decisions regarding whether a batsman is out or not. Each umpire stands close to one of the wickets.

10 As we've already mentioned, cricket at the elite level is played in two forms – the test match and the one-day match. One-day matches are played with 'limited overs'. An 'over' consists of six balls bowled by each batsman. Usually, each team is allowed a total of 50 overs to score as many runs as they can. Then they must swap playing positions. If you and your family are newcomers to the world of cricket as a spectator sport, we highly recommend that you watch a one-day match first. You will learn to grasp the rules of the game in an atmosphere full of excitement and tension, as opposing teams struggle to score the maximum amount of runs in a short time.

11 Test matches are games of strategy. Runs are slower to be scored. Batsmen are more cautious. Bowlers carefully assess the 'bounce' of the wicket and the player they are bowling to. There is an art and science to the test match that is totally different to the one-day match.

12 One of the greatest things about the game of cricket is that it does not have to be played at an elite level to be enjoyed. Anyone can play. Families, groups of friends and groups

of school children. Age and skill level are no barrier to having fun with cricket. Take a cricket bat and ball to the beach and have a hit (use a tennis ball in crowded areas, to avoid hurting others with a hard cricket ball). Any open space like a park can make a fantastic impromptu cricket pitch. And don't forget the great Australian game played by children for generations – backyard cricket!

13 If you or your children wish to play cricket at a more formal level, you are sure to find a local cricket team where coaching in many of the bat and ball skills required to play this game in competition can be learnt. Cricket is a great game for youngsters, teaching them bat, ball and team skills that will stand them in good stead for years to come. And they'll have a lot of fun learning them!

20.12m
(22 yds)

CROQUET

Players: two to six
Age: older children and adults
Equipment: six croquet balls (coloured blue, red, black, yellow, green and orange); mallets for each player; nine hoops and two stakes

1 Croquet was invented hundreds of years ago in France and travelled to England to become the favourite game of house parties in the country in the early 1800s, often known as Pall Mall. Over the last few decades of the 20th century it became increasingly popular again and many people play in clubs and teams, while families enjoy Backyard Croquet described here.

2 The playing area needs to be about 30.5 metres (33 yds) long and half that wide, set up as shown in the illustration. The best surface to play on is close cropped grass, so a good cut with the mower is recommended! Lines need not be drawn for boundaries, as natural boundaries such as fences, trees and shrubs will suffice.

3 A full game with four or six people would take up to two hours to play, so if it does not seem there will be full concentration from all participants for that long, set a time limit and then count the points of each player to that time to see which player wins.

4 The aim of the game is to be the first side to pass all its balls through all the hoops (wickets) and hit both the turning and finishing stakes at the appropriate time with all the balls.

Each ball can score 16 points – one for each of the fourteen wickets and two stake points.

5 A coin toss decides the side which begins and the blue ball always goes first. For the first shot a ball is placed one length of one mallet head from the first wicket. The balls must all pass through the wickets in the order shown on the setting up diagram. At the conclusion of a turn in which a point is scored, the wicket clip of the colour corresponding to the ball should be placed on the next wicket or stake to be scored.

6 Bonus strokes can be earned by scoring a wicket or stake (one point) or by hitting (roquetting) one of the other side's balls. This wins 2 points. Bonus strokes cannot be accumulated. After roquetting a player can choose to:

a) take the two bonus strokes from where the ball has come to rest;

b) place their ball one mallet head's length away from the other ball in any direction and then take the two bonus strokes;

c) place their ball in contact with the struck ball, then strike the ball to send both balls in the desired direction. This is called a croquet shot. There is then one more bonus shot remaining to take; or

d) place their ball in contact with the struck ball and then place their foot on it so it cannot move. The immobilised ball is then struck so as to send the other ball in the desired direction while leaving that ball where it is. There is one more bonus shot remaining.

7 If another player (partner or opponent) puts your ball through its proper wicket or into the turning stake, your side gets the point, but no bonus stroke.

8 Rover balls are balls which have completed the course except for striking the finishing stake. Rovers can be staked out (driven into the finishing stake) with any legal stroke by any player at any point in the game.

9 A ball sent out of bounds should be placed one mallet length inside the boundary line at the point of exit. There is no penalty for going out of bounds.

10 There are various ways of playing shots, but it should be borne in mind that the ball can only be struck with the face of the mallet.

15.24m (50ft)

30.48m (100ft)

Two Croquet grips and stances

FRENCH CRICKET

Players: four or more
Age: any age
Equipment: an old tennis racquet or plastic cricket bat; a large soft plastic ball and a flat playing surface

1 French cricket is a fantastic introduction to the game of cricket for young children. It helps teach ball skills and team participation. It is also a great game to play at the beach, in the park, or wherever there is a family get-together. The aim of French Cricket is simply to get the batsman out. No runs are actually scored.

2 French cricket does not require a pitch or wickets. The player who is batting stands in one place with the bat held in front of his legs. The rest of the players, with the exception of the bowler, form a large circle around him.

3 The bowler bowls the ball and attempts to hit the batsman's legs. The batsman, of course, must hit the ball away. If the bowler manages to hit the batsman's legs, then the batsman is out.

4 The batsman must try to quickly move to a new playing position after he has hit the ball and while a player is running to fetch it. However, if the player fetching the ball sees this move, the batsman is out and another player must take the bat. A fast and furious game that is fun for all!

GOLF

Players: can play alone, but this is unusual – usually twosomes or foursomes
Age: from six years up (with modified clubs)
Equipment: access to a golf course (fees payable but many courses charge a daily fee); minimum set of clubs for young players and beginner adults; up to a full set of fourteen clubs

1 Golf is a fantastic game of skill and patience. The earlier you begin to play the better you will be, even if you are not aiming to become Greg Norman, Tiger Woods or Karrie Web. Anyone can enjoy the physical and social aspects of the game and join a golf club.

Golf can also be practiced in some parks and open fields – as long as it is safe and permissible to do so. For the children, it is also possible to purchase small plastic golf balls from good sports stores. These are safe and fun, and can be played with just about anywhere, without the risk of broken windows or injuries caused by regular, solid golf balls.

2 Golf is not just something you learn from a book. You learn by playing as a family or with friends, where at least one member of the golfing party knows the rules and etiquette of a public golf course. Or you can also learn by attending group lessons with players known as professionals, who are employed by golf courses for just this reason. Or by booking private lessons with these professionals. And you need to practice, practice and practice! Here we will cover the absolute basic golf rules, etiquette, techniques and scoring.

3 When you play golf, you are not only playing against (or with, in the case of team play) other players, you are also playing against the course, too. If you play at a particular course a lot, you will 'learn' that course and can better your score every time. Of course, golf course layouts change too – not where the fairways, bunkers, water hazards and greens are placed, but the course professional will keep players on their mettle by changing the position of where they can tee-off (first hit the ball) and also, the position of the hole on the green from time to time.

4 Let's begin by studying the illustration of the layout of a hole on a golf course, which has every part named (see page 349). The simple aim of a game of golf is to hit a small white ball with a variety of clubs (selection of the correct club is part of learning golf and takes a while), from a tee, down a long piece of mown grass, known as the fairway. The fairway stretches from the tee markers to the green where the hole is placed, and then the player aims to tap the ball into the hole, using a total of the least amount of strokes on every hole.

5 Each hole is a different shape and orientation. It has hazards such as sand bunkers, water hazards, trees and the 'rough' (unmown grass edging the fairway) which will make it difficult for the player to gain a low score. These hazards are to be avoided at all costs!

6 Eighteen holes complete a full round of golf and each hole has a 'par' value, or average, to beat, as well as trying to beat your companions' scores. For instance, a long hole which

may be about 450 metres or so (about 500 yds), could have a par of 5. This means it will take, on average, three strokes (drives) to get to the green and then it will usually take 2 strokes to 'putt' the ball into the hole.

7 To win, you need to take less strokes to complete the hole than your playing companions and by scoring under par, you will also beat the course.

8 Much has been written, filmed and said about the golfing grip and stance – most experts agree it is all important and practice is the only way to improve significantly. If you learn the correct grip and swing the club well, you'll almost always hit the ball well and therefore, score well. There are different grips for the full swing and for putting – see illustrations below.

9 When putting, you need to have your eyes directly over the ball. When judging the putting distance, you need to move the putting head a lot less than when you are swinging, to hit the ball a long way down the fairway. For example, to make a good putt, you may only move the head of your putter 15 cm (6 in) backwards and then 15 cm (6 in) forwards, to stroke the ball the same distance every time. In this case, it would be about 90 cm (3 ft). For longer putts you will need to increase forward and backward movement of the putter slightly. It all takes practice!

10 Use the correct grip for the full swing or drive, when you may be hitting the ball a long way down the fairway. And stand sideways to the target (the green at the end of the fairway). Stand fairly straight with your feet just slightly apart and bend from

the hips, flexing your knees. The back of your left hand faces the target. Look down at your left foot and then look at the target. Now move that foot about 10 cm (4 in) away from the target.

11 The rest of the stroke has parts called the back swing and the forward swing and they are really best taught by professionals, or by looking at a video. You can even get an idea of how they work from watching some golfing computer games.

Some tips though – your head needs to stay level throughout the backswing, and at the top of the backswing your weight should move to your right foot and your torso. Hips and shoulders are turned away from the hole. Then, as you begin your forward swing, your upper body and hips turn towards the hole and your weight transfers to the left foot. As you contact the ball, nearly all your weight should have shifted to your left foot and as you finish the swing, your body should be facing the target.

12 Golf etiquette – you will enjoy your game more and others will enjoy playing you if you follow a few simple, courteous rules when playing on a golf course. Stand quietly and still as another golfer plays a shot; stand out of another golfer's line of vision; play quickly when it's your turn to play and always let faster, more experienced players play through ahead of you; invite another group to play through if you are looking for a lost ball; never hit into the group ahead, be patient and wait for them to play through; after playing from a bunker, rake the sand and repair any damage you've done while trying to

hit your ball out of that sandy hole; avoid making divots (chunks of turf that come clear with a shot, when your club digs into the ground) and if you do, replace the turf and press it back into place; lay your golf bag away from the green; place the flagstick on the green or to one side without damaging the green; if you find any equipment on the course, return it to the golf shop; don't litter; don't talk loudly or yell; leave the putting green as soon as your group has finished; keep your temper if you aren't playing well – remember, golf is a game enjoyed by all levels of player and if you aren't playing well, you can still have a great time.

13 Enjoy yourself!

349

HOCKEY

Players: two teams of eleven
Age: children and adults
Equipment: hockey sticks; hockey ball; shin guards and mouthguards for all players; hockey boots; goalie's equipment – mask, helmet, throat and chest guards, elbow, thigh and knee guards, gloves, box for male players and goalie's boots

1 Hockey (sometimes called Field Hockey) is an exciting stick and ball team game, played on a grassed or artificial pitch. It is played in many countries around the world and is an Olympic sport. Individual men's and women's teams also compete in Commonwealth Games and hockey's World Cup. Hockey is also played in many schools.

2 Similar games to hockey have been played for centuries. Ancient Egyptians played stick and ball games, as did ancient Greeks and Romans. However it is most likely that hockey was adapted from the Irish game of hurling. Modern hockey is definitely an English game and the first official hockey association was formed in the late 1800s, in London. The word 'hockey' is probably derived from the French word *hoquet*, which means 'a hooked stick'.

3 Hockey is played on a pitch 91.5 metres (100 yds) long and 55 metres (60 yds) wide. The pitch is dissected by three lines and there are shooting circles at each end of it. Behind each shooting circle is a goal frame and net (see illustration page 351).

The aim of the game is for each team to score as many goals as they can, by shooting the ball into the opposing team's goal.

4 A game of hockey is played in two 35 minute halves with extra time added to each half if necessary, for time lost due to injury. Players on opposing teams take various positions on the pitch to attack their opponents' goal or defend their own goal. Different attack and defence strategies are used and players are distributed around the pitch according to instructions from their coach or team captain. Players' positions include defenders, forwards and half-backs; these positions are similar to other field ball sports such as soccer and football. Heavily padded goalkeepers defend each of the goal areas.

5 A game of hockey begins at the centre line on the pitch. Players are not allowed to move the ball around the pitch with any part of their body. Hockey sticks have a rounded side and a flat side, and players must move the ball around with the flat side of their stick only.

6 Fouls are called when the rules of the game are not adhered to and we'll mention just a few here. They include interfering with an opponent's play with the hockey stick, or playing dangerously by hitting the hockey ball in such a way that it leaves the ground and travels high in the air. Hockey balls are generally hit so that they run along quite close to the ground.

If fouls are incurred inside the shooting circle they usually result in players from the opposing team getting a shot at the goal, either through a 'penalty corner', at the side of the shooting circle, or a 'penalty stroke', from a special penalty spot inside the circle.

If a player knocks the ball out of play a player from the opposite team usually gets a free hit or a penalty corner.

7 It would be a mistake to think that all the rules in a game of hockey slow the game down, for it is not the case at all. Skilful, athletic players make hockey an extremely fast and furious game.

8 If you or your children think you may be interested in playing hockey as part of a team, there is sure to be a club in your area. Alternatively, older children can enquire at school, as inter-school hockey competitions are regularly held in most places.

9 Hockey can also be played in a much more informal manner. Most good sports stores sell lightweight plastic hockey sticks and balls. They are great fun for young children and adults alike. Why not plan an informal family hockey game, the next time you are having a get-together? Simple goals can be set up using nothing more than a couple of stakes in the ground. Plastic sticks and balls won't hurt anyone and they're so light that even a four-year-old can use them. Teams of three or four players are more than adequate. Informal hockey games with lightweight equipment are a great introduction to the world of hockey. After playing them, your children may wish to go on and join a club or take part in hockey games in a more formal manner.

HURLING

Players: two teams of fifteen
Age: juniors to adults
Equipment: a hurley – a special curved wooden stick approximately 91cm (36 in) long; a sliotar – a small leather and cork ball; access to a playing field marked for hurling or Gaelic football; good quality athletic boots, shorts and jumper if playing with a club; a mouthguard to protect teeth; optional helmets for all players

1 Hurling is an Irish stick and ball game that is similar to hockey. However, the game is much, much older than hockey. There are records of hurling matches dating back at leat 2000 years. Hurling is also very closely related in many ways to the other great Irish national sport, Gaelic football. Both games use the same size playing field and very similar rules. One official sporting body in Ireland governs both sports – the Gaelic Athletic Association.

2 Like Gaelic football, a hurling match is played on a grassed pitch or field, approximately 137 metres (150 yds) long and 82 metres (90 yds) wide. Juniors often play on a smaller pitch. A referee, two linesmen and four umpires supervise the field of play. There are two sets of goal posts at each end of the pitch and they consist of two posts joined by a crossbar (see illustration for Gaelic football page 322).

3 Players in a hurling match move the small sliotar (ball) around the pitch with their wooden hurleys (sticks) in an effort to score points or goals by passing the sliotar over or under the opposing team's goal posts.

The team who scores the most points at the end of the game is, of course, the winner.

Goals are scored by placing the sliotar under the crossbar of the goalposts. They are worth 3 points each.

Single points are scored by placing the sliotar over the crossbar of the goalposts. Each point is worth 1 point.

A green flag is raised by an umpire when a goal is scored and a white flag is raised when a point is scored.

4 When they are on the field, players may pick the sliotar up off the ground with their hurley and transfer it to their hand. They are allowed to run a maximum of four steps with the sliotar in their hand but then they must transfer it back to the end of their hurley.

This can only be done twice before passing the sliotar to another player. However, players can run with the sliotar on the end of their hurley for as long as they like. Players cannot simply pick up the sliotar off the ground – they must use their hurley to do this at all times.

The sliotar is passed from player to player by kicking it, hitting it with the open palm of the hand, or giving it a whack with the hurley. This game is very physical at times and it is not uncommon for players on opposing teams to accidentally hit each other, rather than the sliotar.

5 A hurling match is played over two halves, or periods of 30 minutes at local level.

Championship games are played over two periods of 35 minutes. Extra time may be added by the referee, if there is a draw at the end of the game. Extra time usually runs for two extra periods of 10 minutes each.

6 Each of the fifteen players in a hurling team has a position on the pitch. There are forward positions, midfield positions, back positions and of course, a goalkeeper. Defending players are responsible for contesting the ball in their particular area on the pitch. Attacking players must be careful not to enter the defending player's area before the sliotar when they are playing, or a foul can result and the opponent gets the sliotar!

7 Players tackle their opponents with their shoulders to try to unbalance them and take possession of the sliotar. The game is fast and furious, requiring agility, strength, skill and forethought by the players. As mentioned before, a hurling match can get quite rough. Players can be sent from the field if they behave in a dangerous manner and are 'written up' by the referee twice in a game.

8 There are many ways to 'foul' and lose the ball to your opponent in hurling, such as if the sliotar goes out of bounds, or if players tackle each other in any but the accepted way of using the shoulders. 'Free pucks' or 'sideline pucks' are awarded to the other team if the sliotar goes over the end lines or sidelines marked on the pitch.

9 Although hurling is not a popular game in countries outside Ireland, clubs and teams can often be located in various cities and states. They are often combination Gaelic football/hurling clubs. Hurling is very dynamic and exciting to watch and matches are occasionally shown on television. Once you have seen a hurling match, you will understand why the game has been popular in Ireland for so many centuries. If you would like to learn more about hurling or get involved in the sport, we recommend that you look up your nearest club on the Internet, as many clubs have their own web sites.

ICE HOCKEY

Players: two teams of six, plus substitute players
Age: children and adults
Equipment: ice hockey sticks; ice hockey puck; ice skates; protective shin guards, clothing, helmets and mouthguards for all players; box for male players; goalie's equipment – mask, helmet, throat and chest guards, elbow, thigh and knee guards, gloves, box for male players and goalie's boots

1 Ice hockey is not a popular game in warmer countries of the world like Australia, but it is certainly one of the most popular games in North America. It is a fast, action-packed and sometimes dangerous game that originated in Canada in the mid-1800s.

2 Ice hockey is usually played indoors on a large ice rink, approximately 61 metres (200 ft) long and 25.5 metres (85 ft) wide. The rink is divided into three sections, or zones and there are goals at each end of the rink. The middle of the rink is a neutral zone where players from either team can play, but the two zones nearest the goals are each team's defending zones.

The rink is also marked with 'face-off' circles and a half-circle around the goal, called the 'crease' (see illustration).

3 The aim of ice hockey is for each team to score as many goals as they can by placing the puck inside the opposing team's goal. Play begins with a 'face-off', where the two opposing teams position themselves inside the centre circle and a referee drops the puck in between them.

4 Different players have different positions on the team. Of course, there is a goalie. The remaining five other players are spread out in attacking and defensive positions. There is a centre player, two forward players and two defence players. Coaches regularly substitute players throughout the game.

5 Ice hockey is one of the fastest and most aggressive team sports in the world. There are many ways for players to incur penalties and they frequently do! Charging, elbowing and checking another player's play with the stick are just a few. Players are sent off to sit in a 'penalty box' for certain lengths of time. Then their team is left a player short which of course, makes it harder for them to win. Major penalties may see a player sent off for the rest of the game. Penalty shots may also be awarded to the other team for infringements.

6 Several officials supervise an ice hockey game; there are two linesmen, a timekeeper, a scorer, two goal judges, a video goal judge and two referees.

7 A game of ice hockey is played over three 20 minute periods. At the end of each period the teams change ends. At the end of the three periods, if the score is tied, 10 minutes of extra time is played. The first team to score during extra time is the winner. Extra time is called 'sudden-death overtime' or a 'sudden-death playoff'.

8 Ice hockey teams play at most local ice rinks. If you think you or your children might be interested in taking part in this action-packed sport, we recommend you enquire at a rink closest to you.

In addition, ice hockey is a very exciting spectator sport. It is played at the Winter Olympics and there is always a great traditional rivalry between Eastern European countries and North American countries. Games between these teams are always nail-biting affairs and well worth watching on television.

Goal

Face-Off Circles

Crease

INDOOR CRICKET

Players: two teams of six or eight (generally eight)
Age: children and adults
Equipment: indoor cricket ball (lighter than a regular cricket ball and usually yellow), bat, leg pads for batsmen, good quality sports shoes, batting gloves, protective box for male players, optional helmet or mouthguard for batsman

1 Indoor cricket is a relatively recent variation of the traditional game of cricket and is often played at sports centres. However, specially built indoor cricket venues are rapidly appearing as this excellent game becomes more popular.

2 Indoor cricket is played on a much smaller surface area than regular cricket. The wicket is exactly the same length and width but the pitch around the wicket is narrow, and completely enclosed by a strong net to prevent the ball leaving the playing area. In addition to this, the bowler has a much shorter area in which to run up to the wicket before bowling to the batsman.

3 A limited number of overs are played in indoor cricket. Sixteen overs per side are played in games where there are eight players on each team. Twelve overs per side are played where there are six players on each team. Each player takes a turn at bowling two overs. And each batsman bats for four overs.

4 As in regular cricket, the aim of indoor cricket is for each team to score as many runs as they can. Runs may be scored by:

Running between the wickets, as in regular cricket.

Hitting the ball into the side of the net – 2 points.

Hitting the ball into the back of the net – 4 points.

Hitting the ball full-on into the back of the net – 6 points.

One umpire officiates in a game of indoor cricket.

5 Because indoor cricket is played in a relatively small space with a small number of overs, it is a fast and furious game that is full of excitement for all players. Anyone can form a team – groups of work colleagues, students, neighbours or friends. Teams usually join a competition, competing against other teams every week.

Competitions usually last for twelve to fifteen weeks, with a winning team declared at the end.

6 If you or your family would like to play regular cricket but don't enjoy spending a lot of time out of doors, or don't have a lot of time to practice, then indoor cricket is the game for you. Games are often played at night and on weekends. Why not contact a few local fitness centres in your area and see if they have indoor cricket facilities? Your kids will love it.

Edge of pitch

Leg-side line

Batting crease

Exclusion-zone:
3m (3.2 yds) radius from
centre of batting crease.

Non-striker's crease

Bowling-crease

SOFTBALL

Players: two teams of nine or ten
Age: children and adults
Equipment: softball bat; softball; softball gloves; softball mitts for catcher and first base player; chest and leg protectors for the catcher; helmet and mask for the catcher; helmets for other players; a protective box for male batters; team uniform and shoes

1 Softball is a popular ball game that is very similar to baseball. In fact, many of the rules of the two games are identical.

The game of softball is enjoyed in many countries around the world and is also an Olympic sport. Like baseball, softball is not a game that can easily be played informally with just a few friends or family members. But it is played extensively as a school sport throughout the world and most towns have local teams and clubs available for those who want to learn more about the game.

2 Softball was adapted from the game of baseball in the late 1800s in the United States. It was played as an indoor game and was first called 'Kitten Ball'. The first-ever game was played with a boxing glove as a ball!

By 1933, the modern rules of softball had been fully developed and the first national softball organisation was formed in the United States.

3 Softball is played on a very similar pitch to baseball (see diagram for baseball pitch page 340). However, the pitch is smaller and there is no pitcher's mound in the middle of the field – just a pitcher's plate.

Bases, infield, outfield and foul areas are all similar to baseball.

4 The pitcher in a softball game bowls underarm to his opponent rather than overarm, as in baseball. The softball itself is a large leather and cork ball, a little over 30 cm (12 in) in diameter. Bats used in softball are also smaller and lighter than baseball bats. Juniors often play with special lightweight aluminium bats.

5 A softball game consists of seven innings. During an innings, each team takes a turn at batting and fielding. The batting team may consist of ten players, rather than the nine in baseball. One player is a specialist batter, called a 'designated hitter'. This player takes the place of the pitcher when it is the pitcher's turn to bat.

An innings ends when each team has batted once and all of their players have been got out. Just as in baseball, the team with the most runs scored at the end of the game is the winner.

6 Softball teams must try to hit the ball and travel around the bases, and back home again, just as in baseball. They also try to steal bases, avoid being tagged and hit home runs. There are also several different methods of throwing the ball and batting, which a good coach will be able to explain to you or your children.

7 The game of softball is just as complex and exciting as baseball, which is why it has become an Olympic sport. Many players prefer to play softball, rather than baseball. If you or your children think you might like to try the game or join a team, we suggest you look for local clubs in your area or contact your state association.

SQUASH

Players: two (singles) or four (doubles)
Age: older children and adults
Equipment: squash racket; squash ball; access to a squash court; appropriate sports shoes with non-marking soles

1 The correct name for squash is actually 'squash rackets', but it is generally just called squash. Squash is a very active and athletic sport. If you want to lose some weight or get in shape, then this is the sport for you. It is loads of fun and can be enjoyed simply as a recreational game to be played between friends, or as a highly competitive international sport that is very dynamic to watch. One of the most exciting things about the game of squash is that the ball is able to bounce off walls within the court, where as in tennis it would simply go out of court.

2 Squash was first played in the mid-1700s, in England. It was developed at the famous Harrow school and quickly became very popular, spreading to other countries in Europe and also, the United States. Today the game is still evolving, with rackets and balls made from new materials that improve players' performance, and updates and changes to international rules.

3 A game of squash is generally played between two people although doubles games are also played, especially in competition. The game takes place indoors, on a squash court. A squash court is not like a tennis court at all; it is a large box-like room around 9.75 metres (10.6 yds) long and 6.4 metres (7 yds) wide.

A line divides the court horizontally and other lines in the back half of the court are marked to provide two service areas (see diagram).

4 Squash rackets are much smaller and lighter than tennis racquets, allowing players to use them to good effect in the faster squash court. Different types of squash balls are available, for different types of player. They generally come in four speeds and the speed is indicated by a dot on the ball. Balls with blue dots are the fastest, red dots are medium speed, white dots are slow speed and yellow dots are extra slow. Slightly larger than average squash balls can also be purchased for beginner players or junior players. These travel even more slowly and are easier to control on the court.

5 Like tennis, there are a number of different ways to hit the ball in squash, including forehand, backhand and drop shots. To learn how to play these shots requires the help of a coach. Alternatively, a friend or family member who is an experienced player can show you how. But coaching for beginners is essential to get the most out of this fantastic game.

6 So how is a game of squash actually played? We will concentrate on a singles squash game here.

The server (sometimes called 'hand-in') stands in a service box at the back of the court to serve. The receiver (sometimes called 'hand-out') stands in the other half of the court. The server may choose to start from whichever service box she wishes. If she wins the rally, she must then swap boxes and serve from the other side of the court. But the server always chooses which box she would like to start from. Most players find it easiest to start from the right service box.

The server serves the ball to the front of the court and the ball must hit the wall above the cut line, halfway up the wall. It then bounces away and the receiver must hit it back. The receiver can either hit the ball before it bounces (volley) or hit it after it has bounced once on the floor. If the ball bounces more than once the server has won a point. This is similar, of course, to tennis. However, in squash, the players can bounce the ball off a side wall or the back wall to return it to the front wall, before it bounces back to the opposing player. This does not apply to the service, which must be played straight to the front wall.

7 Provided the receiver gets the ball back to the server, play continues until the ball goes out of play by hitting the 'tin' at the base of the wall, going out of the boundaries of the court, or the opponent being unable to return the ball. If the server wins the point, she continues to serve. If she loses the point, this is called 'serving the hand-out'. Then the receiver becomes the server.

8 Points are scored in this way: Firstly, in the usual scoring system, points can only be won by the server. A squash match is played to the best of five games. Each game is scored to 9 points but if a game reaches 8 all, the receiving player gets to decide how the end of the game is scored. She can decide either to play just to 9 points (set one) or play to 10 points (set two).

A second scoring system is now often

used in men's international competition. This is called the point-a-rally system, or PARS. This system is particularly good when playing doubles.

Games are scored to 15 points and at 14 all the non-server gets to choose whether to go to 15 (set one) or 17 (set three). In this form of scoring, the receiver as well as the server can score, just as in tennis.

9 Most sports centres have squash courts attached to them. Coaching and classes are almost always available at reasonable prices and rackets and balls can also be hired. There is sure to be a squash court in your local area, so why not give them a call and give this game a try?

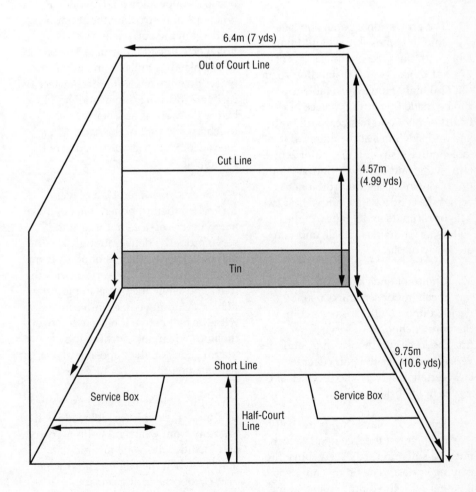

6.4m (7 yds)

Out of Court Line

Cut Line

4.57m (4.99 yds)

Tin

Short Line

9.75m (10.6 yds)

Service Box

Service Box

Half-Court Line

TABLE TENNIS

Players: two (singles) or four (doubles)
Age: any age
Equipment: table, net, bats and balls

1 This is a fast-moving game, which has enjoyed popularity for over a hundred years. It is also known as ping-pong and is now regarded as a highly professional sport, although it can equally be enjoyed played on the kitchen table.

2 The professional game and sets sold in games shops would have a table with the precise dimensions of 274 × 152.5cm (9 × 5ft) standing 76cm (2ft 6in) high. However, a table top can be made by cutting a piece of craft board or plywood to size. Mark both end and side lines at the edges of the table with a strip of white paint 2cm (1in) wide, and a thinner line, say 5mm ($^1/_2$in), down the centre. Add a net across the centre with clamps, find two bats or racquets and a lightweight yellow or white plastic ball, and you are ready to play.

3 Choice of ends and whether receiving or serving is usually decided upon by the toss of a coin. If the winner chooses to serve or receive first the loser can choose ends, and vice versa. In doubles the pairs decide between themselves who receives and serves in the first game.

4 To serve, a player holds the ball in the palm of the free hand, which must be still and easily seen above the playing surface. The fingers are kept together with the thumb free, and the ball is thrown without spin virtually straight up. On descent it is struck to bounce inside the server's court first, then over or around the net into the receiver's court. The ball must be struck on the first attempt, and in doubles the ball must bounce in the right-hand side of the serving court and then into the diagonally opposite court.

5 To return the service, the ball must be struck to pass over or around the net to bounce in the server's court. It must not be allowed to bounce twice, nor is a volley allowed. (A volley is when a ball is struck without bouncing on the playing surface on the volleyer's side of the court.) The ball is out of play if it touches any other object than the net, supports, surface or racquet. Touching the racquet hand below the wrist is acceptable, but touching any part of the hand when the racquet has been dropped is not acceptable.

6 Points are scored by a player when their opponent fails to make a good service; does not return the serve properly; deliberately strikes the ball out of sequence in a doubles game; or touches the playing surface with the free hand while the ball is in play. If a player's clothing comes into contact with the ball before it has passed over the lines when not touching the playing surface, the opposing player scores a point.

7 Unlike in tennis a 'let' has many more meanings in table tennis. It is a rally from which no point is scored and includes the same meaning as tennis – when the ball touches the net or its supports during service (provided the service is otherwise good). Other reasons for calling a let

are: that a service is delivered when the opponent is not ready; a player fails to make a good service or return through interference by spectators or a sudden noise; the ball is broken during play; a rally is interrupted to correct a mistake, such as being at the wrong playing ends; or a rally is interrupted to apply the expedite system.

8 The expedite system is only introduced if a game is unfinished after 15 minutes of play. The umpire interrupts and calls let. The player who is due to serve next begins and the return strokes of the receiving player are counted aloud from one to thirteen by another official. After thirteen good return strokes the point goes to the receiving player.

9 Players or pairs change ends after each game.

10 The game is won by the first player to score 21 points. The only exception is if both players are on 20 points, the game is won by the first person to score two clear points. A match usually consists of one game, the best of three or the best of five.

TENNIS

Players: two (singles) or four (doubles)
Age: any age
Equipment: access to a tennis court
(private, or public where fees are payable
for court hire); tennis racquet for each
player; several tennis balls; good tennis
shoes

1 Tennis is a wonderful ball game. It
is a very active sport that provides
players with lots of healthy exercise
and fun. Players do not need to strive
to be professionals and the game can
be enjoyed by children and adults with
varying levels of skill. It is also a
fantastic spectator sport. Tennis cannot
be learnt from a book, but requires lots
of practice and the 'human touch' of a
tennis coach, or family member or
friend, or sports teacher who is able to
play the game. Today, many children
have access to learning tennis through
their schools. Some also continue to
play after school with private or group
coaching at their local courts.

2 Tennis in its modern form was
first played in England in the
1870s. It was invented by a British
army major and called 'lawn tennis'.
It was probably developed from other
games that were becoming popular at
the time, such as squash and
badminton.

For those unfamiliar with a tennis
court layout, please note the
illustration opposite.

3 A tennis match consists of three
'sets' (or five for some
competitions), in which the winner of
each set is usually the first person to
win six games.

Obviously, to win the match a player
needs to win two sets (in a match of
three) or three sets (in a match of five).

4 You win a game of tennis by
scoring just four points, if you are
lucky. Scoring is as follows: 15-0 (love);
30-0 (love); 40-0 (love); and game.
Game scoring becomes more
complicated when your opponent wins
points too. If you both reach 40 points,
the score is called 'deuce'. The next
point won is 'advantage' to that player.
Then if that player manages to win yet
another point, they win the game. If his
opponent wins, the score returns to
deuce.

Many exciting games between
professional players have gone back
and forth between advantage and
deuce for many points!

5 Sometimes, players win equal
numbers of games in a set. Then
an exciting 'tie-break' must be fought
out between the players, to determine
who wins the set.

Our description of scoring here is very
basic, but it will give beginner players
an introduction to the game.

6 Tennis coaching teaches the grips
for each stroke used in the game –
forehand, backhand, or double-handed
backhand. And a coach can give you a
winning edge by teaching you the right
way to serve, smash, volley, half-volley,
achieve drop shots and the lob.

Group coaching also provides
participants with partners to play with
of a similar standard to themselves.
The game is much more fun if a player
is not matched against someone far
better or far worse than themselves.

7 If your children are interested in tennis, they may be able to get involved through their school. If not, local coaching is also available in most areas.

And don't forget to take a couple of tennis racquets out to the park on family picnics, or other outdoor social occasions with friends. It's always fun just to hit a tennis ball around and helps you practice for more serious time, spent on the tennis court.

Enjoy!

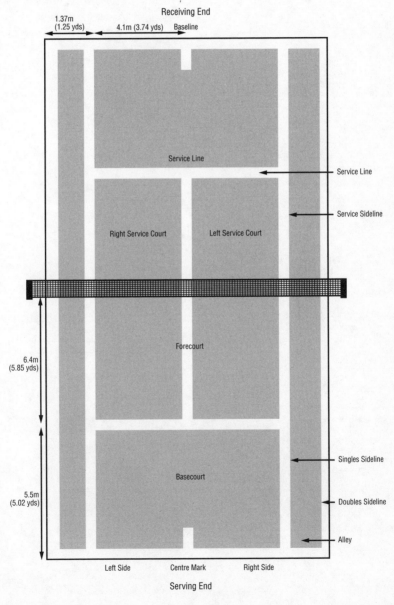

OTHER BALL GAMES

Here, in the final pages of this book, we present three other extremely popular ball games. Team games like basketball are played all around the world and are also very popular as spectator sports. As with many of the games presented in the Active Games section, they can be played formally with a team, or informally with the family at the beach, in a park, or at home in the backyard.

BASKETBALL

Players: two teams of five, plus up to seven substitute players
Age: children and adults
Equipment: access to a basketball court; basketball; basketball boots; shorts and singlet in team colours if playing for a team

1 Basketball is one of the world's most popular indoor ball games and with good reason. It is fast, action-packed and exciting to both watch and play. Professional basketball players seem to fly in the air as they strive to shoot goals for their team. Basketball is also an Olympic sport. Wheelchair basketball is an exciting variation of the game and is a Paralympic sport.

2 The game of basketball was invented in the United States by a YMCA instructor, in 1891. Dr James Naismith was searching for a game that people could play indoors in winter, in between the baseball and football summer seasons. He came up with basketball and the first games were played using a soccer ball and two peach baskets. At first the game was called 'Naismith Ball', but the name was soon changed to its present-day 'basketball'.

3 Basketball is usually played on a rectangular court, indoors. However, it can also be played outdoors on a concrete or asphalt court. The court is usually 25.6 metres (84 ft) long and 15.2 metres (50 ft) wide, but sizes often vary and the court is longer for some games. The basketball court is marked with a number of lines – sidelines, centrelines, baselines, centre circles and free throw lines, which are also called free throw 'lanes' (see diagram page 371). A circular goal hoop or 'basket' with a backboard is positioned at each end of the court.

4 The aim of the game of basketball is for two opposing teams to score as many points as they can by shooting goals through the opposition's basket. Each player has a specific area of the court to defend but they generally move all around the court during a game. Offensive and defensive strategies are played by each team, depending on which has the ball. Offensive teams have control of the ball; defensive teams try to gain control of the ball and stop the opposing team from scoring.

5 The ball is moved around the court in a number of ways:

Passing the ball – players on a team pass the ball quickly to each other and move it up or down the court. This can be done either directly from one player to another, or by bouncing the ball once between two players.

Dribbling – players bounce the ball continuously along the floor as they run along, or when they are standing still.

Pivoting – players often quickly change direction after receiving the ball during a game. They do this while standing still, but skilfully pivot around on their feet.

Shooting – players reach the goal at the opposing team's end of the court and throw the ball up at it. The ball must pass over the top and then down through the basket for any points to be scored.

6 There are a number of different ways to shoot at the basket in basketball and we'll include just three here:

Players throw 'jump shots', when they dribble the ball towards the basket, then jump up and throw it with two hands.

Players throw 'set shots', when they stand still and throw the ball towards the hoop with two hands.

And there is the 'slam-dunk', where players jump right up to the hoop and dunk the ball into the basket.

*A very important word of warning here: it is not recommended that you let a child practise slam-dunking anywhere outside of a controlled court environment, with a professional coach. A number of tragic accidents have occurred in recent years, with children pulling basketball hoops, backboards and even the walls they were bolted to down on themselves by hanging from the hoop after a slam-dunk.

It's always better to be safe than sorry with this move.

7 Players can incur a number of penalties during a game of basketball. They usually result in a member of the opposing team getting a free throw into the court or a penalty shot at the goal from the penalty line. We'll mention just a few of them here:

Players must not interfere with other players on the court by checking their movement, pushing them, tripping them or holding onto them.

Players must not waste time on the court and they must not move out of the boundary lines of the court, or take the ball out of the boundary lines of

the court. There are a number of other ways to incur fouls and violations, and a good coach will teach you or your children how to avoid them.

One referee and one umpire officiate during a basketball game.

8 As we've mentioned, players score points by throwing the basketball through the basket. However, one throw through the basket does not always equal one point.

3 points are scored when a player shoots a basket from outside the semi-circular 3 point line.

2 points are scored when a player shoots a basket from inside the 3 point line.

1 point is scored when a player shoots a free throw after a foul or violation.

9 A game of basketball is usually played over two halves of 20 minutes. However, the clock is stopped during play whenever there is a foul or violation, so the game is often quite a bit longer than 40 minutes.

Professional games of basketball are also played in four quarters of 12 minutes. Some games can even be played to shorter times of 8 or 6-minute quarters for younger children.

If a game is tied at the end of time, overtime is played to determine the winning team.

Overtime usually lasts for 5 minutes, although this can be less. The team who has scored the most at the end of 5 minutes is the winner. If teams are still tied, a further 5 minutes of overtime is played and so on, until a winner is determined.

10 Basketball is generally a team sport but it can be enjoyed informally among friends. Children all over the world love to play 'one-on-one', attacking and defending a hoop in the back yard or driveway of the family home. If you or your children would like to become more involved in the great game of basketball, we suggest you contact sports centres in your local area. Most sports centres have basketball courts available, with coaching available. Basketball is also taught and played in many schools.

25.6m
(84 ft)

side lines

centre circle

centreline

free throw line

basket

baseline

15.2 m (50 ft)

NETBALL

Players: two teams of seven and three substitute players
Age: children and adults
Equipment: access to a netball court; netball; good quality sports shoes; team uniform if playing with a team

1 Netball is a game that is similar to basketball. Netball has been popular with women and girls for many years, but more boys and men are beginning to play this fast and athletic game, too.

Netball was adapted from basketball in the late 1800s and was first called 'women's basketball'. It was widely played in Britain. The new game for women quickly spread to other British colonies and gained further popularity. The game was re-named 'netball' in 1970.

2 Netball is usually played on a rectangular court indoors, just like basketball. However, it can also be played outdoors on concrete or asphalt. A netball court is usually, 30.5 metres (100 ft) long and 15.25 metres (50 ft) wide. It is divided into thirds and has a centre circle, goal circles and a goal ring at each end of the court (see diagram).

A game of netball is played over four 15-minute quarters.

3 The aim of the game of netball is for two opposing teams to score as many points as they can by shooting goals through the opposition's goal ring. Each player is assigned a specific position on court and they are restricted to certain areas of the court.

Players are either Goal Attack, Goal Shooter, Wing Attack, Centre, Wing Defence, Goalkeeper, or Goal Defence.

Each player wears a bib or square over her shirt, identifying her playing position.

In the game of netball, only a Goal Attack or Goal Shooter is allowed to shoot for a goal. One point is scored for every goal.

Offensive teams have control of the ball; defensive teams try to gain control of the ball and stop the opposing team from scoring.

4 Perhaps the biggest difference between the games of netball and basketball is in the way that players move the ball around the court. In the game of netball, players cannot dribble or bounce the ball at all. Nor can players run while they are in possession of the ball. If a player receives the ball after they have jumped for it, their first foot to touch the ground becomes their 'landing foot'. They must keep this foot in the same place on the court or if they lift it off, they must pass the ball to another player before it touches the ground again. If a player catches a ball while standing on two feet, then they can only lift one or the other foot. If they take a step, they incur a penalty. However, they can pivot around on their landing foot. Players must also pass the ball on within 3 seconds of receiving it. This makes the game fast and furious at the elite level, as players become very skilled at manoeuvring and passing the ball quickly between each other.

5 Once the attacking team has the ball in the goal circle, the Goal Attack or Goal Shooter can attempt to

score a goal. The opposing team's defending players will work hard to prevent a goal by obstructing passes between their opponents or shots for goal. They can do this as long as they do not touch or bump their opponents. Like basketball, netball is a non-contact sport.

6 There are around twenty major rules in the game of netball. Obstructions, footwork infringements, players playing off-side (out of their own area of court) and other rule infringements occur regularly. Free passes, penalty passes, throw-ins and penalty shots at goal are then awarded by the umpire. Sometimes the umpire orders a toss-up to recommence play, when two opposing players claim the ball.

Two umpires supervise a game of netball.

7 Netball is played in many schools. It is an excellent game for both boys and girls alike. Many sports centres have netball courts and there is sure to be a local team near you, with coaching available. Playing netball on a local team is inexpensive and fun. Why not give it a try?

VOLLEYBALL

Players: two teams of six for the indoor game, or two teams of two for beach volleyball
Age: children and adults
Equipment: indoor volleyball court (can also be played outside on a flat paved or grassed surface); volleyball; kneepads; loose fitting shorts and top, or team uniform

1 Volleyball is a fantastic ball sport that is popular all around the world. It is also an Olympic sport. The rules of volleyball are relatively straightforward and very little equipment is needed to play. This makes it possible to improvise a net and have a great time with family and friends any time you have a get-together. Rules can be bent in an informal game to accommodate more or less players on each team and the game itself is a lot of fun to play. Volleyball is also a very popular sport in schools.

2 Volleyball was invented in 1895 by a young YMCA instructor in the United States. He invented the game so that some older YMCA members could play a ball game where players didn't have to run around so much! Little did he know that volleyball would become the athletic, high-energy sport it is today. The game was first called mintonette but the following year its name was changed to volleyball because of the way the ball is volleyed back and forth between teams without bouncing on the ground.

3 There are two major forms of volleyball. One is the traditional indoor volleyball, played with two teams of six players. The other is beach volleyball, played out of doors on sand, with two players on each team.

4 Indoor volleyball is played on a court 18 metres (59 ft) long and 9 metres (29.5 ft) wide. A large net is strung across the middle of the court. The net should be 2.24 metres (7.3 ft) high for women and 2.43 metres (8 ft) high for men. Junior and informal games may have a lower net. There are two attack lines also marked on the court.

The volleyball itself is a large white or light-coloured ball – a beach ball is ideal for informal games.

5 The aim of the game of volleyball is for each team to try to score points against the other team. The first team to reach 15 points wins a 'set', as long as the winning team has a clear 2 point lead. If a set reaches 14-all, then the game continues until a team is 2 points ahead, or until one of the teams reaches 17 points. The best out of three or five sets wins an indoor volleyball match. Usually beach volleyball matches consist of one game only.

6 Players are positioned at various places on the court during an indoor volleyball match. Three front court attack players are able to hit the ball into the opposing team's side from between the attack line and the net. This gives them the advantage of being able to smash the ball to the other side of the court with great force. The remaining players defend the back of the court and hit the ball over the net from there.

7 At the start of a game one player serves from behind the back line of the court, into the other team's side. All other players must be in correct positions at this time but after the serve

players may move around the court to get the ball (within reason, as they have their own areas of the court to attack or defend from). If the serving team hits a ball and the receiving team cannot return it, the serving team gets a point. If the receiving team hits a ball and the serving team cannot return it, they don't get a point but they get to have the service – and the chance to score!

At the end of each service the whole team rotates on the court. This means that the next time the team has service somebody else gets a chance to serve.

Indoor volleyball teams swap sides at the end of each set. Beach volleyball teams swap sides after every 5 points.

8 During a game the volleyball is hit or punched back and forth over the net with the hands, fists, wrists and any other part of the body. The ball must be hit cleanly with one or two hands – it is not allowed to be held or carried by players. The ball may also be hit between players on a team three times or less before it is returned over the net. If it is passed between players more than three times a point is given to the other team.

If a player hits the ball and it goes out of the court or doesn't make it over the net, a point is awarded to the other team.

If the ball is hit into a team's side and it hits the ground, a point is awarded to the other team.

9 In many places today, beach volleyball is fast becoming the more popular of the two forms of volleyball. Because there are only two players on a team, players stand anywhere on a court (except for the server, who still stands behind the back line of the court when serving). There are no attack or centre lines on the court and the beach volleyball is slightly heavier and softer than an indoor volleyball. This is so that if there is a light wind on the beach, it doesn't interfere with play. Teams generally play in beach wear rather than shorts and tops.

10 Your children are sure to be introduced to the game of volleyball at school and if they decide to take it up in a more formal fashion, you are sure to find a local volleyball team in your area. Why not give it a try?

ACKNOWLEDGEMENTS

Othello®, Scrabble® and Uno® are the registered property of Mattel Inc and are included in this book with their consent.